For the
LOVE *of* EATING

For the
LOVE *of* EATING

plant-based, vegan recipes for energy, weight-loss and healing

ROANNE LEWIS

LAUGHING RAIN

Dedication
For Brandt and Teakki Rain

Published by Laughing Rain Inc.

Printed in the United States of America

Cover design by Caitlin Legere

For the Love of Eating: plant-based, vegan recipes for energy, weight-loss and healing / Roanne Lewis

1.Vegan cookery. 2. Lewis, Roanne I. Title.

ISBN 978-1-935070-00-9

First Edition

Acknowledgements

Eating well to me, consistently, is the hardest thing for me to do. Many people have helped along the way. I would like to thank:

My mom, Harriet Greene, who started me on the whole foods path, and whose book I contributed to, *The Ashland Whole Food Cookbook*. She edited, simplified, and magically gave order to this book. And Marty Goldman, for his love and support of everything I have ever created.

Michio and Aveline Kushi for introducing me to macrobiotics. Many recipes in this book are based on ones I learned at the Kushi Institute. A few macrobiotic teachers that opened my mind: Wendy Esko, Luchi Baranda, Brodie Boyd, Warren Kramer, Kaare Bursell, Mina Dobic, and especially Diane Avoli – wizards, angels, and magic chefs in and out of the kitchen. Their skills and words changed me forever.

Maggie Jones, my first cooking teacher whose enthusiasm and natural ability were contagious. She made me believe I can teach it if I do it.

Sue Gronberg, whom I worked for in the café of her health food store in Jackson Hole, Wyoming. She allowed me to create to my hearts content and was incredibly supportive and easy-going.

My students and clients whose unending questions have kept me honing my craft and recipes so they will work.

The numerous holistic practitioners I have seen who dropped hints boldly as to how food affects health, " . . . you just have to try it."

Most of our society does not believe in the power of food. Doctors are not taught nutrition, parents don't practice it, and kids are oblivious. It is sad how sick the world is. I believe we can heal whatever is ailing us through change of diet and lifestyle. But as I have always said: food is the hardest to change, it is legal and cheap (relatively speaking). Food habits start at birth, actually in the womb. It takes everything you've got to stick with it long enough, to feel, see and taste the difference whole food makes.

Sweet brown rice rolled in walnuts
and miso chewed forever to relax,
help cope, calm and enlighten,
taste it like a picture, all senses matter
this food, this life, this seed, this path
helps me deal with my childhood wrath.
My organs are tight, my tummy worn out,
so much to remember, so much to think about.
Celery cut in cubes, in a bowl, jade-like jewels,
this food will give me good stool.
When in the kitchen I'm humble, I am sane,
Such is my kin, pots, fire, spoons, and grain.
Steam it, boil, fry or bake, sauté and nabé
cooking is art, for goodness sake.
It's warm, it responds to stirring and salting,
it's exciting when done and the timer starts ringing.
I wash and cut vegetables with ease,
color and taste, crispness – what a tease
anticipate, twenty more minutes to become, to be.
This dish, its taste, fills every corner,
its blush, its flavor, opening the hour

Table of Contents

Introduction

For the Love of Eating is about what and how we eat. It is a way of cooking for health and energy. The "core" of our bodies is where everything is digested and assimilated, and requires good whole food. All symptoms and conditions are the body's reaction to stress and toxins. *For the Love of Eating* helps clear toxins allowing the body to heal and stay healthy. This is not just another book on cooking without eggs or sugar, meat or wheat. It is about taking control of our health.

The essence of *For the Love of Eating* is:
- *whole grains* – prepared properly through soaking (and sprouting)
- *vegetables* – raw and cooked
- *cultured foods* – made at home
- *beans* – soaked (and sprouted) before cooking or eating
- *fruit* – in moderation and good quality desserts, for ideas and recipes see roannelewis.com
- *nuts and seeds* – prepared properly through soaking (and sprouting)

Being brought up on organic whole food gave me a healthy foundation. I have been consulting, teaching, and writing about natural food for over twenty-five years. Addressing health issues through alternative/conventional practitioners and supplements never really helped – there must be a way to heal myself.

In the late 1990's I found macrobiotics, a method of self-healing through cooking and eating, and remarkable results occurred. This made me aware of the power food has to heal. Later, I discovered a leading surgeon, Dr. Caldwell B. Esselstyn, Jr. whose research and practice substantiates the benefits of a plant-based diet. Through these philosophies, my studies, experiences in different cultures and healing regimes, I created *For the Love of Eating*.

After following this way of eating for three weeks, the body begins to retrain itself in what it will accept and how to satisfy cravings. After four months, the red blood cells are completely rejuvenated, and the body is on its way to health. It takes time for the organs to develop the strength and integrity to digest, for taste buds to shed their sticky coating and be able to taste the simple, plain richness of food without over-salting, sweetening, or seasoning. As *For the Love of Eating's* nutrient-dense, fiber-rich foods gently work at moving excess out, our minds will begin to let go of comfort foods and the over abundance of protein, dairy and sweets.

For the Love of Eating is not about depriving yourself, but understanding food, and eating as much as you want . . . that is, of the right kind. *For the Love of Eating* will put the power back in your own hands to heal yourself and get your core strength back (not muscle, but digestion, the root of immune). Being healthy, energetic and focused is how the body was born to be, its innate desire is to heal.

For the Love of Eating's Mac 'n' Cheez is not the typical soy cheese or cashew cream concoction, the Italian Sauce is not another innovative tomato rendition of the classic, the gluten-free steamed Corn Bread is so moist, its ingredients the simplest. Want to eat lots of purple cabbage? Try the Black Soybean Spice Patties, and make Sunflower Dream Cheese to go with them! Simple, everyday cleansing and detox tips are found in Remedies Internal & External, and try the Ginger Mint Lassi or Rye Tonic for a cultured buzz.

Changing what we eat changes our life. What we eat, in over-simplified terms, turns into blood, and blood feeds every cell in our body. Give it a chance – a long, focused, diligent, serious chance – and you will transform yourself.

At the bottom of most recipes I suggest "what to eat it with," and variations with thoughts and/or recipes contained in this book, but did not notate page numbers, be sure to look them up in the index.

get healthy to the core and live simply

How To Cook

"Cooking is the art of life," said the late Aveline Kushi, a prominent macrobiotic sage in whole food cooking and healing. Cooking is easier than you think, it's fun and creative – especially healthy cooking. Blending seeds, grain, and vegetables into creamy concoctions changes the need to use dairy products and keep meals diverse and interesting. And if you don't know anything, it's easy to learn – like riding a bicycle, once you do it a few times, you just get the hang of it and it never leaves you.

Certain tools are needed in setting up your whole foods kitchen:

- pots/pans: high gauge stainless steel, tinted glass, cast iron, enamel-coated, earthenware, corningware. Avoid aluminum, copper, clear glass.
- steaming pot (or steaming basket), baking sheets/pans
- wire cooling racks, bamboo rolling mats
- wooden mixing spoons, measuring cups/spoons
- ice cream scoop, vegetable peeler, slotted spoon
- wooden cutting board, knife (see Resources)
- mixing bowls, large colander, rubber and metal spatula
- mesh strainer (small enough for straining millet, quinoa, sesame seeds)
- blender, food processor, coffee grinder, food dehydrator
- glass containers for storing cooked food (and plastic ones for freezer)
- natural bristle vegetable brush for cleaning root vegetables

Your pantry needs organic choices of grains, beans, nuts, seeds, vegetables, herbs, spices. *Even when not stated in the recipes in this book, I buy organic, fair-trade and local – as long as it is organic, even if not certified – at all times.* There are many foods to choose from other than the ones mentioned here. These are the ones I use most often at home.

For the Love of Eating's guidelines are for a four-season climate. When living in the tropics, obviously different foods are necessary. Certain foods such as oils (even organic extra-virgin varieties) and fermented (and/or sprouted) soy products are suggested primarily in transitioning to a plant-based diet. Even then use in moderation, oils are un-stable and soy foods high in fat, and nutritionally controversial. See Glossary for more information.

WHOLE GRAINS

rice – brown (short, long)   quinoa
    – basmati (white, brown)   buckwheat
    – wild   barley
whole oats   millet

WHOLE GRAIN PRODUCTS

- sourdough or sprouted whole grain bread and tortillas (flour and corn)
- whole grain flours from rice, cornmeal, rye, millet, etc.; rolled oats
- polenta, couscous (if eating wheat), popcorn, whole grain noodles

A note on gluten. All grains contain a small amount of gluten, yet those un-safe for celiac, etc. are: barley, wheat/spelt/kamut, rye, oats. Gluten-free choices are: rice, millet, quinoa, amaranth, buckwheat, corn, teff. Look for gluten-free oats, they can be purchased in health food stores or online. See Cook's Notes for suggestions on gluten-free alternatives.

VEGETABLES

Every day I eat vegetables in soups, stir-fries and salads. I always have cabbage in the fridge (and eat it almost every morning), it lasts for weeks, collards or kale too. Include vegetables in every meal. Try to have a few on hand, from each group, see Vegetables for details:

dark leafy greens   frozen peas and corn
(kale or collards)   Japanese sweet potato
romaine lettuce
carrots   An assortment of others, that
onions   change with the seasons:
green and red cabbage   green beans, snap peas
butternut, kabocha, etc. (squash)   turnip, parsnip, rutabaga
green onions   brussels sprouts, etc.

Keep a space in the fridge for pieces of vegetables: a quarter of a turnip, half a carrot, etc. When cooking often, bits and ends can be used up.

BEANS

The beans I prefer are adzuki, garbanzo, and lentils (green, red, French) which I include in meals weekly. They are lower in fat and higher in protein making them the most gentle on digestion. See Soaking Beans in Cook's

Notes and Beans for proper preparation and cooking. A couple of times a month I include one or more of:

black	navy	split peas
pinto	black eye peas	black soybeans

SEEDS/NUTS

If you have room, store nuts and seeds in your fridge or freezer. The nuts and seeds mentioned here are lower in fat and easier to digest. See Soaking Nuts and Seeds in Cook's Notes.

almonds	sunflower seeds
walnuts	pumpkin seeds
chestnuts	flax seeds, chia seeds
sesame seeds	hemp seeds

CONDIMENTS & SEASONINGS (pg. 189, and Glossary for definitions)

We need salt and seasonings for taste and nutrition, to enhance a food, not drown it. Choose unrefined and organic as much as possible:

unrefined sea salt:
Real, Celtic, Himalayan, Masu
umeboshi vinegar
brown rice vinegar
apple cider vinegar
shoyu or tamari
umeboshi plums and/or paste
dark barley miso
red and light miso (see Glossary)
Sesame Sprinkle (Condiments)

homemade pickle (Condiments)
dill pickle
sauerkraut (see Cultured Salads)
stone-ground mustard
spices & herbs: cumin,
    chili powder, curry,
    cayenne, cinnamon, etc.
    fresh ginger, garlic cloves,
    oregano, dill, basil,
    thyme, etc.

A note on salt: *For the Love of Eating* does not highly season any dishes. Salt is a very concentrated food, use with extreme moderation. Adding salt to food at the table is a habit to break, *now*. The extreme nature of salt and salty seasonings (shoyu, umeboshi vinegar, miso, etc.) is too much of a concentrated food and will lead to cravings and imbalance.

Cook salt into food rather than sprinkling it on top of food for a minimum of 10 minutes; umeboshi vinegar and shoyu, 5-7 minutes; miso, 3-4 minutes. Less will be used, flavor is enhanced and it is incorporated into the chemistry of the dish. In all my recipes I only use unrefined salt. See Miscellaneous for Roasted Salt to be used on popcorn, etc. See Glossary for more information.

MISCELLANEOUS items to complement a whole foods kitchen.

dry shiitake mushrooms	rice papers (see Glossary)
or/and other dried mushrooms	arrowroot starch, kuzu
herbal teas	nutritional yeast
grain coffee	Sea Vegetables:
amasake	nori
apple juice	wakame
molasses (blackstrap)	kombu
barley malt, rice syrup	dulse
pure maple syrup (grade B)	hijiki
stevia or lohuan	arame

FRUIT

Fruit contains high amounts of natural sugars that can create cravings that lead to imbalance when eaten too often. But don't avoid it, an apple, berries, mango in season, or a few dried apricots can give the sweetness needed.

most often:	in season:	dry fruits:
apple	melons	apricot
pear	peach	raisin
berries	nectarine	prune
lemon	mandarin	dates
lime	tangerine	goji berries
	plum	mulberries
occasionally	apricot	mango
avocado	grapes	papaya
banana	mango, papaya	
orange		

Now, your kitchen is set up and stocked. Look through the recipes, read the title page of the chapter, and then choose, or just start with:

Miso Soup
Easy Steamed Vegetables
Simply Brown Rice
Sesame Sprinkle
Rainbow Pressed Salad or
Salt Brine Pickle

Or, dive in with:
Creamy Celery Soup
Millet Patties
Sunflower Dream Cheese
Salad Wrap

Maybe you just want to make Quinoa Muffins and Hot Cocoa? Start with the grain (it takes the longest). See Soaking Grains in Cook's Notes, an important and necessary step to digesting and assimilating whole grains properly. Once the water has boiled and pot of grain is covered and simmering, start with the next longest, Rainbow Pressed Salad and Sesame Sprinkle.

It may seem like this food takes forever to prepare, but as you become accustomed to your new kitchen, it will get easier – having leftovers for lunch and thoughts into motion for the next few days is a relief. A pot of rice, Adzuki Beans & Squash, Sunflower Dream Cheese, Rainbow Pressed Salad, Millet-Quinoa Dosas, and Salt Brine Pickle – an eclectic and exciting assortment of meals can be prepared around that for almost a week.

Wash the vegetables. Begin cutting. Small bowls are helpful to make transfer easy to the cooking skillet but not necessary. Try to prepare only the amount of vegetables needed. I often have leftover cuttings, which I store in the fridge to be used later (soup, stir-fry, etc.).

If not soaking the seeds (but try always to soak them!) for Sesame Sprinkle, then rinse and leave in a mesh strainer to drain while preparing the salad. Once the salad is pressing, start roasting the seeds. While the seeds roast (see roasting in Glossary), cut the vegetables for soup. The rice is cooking, soup simmering, press down on the salad to let those juices rise. Sesame Sprinkle fills the air with nutty goodness . . . think about soaking beans and/or grain for the next day or the day after, soak seeds or nuts to have a Sunflower Dream Cheese or Walnut Cheesy Sprinkle, make Salt Brine Pickle.

The rice is almost done, soup ladled into bowls, steamer set for Easy Steamed Vegetables, and you are cutting radishes and cauliflower for it. Your kitchen smells earthy, steamy, and your belly is ready.

Other things to think about:
When you sit down and have rice or other whole grain – chew, fifty times, then swallow. That chew, that motion, connects our 32 teeth (or whatever you've

got) with 32 vertebrae in our back and a synergistic relaxing energy is created that feeds the nervous system, stomach, spleen and pancreas, and they relax through the natural sweetness whole grain innately contains *when, and only when,* chewed well. The body is fed, optimum fuel – not starchy, processed "carbs" the world is scared of, but complex carbohydrates in their nutrient-dense, polysaccharide form. Chew. Try a hundred times the next bite. Chewing is important for all foods, but crucial for grains. The salivary enzymes begin the digestive process in the mouth – a critical step for proper assimilation.

Use local produce – not tropical fare that is expensive, picked early, and acidic (unless living in the tropics). Try to choose organic, it will be fresher, and much more nutritious. Buy bulk whenever possible.

What's the weather? Mood? In other words, let's not eat a lot of raw foods when it's cold and damp out, or fruit and nuts when feeling scattered and lazy. Raw food is cold by its *nature,* not necessarily temperature. It creates a cooling effect internally and is better to eat more often when it is hot out, or if doing a lot of physical labor or exercise. Nut butter, fats and oils are heavy foods and take a lot of energy to digest. When decisions need to be made, clear thinking is necessary, or perhaps weight needs to be dropped, eat bean soup, cultured salad, whole grains and vegetable stir-fries. If healing from a symptom or a disease, think easy to digest, low seasoning, fresh (meaning eaten within 24 hours of making it) – yet satisfying: Sweet Winter Squash, Miso Soup, Savory Cauliflower & Broccoli, Umeboshi Pickle, or Easy Rice Stir-Fry with steamed corn tortillas, Black & Tan, and Fresh Broccoli Salad.

Center your meals around vegetables. If you have a turnip, and some green or red cabbage, slice them up thin, knead in a dash of umeboshi vinegar and press 40 minutes. In that time, steam a few chopped greens, use up leftover cooked quinoa or millet, and perhaps you have a cup of cooked beans? Blend them with lemon and onion. Set a wet rice paper, steamed corn tortilla or warmed sprouted wheat tortilla on a plate, layer with above preparations and roll it up. Simple, quick, vegetable-rich and chewy.

Be creative. Use up what you have. Eat vegetables at every meal. Include daily: one cup of beans in soups, dips, salads, or wraps; whole grains soaked and cooked for nutrition far surpassing any supplement; cultured salads and homemade pickle for nature's probiotics, and greens, the best health food on the planet. Whole food will save your life, prevent disease, and "cure" just about everything.

get healthy to the core and live simply

Cook's Notes

3-5 days: all recipes last 3-5 days in the fridge. Many will last longer but are best eaten within 24 hours. Vitality and nourishment quickly diminish soon after. Cooked rice and beans last longer (5 days), and can be frozen.

Flax seeds: when a recipe calls for 3 tablespoons ground flax, I measure three tablespoons whole flax seeds and then grind them. See also Glossary.

Garnish: minced parsley, cilantro, basil, leafy tops of celery or carrot, green onion, cucumber, bell pepper, shredded carrots and roasted seeds atop grain, soup, pasta, salad, grain/pasta salads, pilaf, vegetables.

Gluten-free: this book is mostly gluten-free, yet I use ingredients that contain gluten but can be substituted as noted:
- shoyu: use wheat-free tamari or Bragg Aminos
- barley or red miso: use light or chickpea miso
- barley malt: use pure maple syrup, brown rice syrup, or other
- oats: gluten-free are available in health food stores or online
- barley: use any other grain of choice
- udon or soba noodles: use noodles made from rice, corn, or quinoa

Leftover grain called for in recipes: means cooked grain, rice or millet first, they add a creaminess and neutral taste, then oats, barley or polenta.

Matchsticks: thin matchstick cuts; see onion in glossary for techique.

Miso/shoyu substitute: see Seasoning Alternatives in Miscellaneous.

Oils: see Glossary; in recipes that call for olive oil or coconut oil, I mean extra virgin organic, but do not state it to save space. I use *very little* oil.

Optional: truly means it. Or if it was a turnip and you don't have one, but a red potato, parsnip, rutabaga is on hand, use it instead.

Organic: I use organic at all times, and eat the skin on just about everything (even winter squash with the exceptions of acorn and spaghetti).

Plan ahead as much as possible. It takes the pressure off, and helps the ease in preparation. Make a pot of beans and grain for the next few days, use it for quick meals with chopped vegetables: stir-fries, soup, salad or combinations of it all in a tortilla with a Creamy Seed Dip.

Re-heating tortillas: tortillas get soft when steamed, or quickly and directly place it on a gas flame, or heat in a lightly oiled skillet with a dash of water.

Roasting: nuts/seeds, see Roasting in Glossary; Roasted Salt (Miscellaneous)

Simmering: bring ingredients to a boil on high, then turn heat down to a very low heat, or simmer, cover so the mixture is bubbling very gently. If the stove does not simmer low enough, use a flame tamer (see Glossary).

Soaking Seeds, Nuts, Grains and Beans: seeds, nuts, grains, and beans are digested and assimilated much better when prepared properly. The recipes in this book that call for any of these, are soaked before hand, *even* when the recipe does not say to do it. I did not write it in everywhere, so whether it says it or not, soak. Get in the habit of thinking ahead and leaving time for it, and drying/roasting afterwards. Make many cups in advance and store in the freezer. Flax seeds do not need to be soaked unless a specific recipe calls for it (such as Seed Crackers).

Soaking Seeds and Nuts in a salty water solution:
¼ teaspoon at least of sea salt (I use a cheaper grade natural sea salt for soaking, but any will do) for 1 cup of seeds or nuts. Place the seeds/nuts in a bowl, cover with water, add salt, swish around, soak 6-8 hours or overnight. Cashews are not truly raw when purchased, and will get slimy when soaked too long, soak only 6 hours, walnuts can be soaked a shorter time as well. I soak mustard seeds as well. It helps remove some of the bitterness when making mustard.

When the time is up, pour into a mesh strainer, rinse, and set over a bowl to drain, 15 minutes to several hours, even overnight. Then spread onto a cookie sheet or similar, and dry in the sun until crisp, or in a low oven, or near a warm woodstove. I often place soaked seeds/nuts in a skillet on a flame tamer on my woodstove to roast very slowly.

Soaking Grains & Beans in an apple cider vinegar solution:
1-2 cups grain/bean, cover with plenty of water and add approximately 1 table-spoon apple cider vinegar (or 3-4 tablespoons Salt Brine Pickle liquid), soak 12-24 hours. If worried about fungus in general with grains and beans, add a bit of vitamin C crystals or a few drops of grapefruit seed extract to the soaking water. I even soak cracked grains such as polenta, then strain through a very fine mesh strainer when done.

I am a great advocate of sprouting grains, nuts, seeds and beans. See Making Sprouts (Miscellaneous). Sprouting elicits a nutrient-dense food, completely bio-available. I do not remind in all recipes, so take the time to soak and sprout (if you can). It is assumed in *For the Love of Eating* that before simmering grain or grinding seeds, you will have soaked them beforehand.

Steaming "baked" goods: I use a wok to steam cake, bread, cornbread, cookies, pizza, etc. Boil water in a pot first then pour it into the wok. Then set a round stainless steel sheet or grate/cooling rack in the wok, over the boiling water (if steaming cookies, place them right on a round baking sheet in the wok). Set the cake/bread on this rack and cover. Let it steam 5 minutes or so, lift the top, and wipe the condensation off the inside top. Replace top. Do this throughout cooking if steaming cake, cookies, or muffins, but, if steaming bread/cornbread, after a few times (10-15 minutes), the bread is cooked a bit and the top slightly firm, then, place a light cloth over the bread and cover (then no need to wipe the cover anymore).

Vegetable steaming liquid: use the water from steaming vegetables to cook grain/pasta in, as a base for soup, salad dressings or sauces. When a recipe calls for steamed/blanched vegetables and if also cooking noodles, add the cut vegetables to the boiling water, then cook the pasta in this mineral-rich water, saves time, adds nutrition. See also Glossary.

Yield: in general the recipes will feed 2-4 people unless otherwise noted. I do not list the time it takes to prepare the recipe. What takes me five minutes, may take someone else ten minutes; if cooking fresh greens from a garden, or large and often tough ones store-bought, times will vary as does cooking with gas or electric. The ingredients used are the whole plant. Brown rice takes an hour to cook, millet half that time, noodles half that, and with a vegetable dish – a meal can be easily prepared within those times.

Soup

fulfillment . . . embodiment . . . totality . . .

Soup's warming, liquid and slightly salty taste stimulates digestion thus activating enzymes in the digestive tract. It is a great way to start a meal. Soup is an easy way to get an array of different vegetables into one's daily fare. It can be blended into creamy potages, left alone for simple broths, or made into one pot meals. Fewer dishes at a meal are easier on digestion, so one bowl of thick and delicious soup can satiate on many levels. If you don't have what a recipe calls for, substitute. If it needs potatoes and you only have a turnip and a chunk of butternut squash, use that.

Soup is one of the most satisfying meals; simple and easily complete along with using up leftovers. It can be a light beginning, a breakfast, lunch, or dinner. It can hold all the tastes and textures. Make your own stock from root ends and leafy tops (scallions, carrot, onion), peelings from squash, potato, mushrooms, ends of everything, squash seeds/guts, apple peels or any peels (organic only), celery tops, etc.

Using stock or broth as the base is not only nutritious, but tasty – it rounds out flavor and adds richness. If you do not have any stock/broth, leftover miso soup works well, even water from steaming or blanching vegetables (as long as it doesn't taste too strong), or water with a few teaspoons of light miso for lighter soups, red miso for heavier or dark soups such as bean stews. There are recipes for Soup Stock, Squash and Corn Stock in Miscellaneous.

Garnish! adds color, taste, and a bite of raw: white roots of scallions, cleaned and minced, leafy tops of celery, chopped, green tops of carrots, and parsley, chive, green onion, cucumber.

Use what you have – pieces of onion, carrot, peeled broccoli stems, cabbage, beans, grain or pasta . . . simmer, season, blend half of it and you've got a creamy non-dairy sensation. Not only do I get pleasure in eating soup, but in using up anything hanging around in the fridge. Something surprisingly good comes out of very little sometimes.

It's hard to go wrong with soup: gather, chop, boil, season . . .

Any soup (or other recipe) that uses beans, see Cook's Notes for soaking them, How To Sprout in Miscellaneous for sprouting them (if you want to), and Beans, for cooking them.

Miso Soup

Yield: for one person

I have been eating miso soup all my life, but never understood its importance until I worked and studied at the Kushi Institute in Massachusetts. Miso is an age-old ingredient for longevity and health. Its complete protein, enzyme-rich, blood-strengthening quality provides exceptional nutrition; tasty and easy to digest, it adds dimension to a simple vegetable soup. It is made by fermenting soybeans, koji (a natural form of bacteria that provides the culture), barley and/or rice rendering an energy-giving bouillon-type paste. See Glossary. The taste of this soup is subtle, not like most Oriental restaurants whose miso soup is very strong and salty (often made with fish broth as its base).

> 1-1½ cups water
> ½-1 inch piece wakame seaweed
> carrot, diced or sliced in rounds, as much as you want
> onion or leek, a few slices
> cabbage, a few thin slices or diced, or Brussels sprouts, halved
> ½ teaspoon dark miso* see miso in the Glossary

bring above, except miso, to a boil, then simmer 1-10 minutes
The less time, the crunchier the vegetable. Cooking miso soup a longer time until the vegetables are very soft, and still adding the miso at the very end is soothing, as the soft vegetables almost dissolve in the mouth.
scoop a little broth out and into a small cup, dissolve miso in this and then add to soup – or just dissolve miso off the spoon into soup
bring to *barely* a boil for 3 minutes, then take off heat, cover
place garnish, see Cook's Notes under Garnish, in a soup bowl and pour hot soup on top. My favorite is a large, chopped handful of cilantro.

Substitute different vegetables for the ones above. Some favorites:

corn, green onion, cauliflower	grated parsnip, onion, peas
broccoli, onion, shiitake mushroom	carrot, snap peas, turnip
cooked rice or millet, onion, carrot	green beans, celery, broccoli
winter squash, corn, turnip, onion	leek, cabbage, carrot, peas

* in warmer weather use a lighter miso instead of dark miso sometimes.

Creamy Corn

Yield: 2½ cups

smooth and sweet in its own way . . .

Corn is a special vegetable – very simple and light. Its soothing yellow color and sweet garden taste is the quintessence of summer, and when blended into a soup, it's like eating the sun. Adding a potato, diced celery, and a tablespoon or two of oat flour will render a richer taste and feel. If you don't want to blend the soup, grate the corn off its cob into the soup.

> ½ onion, diced, approximately 1 cup
> ¼ teaspoon salt
> 1¼ cup corn nibs (frozen or from 2 ears fresh*)
> 2 cups water or stock**
> steamed cubes of winter squash, or other

simmer above ingredients for 15 minutes (except the squash)
taste this broth, add more salt or 1 tablespoon light miso if needed
blend soup in a blender until smooth
garnish with steamed squash cubes and chopped parsley or green onions

* if using fresh corn, when nibs are cut off, simmer the stalks in the soup base, remove before blending and squeeze liquid into soup, adds good flavor.

** for a creamier soup, add 1 tablespoon flour or 2 tablespoons rolled oats to the vegetables while they cook, and/or replace the water with grain or nut "milk," see recipes in Miscellaneous.

soup is
primeval in nature,
containing the essence
of the sea from whence we came –
and to where we go:
fluid, salty,
ethereal

Simply Squash

Squash is an integral part of my diet. Its low natural sugar content, high fiber and complex carbohydrate profile make it an ideal food for everyone. It is rich in vitamin A, C, potassium, B-vitamins, iron, zinc, calcium. My favorites are Kabocha, Hokkaido, Butternut, and Delicata, especially the first two, they have an incredible rich taste and dense texture. Leave the skin on unless it's acorn (often tough skin), or if it is not organic.

2½-3 cups winter squash, cubed (3 cups if you like it thicker)
½ onion, diced (about 1 cup)
2½ cups water or vegetable stock
juice of ½ a small orange + 1 teaspoon orange zest, both optional
fresh grated ginger, pinch cinnamon
minced parsley and/or green onion, Creamy Seed Dip, optional

bring first 3 ingredients to a boil, simmer covered 10 minutes
add the orange juice/zest, ginger and cinnamon if desired
purée in a food mill, blender, or mash by hand
garnish with parsley/green onion, and dip if using

If you would like the soup thicker: mix 2 teaspoons kuzu or arrowroot starch into the orange juice or a splash of water and whisk into the soup, simmer a moment. If the squash isn't very sweet, add 1 teaspoon barley malt if desired.

Alternate:
3 cups broth, stock, or water
1½ cups winter squash (diced)
3 tablespoons cornmeal
½ cup corn, optional
1 teaspoon fresh ginger, pinch each cumin and cinnamon

simmer first 4 ingredients (or add corn in later) for 20 minutes
blend until smooth, pour back into pot
stir in ginger and spices, simmer a moment
add corn, cooked beans, or steamed and cubed vegetables if you like.

Mushroom Leek Soup

Sautéed leeks together with mushrooms in broth emit an aroma that brings me back to some ancient time. This delicate soup goes well with everything, or simply with Creative Chef Salad and Sweet Winter Squash.

>
> 2 cups crimini mushrooms, slice in half, then slice thin
> ½ cup water
> 1 leek, cut in half, wash well, then slice thin
> ¼ teaspoon salt
> 3 cups water or preferably vegetable broth/stock

sauté mushrooms and water in a pot for 15 minutes, stir often
add leek and salt, sauté a few minutes
pour in water or stock and bring to a boil, simmer 10 minutes
if additional seasoning is needed, simmer in 1 tablespoon light miso or shoyu

For variation:
- whisk in 3 tablespoons cornmeal, cook until thickened, 10-15 minutes, stir often, then add cooked lentils, ½ teaspoon thyme and cayenne to taste

What to eat it with:
- ladle over cooked noodles, millet or rice
- use leftover soup broth to cook rice or quinoa in
- cornbread and Cashew Cream Cheese with steamed and raw vegetables
- Rice Flat Bread or Millet-Quinoa Dosas with Sunflower Dream Cheese, steamed greens or Savory Cauliflower & Broccoli with Lemon Sauce
- Garlic Bread, Seed Crackers with Quick Avocado Dip
- noodles with Walnut Cheesy Sprinkle (see Condiments)

Lemon Coconut Velvet

Yield: 1½-2 quarts

satin spiced & tangy warmth...

For some reason spaghetti squash has the flavor for this soup. I have never tried it with any other kind, though any would work – butternut, delicata, acorn, etc.

> 1 spaghetti squash, cut in large chunks
> ¼-½ teaspoon salt
> 1 can coconut milk
> 1 lemon
> cilantro, minced
> dash cinnamon, cayenne

simmer squash in 1 inch of water + salt for 15 minutes, until soft
when done, remove squash out of its hard shells to equal 5-6 cups
place cooked squash and coconut milk in a blender, blend until smooth
add a bit of the cooking squash liquid to the blender if needed to get it smooth, or just blend half the squash and hand mash the rest for texture
add it to the rest of the squash cooking liquid, stir, pour into serving bowls
add a lot of fresh lemon, minced cilantro, cinnamon and cayenne

For variation:
- instead of coconut milk, use almond, oat or homemade rice milk (see Miscellaneous)
- instead of coconut milk use broth or water and 3 tablespoons oat or rice flour whisked in and simmered with the squash and water

What to eat it with:
- Simply Brown Rice, Quinoa Pilaf, or Noodles Quick & Easy
- cultured salad: Crunchy Cabbage Salad or Pressed and Fresh
- Dark Ginger Medallions (see roannelewis.com for recipe) with a cup of tea at the end
- Skillet Greens, steamed kale, or Easy Steamed Vegetables
- Rice Flat Bread and Hummus

Creamy Celery Soup

Yield: 3 cups

This is a special soup. It holds its own nicely, but ladled over steamed or braised vegetables, Savory Cauliflower & Broccoli, or noodles becomes something like a white sauce, or a likeness to a cheese sauce.

½ onion, diced
½ cup cooked grain (millet, rice or oats) or red potato*
1 tablespoon flour (rice flour or other)
2 cups water or stock
3-4 celery stalks, cut in chunks, and set aside ¼ cup minced
2 teaspoons parsley, minced
¼ scant teaspoon thyme
2 teaspoons nutritional yeast
mirin and/or fresh lemon juice, optional
green onion, minced and roasted pumpkin seeds

simmer the first five ingredients + ½ teaspoon salt, 15 minutes
pour into a blender and blend until very smooth, return to pot
add the ¼ cup minced celery, herbs and yeast
stir in *a splash of mirin or lemon and a pinch of cloves* if desired
garnish with green onion and pumpkin seeds, roughly chopped

For variation:
- sauté 1 burdock root (diced small or shaved, see Glossary) in ½ teaspoon toasted sesame oil + ¼ cup water, 10 minutes. Add at end.

Also: you can use celeriac root along with or instead of the celery.

* or rutabaga, cauliflower, peeled broccoli stems

What to eat it with:
- over noodles, cubes of Corn Bread dipped into it
- with Tangy Beet Side, Cornbread & Salt Brine Pickles
- Jade Green cultured salad, Greek 'n' Tangy Cuke 'n' Carrot
- Collard Green Wrap, Tempeh Sandwich, or Seaweed Salad

Creamy Broccoli

beautifully green and lush . . .

Yield: 3 cups

2-3 stalks broccoli, separate florets (4 cups or so) from the stems
1 cup turnip, zucchini, leek or onion, diced (or more broccoli stem)
½ cup cooked grain (rice, millet, oats) or diced red potato
2 cups water or stock
¼ teaspoon salt
1 tablespoon fresh or ½ teaspoon dry dill

slice off the hard end of the broccoli stem, then peel and cube (1½ cups)
place cubed stalks in a pot with choice of vegetables and grain or potato, and water or stock
bring to a boil, add salt and simmer 10 minutes
add half the broccoli florets, simmer another 4 minutes
cut the rest of the broccoli into small florets and steam 2-3 minutes
when the soup is done, pour into a blender and purée until smooth
place soup back into the pot, add the steamed florets and stir in the dill

It is thick, add more water or stock if desired to thin it out.

For variation:
1½ cups crimini mushrooms, diced
1½-2 cups broccoli florets (the steaming half)

sauté mushrooms in a skillet with dash of water and 1 teaspoon shoyu
cover during cooking, stir often, cook 5 minutes, add water as needed to keep from drying, add broccoli, cover and cook another 2-3 minutes
stir in this mushroom/broccoli sauté to the blended soup
taste and adjust seasonings

What to eat it with:
- Stuffed Squash or Sweet Winter Squash
- Quinoa & Portobello Patties and Crunchy Cabbage Salad
- steamed Japanese sweet potatoes and Golden Tofu with lemon
- Wilted Kale or steamed greens, Cultured Confetti with Arame

Minestrone Soup

Minestrone means "big soup." Macrobiotic means big life. Eating hot soup on a hot day actually cools the body . . . the Italians knew this, so did the Japanese. This is a great meal in itself anytime of year.

> 2 cups carrots* (3-5 carrots depending on size), diced
> ½ onion diced
> 1 turnip, diced small, or peeled broccoli stem (1½ cups)
> 1 cup green beans, cut in ½" pieces + green peas if desired
> 2 teaspoons light miso
> 2-3 tablespoons umeboshi vinegar, to taste
> 2 cups (½#) cooked elbow or penne pasta, or any leftover pasta
> 1½ cups cooked navy beans or kidney beans (or 1 can)
> 2 cups soup stock**

simmer carrots (squash) in 1 cup water for 15 minutes in a small pot
sauté onion, turnip, green beans, miso in ½ cup water in a soup pot
blend the cooked carrots in their cooking liquid until smooth, set aside
add stock, beans and umeboshi vinegar to the soup pot
simmer until just soft, then add the carrot puree
(as well as 1 cup chopped kale, collard or bok choy greens, optional)
stir in the pasta, taste and adjust seasonings
add one large clove garlic very finely grated or minced right at the end

For a more satiny and thicker soup, combine 2 teaspoons arrowroot mixed into 2 tablespoons cool water, whisk into simmering soup.

* for the carrot base, use half winter squash (butternut, kabocha) with the carrots (2 cups total) – my favorite, and a few tablespoons beet while simmering for a "tomato" color.

** if you do not have stock, do the following (or just use water or any broth), simmer all in 3 cups water, 20 minutes, strain, use for soup base:
> 2 shiitake or other mushrooms (dry or fresh)
> chunks of vegetables, any kind, optional
> 1 inch piece kombu

Creamy Mushroom

Yield: 3 cups

velvety warmth with oats & onion . . .

2/3 cup cooked oats, rice or millet, or 1 cup thick oat cream*
¾ cup onion, diced
¼ teaspoon salt
½-inch piece kombu seaweed, optional
2 cups stock or water (if using oat cream, use 1 cup water)**
3 cups mushrooms: crimini, portobello, shiitake and/or others
pinch nutmeg, freshly ground if possible
1 clove garlic, minced, optional
fresh or dried tarragon, chives, thin lemon wedge

simmer grain/oat cream, onions, salt, kombu and stock or other, 10 minutes
blend until very creamy, set aside. Meanwhile,
wash and slice mushrooms, or a mix including white button if desired
(or grate mushrooms and onions for a different texture)
sauté in ¼ cup water with the nutmeg, 5 minutes, add fresh garlic if desired
add cooked mushrooms and their liquid to the soup base
garnish with tarragon, chives or green onions, and lemon if desired

If the soup is too thin for your liking, before adding the garnish, whisk in 1-2 tablespoons flour, and simmer 5 minutes, stir often

* oat cream is the creamy topping of cooking oatmeal (or whole oats), or barley flakes. If you've made hot cereal that morning, spoon off the top thick and creamy liquid and use in this soup recipe, or try:
    - or 3 tablespoons rice or oat flour in with the stock
    - or ¼ cup rolled oats, cook in with the stock and then blend

** if you have no stock, use water + ½ teaspoon shoyu or red miso; or see Soup Stock in Miscellaneous. I often use just water as the base with no extra seasoning, and it is delicious.

For variation:
    - add half the cooked mushrooms and then blend for a creamier version. After blending mix in the other half of the cooked mushrooms.

Leek Potato Soup

Yield: 4-5 cups

blended smooth, thick and hearty . . .

I like this soup so much, I went through a phase of eating it twice a week for several months (when I was pregnant). It is simple, soothing, and delicious.

> 2 red potatoes, 2-2½ cups diced
> 3 cups broth/stock or water
> ¼ teaspoon salt
> 1 leek, green and white parts, chopped (2-3 cups)

simmer potato in broth/stock or water and salt, 10 minutes
cut leek in half lengthwise, clean out each rib, dice white part
add white part of leek to potatoes, simmer 5 minutes
chop the green of the leek and add to soup, simmer another 5 minutes
blend all in a blender until very creamy. Leave out a few chunks of potatoes and leeks for texture if desired

If it is too thick, just add a bit of water or broth.

For variation:
-   add dry or fresh dill at the end
-   add lightly steamed or sautéed diced zucchini
-   instead of salt, use 2 teaspoons light or red miso

When I prepare soup, it is often the only dish I can handle, and so the rest of the meal can be as simple as noodles or grain with Sesame Sprinkle, Salt Brine Pickle or leftover cultured salad and some beans or Golden Tofu, or a platter of steamed greens/vegetables with or without a Creamy Seed Dip.

Creamy Onion Soup

Onions are a great vegetable for many reasons. They are inexpensive, provide wonderful flavor and texture, even a creaminess when cooked and blended, and have serious healing qualities. They help clear congestion, relieve allergy conditions, contain immune enhancing and cancer-fighting compounds. I put a grated raw onion compress over my ear once and it took an earache pain away. Whether cooked or raw, eat them often. This soup can be simple and soothing as is, or decadent with the variations below.

>   2 red (or yellow) onions, sliced in thin half moons, 4-5 cups*
>   ¼ teaspoon salt
>   3 cups stock or vegetable broth (or water)
>   ¼ cup rolled oats or 3 tablespoons rice or barley flour (or other)
>   1 teaspoon shoyu, optional
>   minced green onion, parsley; Creamy Seed Dip or Tofu Sour Cream

sauté onion and salt in ½ cup of the stock (or water) for 10 minutes
add rest of stock, oats (or flour – whisk it in), bring to a boil
cover and simmer for 15 minutes, stir often
blend half the soup (or all) and return back to pot
add shoyu if additional seasoning is needed and simmer 5 more minutes
garnish with green onion, parsley, Creamy Seed Dip or Tofu Sour Cream

* see onions in Glossary on how to cut them

For variation, add:
-   fresh basil or cilantro, garlic or ginger

What to eat it with:
-   cubes of Pan-Fried Mochi into each bowl of hot soup
-   a piece of Garlic Bread on top of each full bowl of soup
-   Sweet Winter Squash and Fresh Broccoli Salad or Rainbow Salad
-   steamed broccoli or other steamed green vegetable

Also see the recipe "Creamy & Sweet . . . a different take," in Breakfast for a simple and soothing onion-type hot cereal, try it, it's not really "oniony."

Split Pea Soup
dense nutrition, powerful protein

When cooking split peas, I soak them overnight first, even though they do not necessarily need it. I think it helps in their digestion. In the morning, drain and cook in fresh water until very soft. This soup freezes well.

> 1 cup split peas (I use green)
> 4 cups water
> 1 inch piece kombu
> 1 onion, diced small
> 1 cup winter squash or/and carrots, diced
> 1/3 cup *each* corn and peas
> 4 shiitake mushrooms (or other), chopped roughly
> 4 cloves garlic, chopped
> 1 teaspoon toasted sesame oil, optional
> ½ teaspoon salt
> 1 teaspoon dry basil

boil peas and water, skim foam off, add kombu, simmer 1-1½ hours
sauté onion, squash/carrots, corn/peas, mushrooms, garlic and salt in the oil for 10 minutes, stir often
add sauté to the split peas, take out several cups and blend until smooth
stir together and add the basil, simmer a moment more

For variation add:
- cubes of Spicy Tempeh after part of soup is blended
- cooked rice in each bowl, ladle soup on top
- handful chopped greens in the last few minutes of cooking

What to eat it with:
- salad: cultured or fresh
- Easy Steamed Vegetables or Quick Blanched Vegetables
- platter of raw and steamed vegetables
- warm millet, noodles, couscous, or a tortilla
- steamed carrots and raw cucumber slices with lemon
- hot tea afterwards such as green, kukicha, or peppermint

Vegetable Chowder

½ onion, diced
1 small turnip or rutabaga, diced
½ cup winter squash, diced
1 small red potato, diced, optional
1 small carrot, diced
¼ cup *each* peas and corn
½ cup mushrooms, sliced
½ cup green beans, sliced in ½" pieces
2 tablespoons cornmeal or flour (rice, barley, or oat)
3 cups water or stock
½ cup broccoli florets, optional
½ cup chopped collard, kale or bok choy greens

sauté the first 8 ingredients in ¼ cup water + ½ teaspoon salt, 5 minutes
sprinkle in cornmeal or flour, sauté 10 seconds
add water/stock, cover and simmer 20 minutes, stir occasionally
toward end of cooking, add broccoli and greens
fresh or dry herbs are nice: pinches of sage, thyme, savory or chervil
stir in at the end 1-2 heaping teaspoons nutritional yeast

Garnish with minced green onion.

Serve as is, or blend for a creamy green chowder.

For variation add:
- cubes of polenta or Magic Millet
- cooked beans, grain, pasta
- minced burdock, cauliflower florets, okra, zucchini
- finely ground roasted pumpkin seeds at the end

What to eat it with:
- Rice & Adzuki Bean Patties with stone-ground mustard and Carrot Ketchup
- Corn Bread and add fresh minced garlic to your bowl of soup

Lentil Soup
a hearty and healthy satisfying soup . . .

There must be thousands upon thousands of versions of lentil soup. It is quite simple and can be so delicious and satiating, its simplicity is a meal, and lentils are an easy bean protein to digest. I often make extra lentils or any beans (and sprout them), they are good in so many things, they freeze well, and can easily be added to soup at any time. See Cook's Notes for soaking beans.

> 1 cup lentils, green or red, soaked and sprouted if possible
> 1-inch piece kombu seaweed
> 1 onion, chopped, about a cup or so
> 1-2 carrots, diced
> 1 cup winter squash, cubed, or leftover Sweet Winter Squash
> 1-2 ribs celery, diced
> handful mung bean sprouts, optional (see Making Sprouts)
> 3-5 crimini mushrooms, roughly chopped
> ½ cup peas or corn, optional
> ¼ cup finely grated red beet, optional
> ¼ teaspoon salt

soak the lentils overnight, or just cover with water and bring to a boil
scoop off foam, add kombu, cover and simmer 10-45 minutes*
prepare the vegetables, set aside, watch lentil water, may need more
when the lentils are almost soft, add the salt
mash in the squash if using Sweet Winter Squash
bring back to a boil, then add all the vegetables (including raw squash)
simmer 15 minutes, stir occasionally. Taste and adjust seasoning if necessary.
Ladle into bowls with minced green onion, cilantro, and/or parsley.

* sprouted lentils take 10-15 minutes to cook, soaked lentils longer, etc.

For variation add:
- leftover Italian Sauce or Mac 'n' Cheez sauce at the end
- ¼-½ teaspoon each: cayenne, cumin, or curry when adding vegetables
- add 1 teaspoon rosemary or thyme in the last 15 minutes

Black or Adzuki Bean Soup   Yield: 4-5 servings
carrot, celery, squash & corn . . .

The most basic recipe is often the best. Remember, nothing fancy here, just tasty and good for core health. Variations can be done to suit taste and season. Cold weather is balanced by hearty warming dishes and longer cooking to help keep heat in the body; beans with squash and ginger are ideal. For warmer weather, beans work in salads, light soups for dinner, and spreads. Try using different beans, spices, and vegetables such as black-eye peas with parsnip, leek, and broccoli or garbanzo beans with green beans, onion and carrot.

> 1 cup onion, diced
> 1 stalk celery, diced
> 2 cups water or stock
> 1 cup carrot or/and winter squash, diced small
> 2 tablespoons cornmeal or polenta, optional
> 3 cups cooked black or adzuki beans* + 1 cup of their liquid or water
> 1 teaspoon red miso, optional
> ½ cup corn nibs or frozen peas
> 1 teaspoon fresh ginger, peeled and finely grated or minced
> green onion, cilantro, lemon or lime as garnish

sauté onion and a ½ teaspoon salt in ¼ cup water in the soup pot, 5 minutes
add the next 4 ingredients, stir well, bring to a boil and simmer 10 minutes
add the beans, liquid/water, (miso), corn, ginger, simmer 5 more minutes
garnish with green onion, cilantro, and a squirt of lemon/lime if desired

* see Cook's Notes for soaking beans, and Beans for cooking them

For variation:
- add jalapeño pepper or cayenne pepper, ¼ cup arame, ½ teaspoon chili powder, cumin, and oregano in the last 5 minutes of simmering
- add 2 more cups of water/stock (or bean liquid), ½-1 cup each of diced rutabaga and daikon and whisk in ¼ cup rice flour (or other, along with the cornmeal if using, or just all cornmeal), simmer 15 minutes, stir often. In the last 5 minutes of simmering, add 1 cup broccoli florets and if desired ¼ teaspoon of each: cumin, thyme, cayenne.

Vegetable Soup

Yield: 2-3 generous portions

creative, quick, satisfying . . .

Here is another simple recipe I prepare a few nights a week for supper. Sometimes just thinking about what to eat, what to cook, what to do is exhausting, especially when I just want something good and easy. This is it: basic, throw it together, usually turns out to be the best soup recipe.

begin boiling 3 cups water with 1-inch piece kombu or wakame seaweed
add ½-1 cup cooked winter squash, and mash it. If you do not have
cooked squash, add it raw, simmer 10 minutes and mash it in the water
season with ½ teaspoon salt, cover, bring back to a boil
add 4-7 different cut vegetables, ½-1 cup of each, simmer 10-15 minutes:
carrot, daikon or radish, parsnip, turnip, rutabaga, winter squash, cabbage,
onion, leek, green beans, corn, broccoli, collard, kale (if using any of last three,
add in the last 3-5 minutes of simmering because they cook up fast)
ladle into soup bowls, garnish with chopped green onion or parsley—side
it with steamed corn tortillas and slices of avocado or Seed Crackers

This is a great way to use up bits and pieces of many different vegetables.

For variation:
- add cooked beans or/and cooked grain or noodles
- ½ teaspoon curry, cumin and ¼ cup cilantro or/and ginger and garlic
- blend half and add it to the rest for a thicker soup
- whisk in 2 tablespoons flour or cornmeal while simmering to thicken
- use coconut milk, or other grain or nut "milk" for part of the water

What to eat it with:
- ladle onto a bed of chopped lettuce and other raw grated vegetables
  with a drizzle of Sesame or Ranch Dressing (see Salad Dressings).
- make it thick by simmering in ¼ cup of flour and 2 cups of beans, then
  pour onto a crust of Magic Millet or polenta, smooth mashed potatoes
  on top and bake 30 minutes.

Barley Stew
soothing vegetables, healing shiitake . . .

Hippocrates recommended barley soup, or ptisan, to restore health, changing its strength and vegetable combination depending on the issue. It has a soothing, mild taste, chewy texture, and emollient quality making it easy to digest. Hulless or whole barley is better than its pearled variety, yet takes a long time to cook, so I prepare a few cups and freeze it for quick use.

> 1 cup whole barley*, see Glossary for more information
> 1 inch piece kombu or wakame seaweed, broken up
> ½ onion, diced
> ½ turnip or rutabaga, diced
> ½ cup corn nibs
> ½ cup daikon radish, diced
> 1 carrot, diced
> 2 dried shiitake mushrooms, or other, dried or fresh
> 1/8 teaspoon salt or/and 2 teaspoons dark or red miso
> parsley and green onion, minced

rinse barley, simmer it with the seaweed in 4-6 cups water for 2 hours
watch the water, it may need more. Pressure cook if time is short. If using pearl barley, cook less time in less water. Cook until soft, then,
add vegetables + additional 2 cups water/broth, simmer 15 minutes
season with the salt, more may be needed, simmer 10 more minutes
add the miso (simmer it in 3-4 minutes) if desired, garnish with parsley and green onion

For variation add:
- different sea vegetables and different fresh vegetables
- cumin, ginger, garlic, and cilantro or oregano, basil, and thyme
- cubes of polenta, cooked black-eye peas, split peas or lentils

* whenever possible, soak the grain, see soaking grains in Cook's Notes. I often soak whole barley, blend it with fresh water and cook it (see Soothing Barley in Breakfast), it reduces time and is easier to chew. If sensitive to gluten, use millet or quinoa, or half the amount of amaranth or teff.

Noodle Soup
a witty brine with greens & roots...

I love noodles. They are one of the most satisfying foods on the planet, quick and easy to prepare, easily seasoned, and just about everyone enjoys them. They are delicious with soup or broth, and since I can consume noodles way too fast, this combination slows me down.

> 1 packet udon, somen, soba, rice noodles, or other
> 1 inch piece wakame or kombu seaweed
> 2 shiitake mushrooms, sliced, if dried soak in water and then slice
> 1 small carrot or turnip, diced
> ¼ onion or 2 green onions, sliced thin
> 1 leaf collard or kale, or ½ cup cabbage, chopped or thinly sliced
> 1 carrot, diced small or other vegetable of choice*
> 1 tablespoon shoyu or any miso (see Glossary for kinds and when to use which ones)
> green onion, parsley and/or cilantro, minced as garnish

cook pasta according to directions, set aside
place seaweed and mushrooms (+ their soaking water) in a pot
add 3 cups water, bring to a boil, simmer 10 minutes
slice kombu seaweed thinly, add back to pot
add all vegetables and shoyu/miso, simmer 5 minutes
taste and adjust, add more shoyu/miso if desired, cook it in 4-5 minutes
place a serving of noodles in a bowl, ladle soup over noodles
garnish with minced green onion, parsley, fresh grated ginger

* try leek, rutabaga, parsnip, corn or peas, bok choy, green beans, daikon or red radish, kale or any greens sliced.

Also nice with roasted pumpkin, sesame or sunflower seeds or torn pieces of nori seaweed. You may need to season a little more with the shoyu, but cook it in and don't just pour it on top.

Chunks of Golden Tofu, Spicy Tempeh, beans, or polenta squares are a rich and filling addition.

Wellness Soup

I created this healing, warming soup during cold season when everyone was coming down with something. There are many recipes that are great for boosting one's system, more could be added to this one certainly, so play with it.

8 cups water or stock
1 large carrot, cut in ½ inch rounds
1 onion, diced
1 cup rutabaga, daikon or turnip (or a mix of all), diced
1-2 stalks celery, cut in ½ inch pieces
6 shiitake mushrooms, diced (if dried, soak in water, keep the water)
2 cups cooked lentils (or one can) or other cooked bean
¼ cup *each* polenta (or cornmeal) *and* amaranth (or teff)
1 red potato or Japanese sweet potato, diced
6-12 cloves garlic, roughly chopped
1 inch piece ginger, peeled and sliced
1 inch piece kombu seaweed (or wakame) broken in small pieces
¼ cup *each* corn and peas
1 inch piece fresh turmeric root, minced
2 tablespoons miso: dark barley or red
4 scallions, sliced thin on the diagonal + minced parsley

boil the first 12 ingredients in a large pot + the mushroom soaking water
cover and simmer 30 minutes, stir often
add corn, peas, turmeric and miso, simmer another 3-4 minutes
serve with scallions, parsley, a dash of cayenne, and a squeeze of fresh lime

For variation add:
- burdock root diced or shaved (see burdock in Glossary)
- rosemary or/and cilantro
- greens: arugula, kale, collards, etc. added with the corn, peas, etc.

When ladled into bowls, squeeze a dropperful of any herbal tincture:
- Angelica, Echinacea, Astragalus
- medicinal mushrooms such as reishi, maitake, etc.

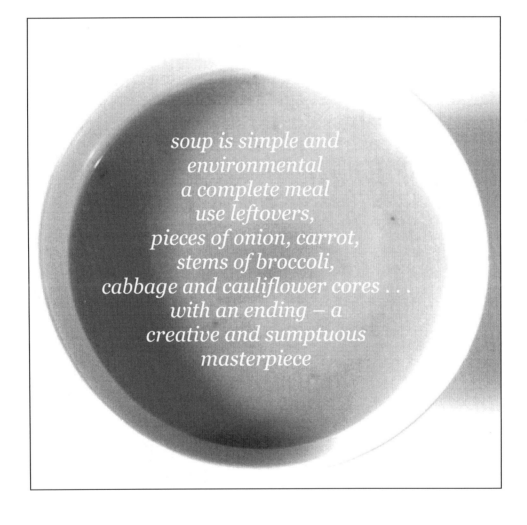

*soup is simple and
environmental
a complete meal
use leftovers,
pieces of onion, carrot,
stems of broccoli,
cabbage and cauliflower cores . . .
with an ending – a
creative and sumptuous
masterpiece*

Vegetables

roots . . . round . . . leafy green . . .

There are three categories of land vegetables: root, round, and leafy. Include at least one from each category in your daily fare. Below are examples:

- *root*: parsnip, burdock, carrot, turnip, rutabaga, daikon, beet, radish.
- *round or sweet*: cauliflower, onions, cabbage, winter squash, Japanese sweet potato, garnet yam, corn, (sweet is also daikon, carrot, parsnips, green cabbage when cooked/braised).
- *leafy or green*: kale, collards, bok choy, mustard greens, arugula, leeks, watercress, green onion, celery, broccoli, parsley, cilantro, green peas, green beans, napa cabbage, spinach (best eaten raw primarily), Brussels sprouts, celery, zucchini, romaine lettuce, radish/turnip greens, etc.
- *occasional use:* red potato, peppers (red bell and hot), swiss chard, cucumber, artichoke, sunchoke, asparagus, tomato (in-season, local).

If buying organic, leave the skin on most vegetables, even winter squash. Rinse the vegetable, scrub roots and some of the round vegetables with a vegetable brush. The skin usually steams/cooks up soft and contains important minerals, fiber, nutrition – unless you want a very orange colored soup, pie, etc. Acorn and spaghetti is the only squash whose skin tends to be tough but works on the half shell for stuffed squash.

Vegetables come in all different textures, sizes, and therefore different cooking times: winter squash, turnips, parsnips and rutabaga may take longer to cook than summer zucchini, mustard greens, broccoli or leeks. Such vegetables as carrots, radish, or cabbage can be cooked short or long depending on season, mood, texture desired and taste.

Cut vegetables in pieces depending on the recipe: for a quick blanch or steam, cut smaller such as thin rounds or half moons, matchsticks, small cubes or thin spears. For long sautéing, braising, or for a stew, larger pieces work well, such as cutting a radish in half or even leaving whole. Stems of broccoli can be peeled and sliced, the florets broken into pieces. Stems of collard or kale can be cut small and added or sautéed separately. See onions in glossary on how to cut

Vegetables not as favorable are the nightshades: tomato, potato (red skinned are okay on occasion), cooked spinach/chard (best to eat these raw), peppers, eggplant. They tend to be acid-forming and may inhibit the absorption of calcium (and other minerals). When the blood becomes imbalanced from excess acidity by these and other foods: sugar/sweets, caffeine, processed foods, meat, and dairy, tobacco, stress, etc., then it will take minerals from the blood first, then the tissues and bones to balance and buffer this acidity. This is not to say never to eat them. Tomatoes in season, locally grown and picked when ripe are a delicacy. Just use discretion, if dealing with inflammation or disease of any kind, avoid them until you get your body back into balance and symptoms dissipate.

Not all vitamins and minerals are lost in the process of cooking, beta-carotene actually becomes more available through cooking. If one is eating a healthy, whole and primarily plant-based diet packed with vegetables and virtually no processed or refined foods, dairy, meat or sweets, then any loss of nutrients through cooking is not a big deal – unless over-cooking it. Keep it crunchy through light cooking most of the time. But slow braising and sautés are soothing, easy to chew and digest, especially in the cold season.

It is controversial whether we need to obtain enzymes through what we eat, or does the body produce enough? If food is chewed very well, then the amount of salivary enzymes produced in the mouth is more than enough. However, most of us can barely slow down to chew. I generally follow the rule of chewing whole grain, very well and the rest, I chew as well as I can. There are other sources of enzymes, vitamins, and minerals included in a whole food diet such as: cultured salads, homemade pickle, sauerkraut, fermented grains, sprouts and other concentrated foods.

The difference between cooked and raw vegetables is another issue and can be discussed ad infinitum. How plants and vegetables are prepared, cut, and eaten affect the body in different ways. Both cooked and raw (and cultured) are very important. Include all in your daily fare.

A note on greens (kale, collards, etc.). They are as fickle as the weather. One bunch will steam up soft and delicious. Another may be bitter and tough. Don't be discouraged. Try to eat them as fresh as possible, and blanching them often renders a much tastier green than steaming.

Easy Steamed Vegetables

Eat steamed vegetables everyday. They are easy, quick, and are an enormous benefit to health – not just from eating vegetables. Quick steaming is light, keeping the vegetables slightly crunchy. It breaks down the cellulose fibers just enough to make chewing easier, deeper nutrients are released, and natural sugars subdued.

Use the following vegetables **or** others of choice:
>1 cup cauliflower or broccoli florets
>1 carrot, sliced in ¼ inch rounds or green cabbage
>red radishes, sliced or quartered or daikon

fill steaming pot or regular pot with a ½ inch of water
set a steamer basket inside if not using a steaming pot, turn heat on high
prepare vegetables and place in the steamer in sections
cover, steam 1-3 minutes, transfer vegetables to a plate; enjoy plain or with Hummus, Sunflower Dream Cheese, Easy Umeboshi) or fresh lemon

Steamed Greens: as above, yet set sliced cabbage in steamer first, then chopped kale or collards (or other dark leafy greens), steam 1-4 minutes.

Steaming time can take anywhere from 30 seconds to 10 minutes or more depending on vegetable and size of cut. Just picked garden greens only take 30 seconds, store-bought hardy leaves of collards or kale take 3-5 minutes usually. If steaming longer, start with more water, and check part way through. When done, use this water (vegetable steaming liquid) as soup stock, for cooking noodles, grain or added to dips, dressings, sauces, etc. Just check before using that it is not bitter.

If cooking/steaming more than one kind of vegetable, put the longer cooking, say peeled and cut broccoli stems or winter squash, on the bottom of the steamer basket or just in the bottom of the pot if you do not have a steamer basket. Add ¼-½ inch water, steam/cook a minute or two, then layer carrots, radish, etc., and then leafy greens on top. Cook until the color turns bright and they are still crisp to the bite (except winter squash, cook until soft). Do not crowd the steamer or the vegetables will not cook evenly.

Quick Blanched Vegetables

Blanching is another easy method in which to eat vegetables daily. Quick cooking breaks down the tough fiber or cellulose of the vegetable making it easier on digestion, deeper nutrients are unlocked and released, and they still retain nutrient, color and taste. It is easy to chew and digest.

>   1 cup broccoli florets
>   ½ cup daikon, cut in rounds or half moons, or turnip
>   2 cups bok choy, cut in large pieces (stem and greens)

fill a pot with two inches of water and bring to a boil
place the bok choy into the boiling water
allow the water to return to boiling, then cook 1 minute or less
remove with a slotted spoon or bamboo skimmer and set on a plate
let the water return to a boil, add the broccoli, cook 1 minute then remove
repeat with the radish or turnip or any other vegetable of choice

In general, blanch sweet vegetables first so the water isn't heavy or bitter when getting to the last vegetables being cooked. See Vegetables chapter page for which ones are categorized as sweet.

This water works nicely for cooking pasta, as soup stock or a base in sauces, dressings, blended in dips, fed to plants or pets. This is a delightful light side dish, or main dish when eaten with hummus, Sunflower Dream Cheese, Lentil Walnut Paté, or tossed with a light dressing such as Juniper Berry Splash, Easy Umeboshi or Miso & Fresh Herb.

All vegetables cooked in any of these methods should be slightly crisp and colorful, yet cooked. Enjoy greens and vegetables like this weekly.

> *Without vegetables, would there be life? For every color,*
> *texture, taste, nutrition. Essence of earth, sky, water, air*
> *we owe allegiance - health and reverse of all disease.*
> *Yes, victory through sustenance*

Nourishing Root Braise

Yield: 4-6 servings

sensuous, nourishing, and strengthening . . .

Slow braising (or nishime) is cooking vegetables in a small amount of liquid for an extended period of time rendering a soft, sweet, and rich vegetable dish. The deep nutrients and natural sugars from the vegetables cook in their own juices. This taste is loved by the pancreas, stomach, and spleen (the digestive organs), and is helpful to keep them relaxed and satiated.

> ½ inch piece kombu or wakame seaweed
> 1 burdock, cut in thin rounds, about 1 cup
> 4-6 dried shiitake mushrooms, broken in pieces, optional
> 1 carrot, cut in large rounds, 1 cup
> 1-2 Jerusalem artichokes, cut up, optional
> 1-2 broccoli stems, peeled, cut in chunks, 1 cup or so
> 1 small turnip, rutabaga, and parsnip, all large diced
> 1 cup green cabbage, cut in small chunks
> ½ cup corn or cut green beans or green peas, or all
> 2 teaspoons red or light miso, or an 1/8 teaspoon salt
> fresh herbs such as dill, parsley and green onion

boil 1 cup water (or stock) in a medium pot, with the kombu/wakame
add the burdock, then the next 5 ingredients, do not stir, just layer
cover and simmer 20 minutes (if using salt, add it now as well)
layer the green beans, cabbage, and peas/corn
mix the miso into a bit of cooking liquid and add, if using
cover and simmer 5-6 minutes, until the cabbage is just soft
garnish with minced green onion and fresh dill

All above vegetables are optional, use combinations you like. Miso or salt can be replaced by shoyu or umeboshi vinegar, or use nothing. Enjoy with Nachos (Snacks), Sweet Rice Balls (Grains), add beans for a rich stew, or just as is with noodles or quinoa and homemade pickle.

For a simple variation I do the following at least once a week:
- braise ½-inch rounds of daikon or slabs of turnip alone or with winter squash or green beans with no seasoning 10-20 minutes, until soft.

Sweet Winter Squash
kabocha, hokaido, butternut, delicata . . .

Winter squash is one of my favorite vegetables, and when very sweet and richly textured squash is available, perhaps through a farmer's market and in the fall, this quick and simple dish is almost like a muffin or worldly pastry in a strange and country way. When you have taken a break – a long break – from sweets, syrups, natural cookies and baked goods, etc., steamed or baked winter squash is a treat!

½ organic Hokkaido or Kabocha winter squash

rinse the squash, cut in half with a sturdy knife
remove seeds in one half, store the other in the fridge for another use
lay the squash cut side down cutting off any knobs or rough spots
cut in ½ inch slices, leaving the skin on and cut in half again
place in a steamer, steam 10 minutes or so, depending on size of cut
poke with a knife or fork, it should be soft but not mushy

This is delicious plain. It can replace the craving for cookies and muffins and cake *just* about anytime. You can soak the seeds a few minutes (or overnight), clean them, let them dry on a plate, then dry roast for a fun snack while reading this book (butternut and delicata seeds are the best), or put away for spring planting!

With deep orange flesh, Hokkaido, Kabocha, and delicata are the sweetest (I think). But try others such as butternut, turban, etc.

What to eat it with:
- complement with steamed or Skillet Greens
- dice and add to Creamy Corn Soup, Vegetable Soup or any soup
- toss with salsa and beans for a hearty dip
- roll in a tortilla with warm rice, sliced lettuce and a Creamy Seed Dip
- with morning hot cereal
- diced with corn, peas, steamed diced turnip and daikon
- mashed on a corn tortilla with avocado
- on a platter with other cooked and raw vegetables and a dip

Calming Onions

Yield: 2-3 servings

Onions are a miraculous vegetable. They have the ability to become very sweet and soft when cooked slow and long - the natural sweetness the body craves. This dish is calming and gives me mellow, balanced energy.

> 2 medium onions, cut in half from end to end and peeled
> 1 tablespoon light miso, optional

set each onion cut-side down, from end to end slice in 4 large sections
set the onions in a small skillet or pot
add ¾ cup water, may need to add more water later
with your fingers make little pebbles with the miso and dot the onions
cover, bring to a boil, then simmer on *very* low for 30-40 minutes
add water if needed, small amounts at a time to keep from burning, and then a little browning at the end is the best
serve with minced parsley and fresh lemon if desired

For variation:
-   at the end, stir in well-cooked beans such as navy or pinto, simmer in mustard and barley malt, molasses or apple juice, let cook and bubble, garnish with fresh herbs

The longer onions cook, the sweeter they get. Onions nourish the stomach, spleen, pancreas (because of that natural sweetness), as do cabbage, winter squash, parsnip, carrot, and sweet potato. These vegetables (and others) help soften and relax these organs giving them the sweet taste they naturally crave.

What to eat it with:
-   Sweet Winter Squash, steamed broccoli, Black or Adzuki Bean Soup
-   Hijiki Mushroom Sauté and warm quinoa or millet
-   Nutty & Nice cultured salad, Roasted Sesame Rice with Peas
-   beans and rice, or see Quick Avocado Dip to use leftovers with, and Seed Crackers
-   sprinkled with Pumpkin Parmesan, Classic Green Salad

Roasted Roots with Tarragon & Garlic

      1 onion, cut in half then in half again, and in thick slices
      1 sweet potato *and* 1 red potato, cut in large dice
      rutabaga *and* turnip, diced or cut in spears
      parsnip, thin rounds or spears
      2 tablespoons shoyu or 1 teaspoon salt
      3-4 tablespoons steaming liquid from the potatoes/vegetables
      2 tablespoons apple cider vinegar or rice vinegar or other
      1 teaspoon tarragon and 2-6 cloves garlic, roughly chopped

wash the vegetables, cut in 1 inch chunks or as written above
place in a steamer one vegetable at a time and steam, 8-10 minutes
transfer all to a bowl, toss with the last 4 ingredients
place in a shallow 9x12 oven pan (or cookie sheet with sides)
bake in a 400° oven, 20 minutes, then gently flip the vegetables
cook until golden, turning the vegetables so each side gets roasted

What to eat it with:
- steamed greens and Minestrone Soup or Lentil Soup

Easy Roasted Potatoes

      5-7 red potatoes, slice in large, thick shoestrings (5-6 cups)
      2-3 tablespoons steaming liquid (from the potatoes)
      1 teaspoon salt *and* shoyu
      paprika, dill and a dash of cayenne, or prepared mustard, optional

steam potatoes 10 minutes
mix steaming liquid, salt and shoyu in a bowl, add steamed potatoes
toss to coat, place potatoes onto 2 cookie sheets in a single layer
bake at 400°, 20 minutes, then turn each potato (time-consuming
I know but worth it), bake, turn again, check every 10 minutes
when potatoes are puffed and golden on most of the sides
transfer to a glass container, toss with seasonings if using
cover (softens them slightly so they are not so dry) . . . delicious!
Dip or coat in mustard if not using the seasonings, and steamed greens.

Whipped Root Vegetables

Instead of mashed potatoes, this decadently eclectic blend of root vegetables is outstanding for a light and smooth side dish. If using organic vegetables, leave their skins on, otherwise peel them.

> 1 rutabaga or small parsnip, diced
> 2-3 cups butternut or kabocha squash (or more sweet potato), diced
> 1-2 sweet potatoes, 2-3 cups diced

cut the vegetables in large dice
prepare a large steamer or pour 1 inch of water into a medium pot
layer the vegetables, first rutabaga/parsnip, salt them, then squash/sweet potato, salt them, then sweet potato, salt them (salt *lightly*)*
steam/simmer 15-20 minutes, until soft, check by poking with a fork
transfer to a bowl and mash or place in a food processor (or food mill)
add small amounts of the cooking liquid as needed while blending
blend well, taste and adjust seasonings
scoop into a bowl, sprinkle with paprika and minced green onion

* lightly salting each layer means less than an 1/8 of a teaspoon

Serve as is, or place into a baking dish, drizzle with almond, rice, or coconut milk, sprinkle with paprika and brown the peaks under a broiler.

Enjoy with Easy Steamed Vegetables or steamed greens, grain pilaf or a bean soup and a cultured salad. Leftovers can be smoothed into small cups, placed in a steamer, and warmed, then topped with either:
-   Sunflower Dream Cheese, Creamy Seed Dip or Hummus
-   Ranch Dressing, Sweet Bean Sauce, Walnut Cheesy Sprinkle
-   Creamy Greens, Matchstick-Cut Stir-Fry

Use this for a layered casserole such as: a base of Magic Millet or polenta, then a layer of Adzuki Beans & Squash or Vegetable Soup (just make it thick, check out its variations), grated mochi, chopped greens, and then spread thickly Whipped Root Vegetables on top, bake 30-40 minutes for a creative Shepard's Pie.

Matchstick-Cut Stir-Fry

Cutting vegetables into matchsticks (see glossary under onion) is fun, lively to look at, and has an energetic quality that resonates with the large intestine cell shape. How food is naturally formed, cut, and/or prepared can help with the healing quality: root vegetables grow in the ground and in general nourish the lower body, green leafy vegetables grow up and nourish the upper body, round vegetables nourish the middle organs, or the stomach, spleen and pancreas.

> 1 turnip or rutabaga, cut in thin matchsticks, about 1 cup
> ½ onion, cut in thin half moon slices, see Glossary under onion
> 1 small parsnip, cut in matchsticks, optional
> 2 carrots, cut in matchsticks, 1½-2 cups, see Glossary under onion
> dash toasted sesame oil, optional
> 1 lotus root, cut in half moon slices, if you can find it, optional
> 1 teaspoon shoyu, fresh ginger juice, parsley or green onion

layer the turnip/rutabaga, onion, parsnip if using, and carrot in a skillet
add 1 cup of water, bring to a boil, then cover and simmer 15 minutes
drizzle sesame oil if using and shoyu, cover and simmer 5 minutes
toss lightly, cook uncovered on high until liquid has almost cooked off
toss in fresh ginger juice (see Glossary), chopped parsley or green onion

For variation try different vegetables such as:
- burdock, carrot, onion; sauté the burdock first in water to cover until almost soft, then add other vegetables
- daikon radish, carrot, and butternut squash
- dried daikon (see Glossary), carrot, and hijiki or arame
- carrot and snap pea matchsticks or frozen peas (I eat this combo with soft cooked rice or millet for breakfast, with Salt Brine Pickle)

As a side dish to any meal, or:
- with grain or pasta, polenta, pilaf, a bowl of bean soup
- mixed into a raw or cultured salad; rolled in a tortilla with grain
- rolled into Nori Rolls or raw or steamed greens with Sliced beets (see Tangy Beet Side), Creamy Seed Dip, House Dressing, or Ranch Dressing

Easy Vegetable Sauté
creative and light daily fare . . .

I eat a vegetable sauté at least once a day. It is quick, easy and satisfying.

Choose one or several longer-cooking vegetables (1-2 cups):
> rutabaga, winter squash, green or red cabbage, green beans, parsnip, burdock, broccoli stem (peeled), turnip, daikon

Choose one, or several quick-cooking vegetables (2 cups):
> leek, napa cabbage, bok choy, kale, collard, broccoli florets, bean sprouts, zucchini, celery, carrots, snap peas, frozen peas, corn, onion

Wash the vegetables, slice in thin diagonal pieces, small dice, quarter or half moon slices. Keep in mind that longer-cooking vegetables need to be cut thinner or smaller so they don't take up more time cooking with the others.

heat ¼ cup water in a skillet, add the longer-cooking vegetables
cook for a few minutes, covered, add more water if needed
sprinkle a bit of shoyu, umeboshi vinegar, or salt to taste or not at all
then add quicker-cooking vegetables, cover and cook for a moment
toss gently for 1-3 minutes, add small amounts of water or broth *if* it's getting dry, or if too wet, leave lid off and let the excess burn off

- use vegetables alone or in any combination, use what you have
- the vegetables should be cooked, yet still have a crunch when chewed

The cooking time depends on the vegetable used and the size of the cut – if not sure, undercook it, can't go wrong with vegetables, and after they are served, they soften a bit more anyway.

For variation add:
- minced ginger, garlic, grated fresh turmeric root or fresh lemon or lime
- roasted nuts or seeds, cooked beans, Golden Tofu or Spicy Tempeh
- great with grain, noodles, in a tortilla with a dip (Snack, Spreads & Dip)

Skillet Greens

Greens are a huge part of my diet. I eat them everyday, not because they are good for me and I feel I have to. I love them. The high mineral content in their chewy "salty" taste and texture often fulfills that need or feeling to want to eat more after a meal, or feel like something is missing – greens are missing. Quick cooking does not negate their incredible nutrition but aids digestion, ease of chewing, and absorption.

It is key to cook them no longer than a few minutes, until soft, yet still have a crunch when chewed. If your teeth are not sound, still do not overcook, either blend or food process them after cooking. Or cut them smaller.

Use one green or a combination. Sliced green cabbage is a staple in our house. This amount makes approximately 2 cups cooked, depending on the size of the leaves.

> 4-6 green leaves: collard, kale, mustard, bok choy, napa cabbage
> shoyu or umeboshi vinegar to taste
> dash olive or toasted sesame oil, optional

wash the greens (use one kind or a combination), cut them in half along the middle vein, lay the halves on each other, then cut in ½ inch strips
heat 3 tablespoons water and the shoyu/umeboshi vinegar in a skillet on high
toss the greens in the pan, cover and cook for 30 seconds
add the oil if using, toss often, another minute or two, or until just soft

For variation, add:
- thinly sliced ginger or its juice (see Glossary), or garlic
- slivered almonds, sliced Bosc pear, dried cranberries or currants
- a pinch of cinnamon, and fresh lime or lemon juice

I sauté greens more often if they are old and a little bitter, or for a change. However, I eat steamed greens (see Easy Steamed Vegetables) daily, with breakfast or as a 10 a.m. snack if I am at home and again at dinner.

Green Bean Vinaigrette

Vinaigrette is a dressing traditionally made simply with oil and vinegar and can include salt, pepper, and herbs. Prepared mustard is often added to keep it from separating as well as lending a superior texture and taste. Play around with different vinegars, and I omit the oil. See Salad Dressings.

> 1 pound fresh green beans, cut or snap the stems off
> 1 recipe Quick & Easy Dressing or Lemon Sauce

place the beans in a steamer, steam until just soft, about 10 minutes
prepare Quick & Easy Dressing, omit the dill and use minced green onion
set on a platter, drizzle the dressing
This is a very delicious and easy recipe to be used on many different vegetables: cauliflower, broccoli, carrot, zucchini, etc.

Asparagus Vinaigrette

> 1 bunch asparagus, cut off tough ends

place two forks opposite ends on top of each other at the end of a skillet
set the tops of the asparagus on the forks to raise them out of the water
leave the tougher ends in the skillet
add ¼ inch water, cover and simmer until just soft, 6-8 minutes
drizzle with dressing (Green Bean Vinaigrette above) or Lemon Sauce

Artichoke Vinaigrette

Use as many artichokes as you like. Slice a half inch off the stem, place stem up in a steamer, or in a pot with two inches of water in it, or in a pressure cooker (takes least amount of time) with a couple inches of water in it, but steaming gives the best flavor. Cover and cook until tender, anywhere from 25 minutes (pressure cooker) to 45 minutes (steaming), dependant on size of artichoke. Set on a platter, place the dressing in a bowl and dip the tender leaves into it. Then clean out the fuzzy choke and dip the heart in vinaigrette (as above) or our favorite is Lemon Sauce.

Daikon Medallions

Daikon, or Japanese white radish, is a long root vegetable with a radish taste. Its pungency has great healing qualities by reaching deep into our system and clearing out mucous, old fats and proteins. Its bite is intense when raw (yet easily cut with fresh lemon and a splash of shoyu or umeboshi vinegar) or cook into stir-fries and soups, its sharpness subdued and its healing action goes deeper. Enjoy it often in many different dishes.

> 1-2 daikon roots, cut in ½ inch rounds, 2 cups
> 1 tablespoon rice syrup* optional

place the daikon in a small pot or saucepan
add a pinch of salt, then add a ¼ cup of water, bring to a boil
cover and simmer 5 minutes**
drizzle the syrup, cover and simmer another 5-8 minutes
turn up the heat and slightly brown the daikon
serve as is or toss with crisp diced Bosc pear and thinly sliced red onion

* or 1 cup apple juice. If using juice, do not use any water, simmer just the juice and a pinch of salt in a saucepan for 15 minutes until reduced to less than half. Then add the daikon and simmer 10-15 minutes, until soft and slightly sticky, almost a bit browned.

** if not using sweetener, which I rarely do because I love it plain, just simmer it for 10-12 minutes and then a bit more if needed to burn off any remaining liquid. When cooked, daikon becomes "sweet" on its own.

For variation add:
- other vegetables: onion, parsnip, butternut squash, rutabaga, or Japanese sweet potato

Eat with:
- Sweet Winter Squash and Indian Lentils & Greens
- Fresh Broccoli Salad or as a layer in Layered Salad
- on a combination plate with other vegetables
- mixed in with beans, corn, rice, with Sesame Sprinkle
- as a side dish with others such as: Wilted Kale Salad, Jade Green or Rainbow Pressed Salad and Millet Patties

Savory Cauliflower & Broccoli

Takes two minutes to prep. The delicacy of light miso lends a light, seasoned taste but I make it without as well. Best eaten all at once with Sweet Winter Squash, Corn Bread, and Quick Beans.

> 1 teaspoon light miso mixed into ½ cup water
> ½ head cauliflower, cut in medium florets, stem too
> 1 broccoli, top and stem, cut in medium florets
> ½ inch piece wakame or kombu seaweed, broken up

set a skillet or glass pan (stove-top safe) on a burner, add the miso/water and wakame/kombu, turn heat on high
prepare vegetables, peel broccoli stem, cut in large dice
add the broccoli stem, then cauliflower and broccoli florets
bring to a boil, cover and turn heat down, simmer 8-10 minutes
add another ¼ cup water or broth if necessary, then place on a plate

Plain is delicious or drizzle with lemon/lime juice, dip into Lemon Sauce and/or sprinkle with Walnut Cheesy Sprinkle or Pumpkin Seed Parmesan.

For variation: use thickly sliced turnip instead of cauliflower/broccoli.

Seared Zucchini & Onion

This is just easy and great with grain or noodles, Tempeh Sandwich, rolled in the Salad Wrap . . . any wrap or sandwich. Substitute zucchini with peeled and sliced broccoli stems if desired.

> 1 zucchini, cut in half lengthwise, then in thin slabs on the diagonal
> 1 onion, in very thin slices, see Glossary under onion (for how to cut)

place onions then zucchini in a skillet, season with salt/ume vinegar or not
sauté on medium-high until just browned, about 10-15 minutes
add dashes of broth or water if needed to keep from burning

For variation, add towards end of cooking:
- 1 heaping cup cooked kidney beans (or other), cumin, chili powder
- add on top of onion and under zucchini, parsnip or rutabaga matchsticks, and a bit more water so they cook. Top with roasted seeds.

Tangy Beet Side

2-3 red beets, scrubbed, leave skin on, dice*
1 inch piece kombu or wakame seaweed, rinsed
umeboshi vinegar to taste
1-2 tablespoons brown rice vinegar or apple cider vinegar
1 green onion, chopped finely *and* fresh dill (if you have it)

simmer beet and kombu in ½ inch water for 15 minutes – or steam the
beet, soak the kombu in water, then cut it up and steam it with the beet
transfer to a bowl, chop kombu and add it back to the beet (if boiling)
mix some of the beet cooking liquid with vinegars and onion and,
add it to the beets, kombu, and garnish with fresh dill

* if you have the greens with the beets, wash them well and chop. Add
them to the cooking beets in the last 2 minutes and include in the dish.
It gets better as it marinates. Also tasty with leftover Pesto mixed into it.

Save a bit of the red juice from cooking the beets to mix into Quick & Easy
Dressing for Rouge Vinaigrette.

Sliced beets: cut beet in half, then slice thinly in half moons. Steam until
tender, about 5 minutes. Set on plate, slice in matchsticks.

Sweet Potato & Zucchini Tumble

1 large Japanese sweet potato, cubed, leave skin on
2-3 zucchini, trim off ends then cut in half – not lengthwise
½ yellow or red onion, diced or 3 green onions, chopped
¼ cup fresh parsley, minced + ½ teaspoon red pepper flakes
Papaya Seed Dressing or Spring Onion Vinaigrette

steam potato 5 minutes
shave zucchini with a vegetable peeler in thin flat strips
place onion on top of potatoes to steam, then the zucchini, 1-2 minutes
transfer all to a bowl, toss in parsley, pepper and dressing

For variation:
- instead of potato, use rutabaga, parsnip or Jerusalem artichoke
- leave zucchini raw, or instead of shaving it, cut in matchsticks

Wilted Kale Salad

kale, leek, shallot & tangerine . . .

I could eat this everyday.

>8 cups chopped kale, 1-2 bunches
>1 small leek or red onion or 4-6 shallots* (about 2 cups cut)
>¼ cup water
>2 teaspoons shoyu and dash of umeboshi vinegar
>¼ cup apple or tangerine/mandarin juice

wash kale, then cut down its main vein, lay halves on each other, slice in ½-inch strips. Thinly chop the stems, add them with the leeks
cut leek lengthwise, wash well between the ribs, thinly slice
simmer water, shoyu, vinegar in a saucepan, add leek and kale stems
sauté leek/stems, toss and cover for 2 minutes
add kale and juice toss and cover, simmer 2-3 minutes
uncover, toss and cook on high until liquid is almost gone

* if using red onion, cut in thin ¼ moons, shallots, cut in half and thinly slice, see how to cut in Glossary

For variation:
- add fresh lemon juice
- add 1 tablespoon currants, minced dry apricot or raisins to leeks
- use kale and collards, or kale and mustard greens – any greens
- instead of simmering the kale, knead it with ¼-½ teaspoon salt until wilted and wet, then knead a moment more. Quickly rinse with hot water, mix in the cooked leek or onion and rest of ingredients.

. . . warm, sensuous, and green . . .

It takes ten days for the blood plasma to change, three weeks to change a habit (or so it is said), four months for the red blood cell to completely rejuvenate itself, and, if you can last that long, complete regeneration . . . in 7 years

Potato Salad

a picnic – get out of the house . . .

4 cups red (and/or yellow Finn potatoes), cubed
½ - 1 cup peas, optional
1-2 green onions OR ¼ cup red onion, minced
1 small carrot, finely grated, optional
1-2 ribs celery, finely diced
2 dill pickles, diced or ¼-½ cup black olives, sliced
Quick & Easy Dressing or House Dressing

steam the potatoes 8-10 minutes or until soft but not mushy
place the peas on top to warm in the last minute
scoop all into a large bowl, add other ingredients if desired,
dressing of choice and toss gently

For variation:
- set the celery and onion on top of the peas in the steamer in
  the last minute to just take the raw edge off
- see also Steamed Salada
- I like to use Japanese sweet potato and/or garnet yam mixed in

What to eat it with:
- Nutty & Nice cultured salad, Miso Soup
- A steamed vegetable platter with Ginger Glaze or White Bean Dip

The controversy of raw versus cooked has never affected me. I believe both are
necessary. All methods of cooking have their place. There are people who
cannot chew or digest raw vegetables, some cannot get energy from cooked
food, many cannot keep warm with a raw diet, and many do not have time to
cook. Though a raw diet may not use fire, it takes a lot of preparation. Any
change takes time to learn, to allow the taste buds to change, and get beyond
old habits. Cooking creates an energy not found in raw foods. All forms of
preparation are necessary, try not to get stuck on one only unless specifically
going through a healing or cleansing time.

Steamed Salada

olives, cucumber, spring onion . . .

1 cup broccoli florets
1 cup cauliflower florets, or 2 cups broccoli
1 small carrot, cut in ¼ inch rounds
1 cup *each* red potato and Japanese sweet potato or other
½ cup black or green pitted olives
¼ of a cucumber, cut in thin ¼ moons or 1 stalk celery, diced
umeboshi vinegar or salt to taste
2 tablespoons fresh tangerine or orange juice
1 tablespoon lemon juice
1-2 green onions, minced, or ¼ cup red onion, minced

steam broccoli, cauliflower if using and carrot, see Easy Steamed
Vegetables, about 5 minutes
cut potatoes in ¼ moons or large dice about ¼ inch thick
steam potatoes until just soft, 8-10 minutes
place olives and cucumber/celery in a bowl, add the steamed vegetables
toss with 2 teaspoons vinegar or salt and the citrus juices
scoop onto serving platter, sprinkle with chopped green onion

If using minced red onion, place atop the steaming vegetables in the last
30 seconds or so – unless you like them raw.

For variation, try other vegetable combinations:
-   red radish, rutabaga, yellow onion, summer squash
-   turnip, celery, golden beet, green bean, and use grapefruit juice
    instead of lemon, and cilantro instead of green onion

What to eat it with:
-   greens, always greens
-   any grain or bean burger
-   Hummus with Rice Flat Bread, Sour Millet Bread, Seed Crackers
-   Quinoa or Millet Pilaf, Sprouted Sourdough Bread, Garlic Bread

Coconut Vegetable Curry
a spicy creamy satiating adventure . . .

Coconut is creamy and satisfying, though rich, fatty and heavy, so balance with a light salad that has radish in it and greens. Coconut contains lauric acid that has anti-bacterial, anti-fungal, anti-microbial, and anti-viral properties.

> 1 cup winter squash (butternut, kabocha) OR Japanese sweet potato
> 1 turnip or parsnip, diced (1-1½ cups)
> ½ teaspoon salt
> 1 cup cauliflower and broccoli florets
> ½ cup peas
> 1 cup onion, diced
> 1 can unsweetened organic coconut milk or other*
> 2 teaspoons curry powder
> 1 teaspoon cumin powder
> cayenne to taste
> 1 cup cooked garbanzo beans, red lentils, (or other), optional
> 1-2 cups cubed polenta, optional
> large handful chopped cilantro, optional
>
> cooked basmati rice or noodles, and steamed greens
> minced green onion, roasted sesame seeds and lemon or lime

clean the squash, remove seeds and dice, or sweet potato if using
place in a skillet or pot, add the turnip/parsnip, salt and 1 cup water
bring to a boil, cover and simmer until just soft, 8 minutes
add cauliflower, broccoli, peas, onion, coconut milk (or other milk/flour mixture), spices, simmer 10 minutes, stir occasionally
add beans/lentils, polenta and cilantro if using, simmer 2 minutes
stir often. If it is too loose, add more rice flour and simmer it in 5 minutes
serve over Basmati rice or rice noodles, or any kind of noodles
garnish with minced green onion, roasted sesame seeds and lemon or lime

* instead of coconut milk, use 1½ cups nut or grain "milk," (see Miscellaneous) and 2 tablespoons rice flour. Whisk the flour into the milk before adding.

Creamy Greens

As a kid I used to love a frozen creamy spinach that came in a box. Well, this is even better.

>   2 inch piece wakame seaweed
>   1 leek, cut in half, rinsed between the layers, diced, 2-3 cups
>   4-6 collard or kale leaves, washed, roughly chopped, trim the stems
>   1 cup broccoli florets or diced zucchini
>
>   ½ recipe Tofu Sour Cream (see Spreads, Dips, Salsa)
>   Pumpkin Seed "Parmesan" (see Condiments & Seasonings)

layer the wakame, leeks, greens, and broccoli/zucchini in a skillet
pour in ½ cup water, and a large pinch of salt
cover and simmer until vegetables are tender, 5-8 minutes
meanwhile prepare the Tofu Sour Cream
roughly blend the simmered vegetables in a food processor, set in a bowl*
fold the sour cream into the greens, sprinkle with Pumpkin "Parmesan"

* if there is a lot of liquid in the pan left from cooking, drain (and keep to use in another recipe) or add to this one if needed.

For variation:
-   after folding in the sour cream, add chopped artichoke hearts and serve as a dip with Seed Crackers or sourdough bread
-   substitute the Tofu Sour Cream with ½-1 cup Creamy Seed Dip, Sunflower Dream Cheese, Bean-Naise, or White Bean Dip

One way to create alkalinity in the body is through the breath. Deep breathing removes acids if done often, as well as regular exercise. Acid tends to build up when it gets to a level the body cannot handle by the eliminative organs (lungs, skin, kidneys, bowels). It accumulates and localizes in the body in the form of cysts, tumors, pain and inflammation, and in time, degenerative disease. Greens help create an alkaline system. Eat them everyday.

Sea Vegetables

Natural minerals, incredible healing qualities . . .

Most traditional cultures harvested seaweeds or sea vegetables as well as other plant foods from the ocean, and for good reason. They are high in minerals, and easily absorbed. They help the body deal with radiation, aids in reversing hardening of the arteries, provides fiber, helps with weight-loss and lowering high blood pressure, and the list goes on.

Sea vegetables have a strong taste, some more than others. See the Glossary for explanations of individual ones. In general, wakame, arame, and kombu are mild tasting while hijiki, dulse, and nori are stronger tasting.

Most seaweed is soaked or rinsed before using. Others such as nori, which comes in large sheets and is used to wrap rice and other ingredients for sushi vegetable rolls (see Nori Rolls), needs no soaking. In fact, running a sheet of nori over an open flame or hot burner a few seconds on the shiny side makes it crispy and tinted green, and can usually nip the bud of a sweet attack (as well as a few rinsed Salt Brine Pickles!).

Include seaweeds daily: wakame in miso soup; arame or hijiki (1-2 servings per week) in a dish or salad; kombu cooked into beans, grain, soup; dulse, wakame or arame fermented in a Cultured Salad or ground in Sesame Sprinkle. They are an important addition to a whole food diet . . . to any diet!

Only use cold water for rinsing (rinse it a few times) and soaking seaweeds. The last rinse or soaking water can be used in cooking if desired, otherwise, use the soaking water to water plants or mix into pets food.

Other recipes that include sea vegetables:
- Noodles with Arame & Hemp seeds, Cultured Confetti with Arame
- Cultured Salads, Rice Wraps with Tofu & Arame
- Nori Rolls, Creamy Greens
- Barley Stew (Soups) and Miso Soup both use wakame
- Nori Crackers, Sesame Sprinkle, Popcorn

Wakame & Onion Sauté

When I worked at the Kushi Institute we would make this all the time. I loved it. I am one of those people who instantly liked natto (see Glossary). This dish is unique in its texture and taste. It is a delicacy. The calcium content in seaweeds is extraordinarily high. Split this dish into a few sides to last a few days.

    ½ cup wakame seaweed
    2 onions cut in thin slices (see Glossary under Onion)
    dash toasted sesame oil, optional
    ½ cup natto, or cooked navy or adzuki beans, optional
    1 tablespoon shoyu, to taste

soak wakame in 1 cup cool water for a few minutes
sauté onions in a skillet in ½ cup water, 10-15 minutes
cover onions, stir often
strain and add wakame, oil if using, and shoyu
sauté 5 minutes, add natto or beans if using
cover and simmer a few moments
garnish with minced green onion and/or parsley

For variation:
- use arame or sea palm seaweed instead of the wakame
- use leeks instead of onions (and sauté initially 8-10 minutes)
- add other vegetables to the sauté: winter squash, Japanese sweet potato, broccoli, burdock, snap peas

What to eat it with:
- Creamy Corn Soup
- Sweet Winter Squash and Quinoa Pilaf
- Mushroom-Leek Soup, Rice & Carrot Patties, or just mixed into some warm cooked beans (if not added already)
- brown or white basmati rice, a salad or soup and steamed greens

Mystic Arame

Yield: 3-4 servings

Arame is one of the milder tasting seaweeds, with a slight bitter-sweet taste when cooked with carrots and onion. It is easy to prepare and can be mixed into just about anything. One dry ounce (¾ cup), and when reconstituted turns into almost 2 cups. Arame can be cooked for a long or short period, such as in the first variation below, it is added near the end for a few minutes only.

> 2 tablespoons currants, raisins or dried chopped apricots, optional
> ½ cup arame seaweed
> 1½ cups carrot, cut in thin rounds or half moons
> 1 cup *each:* red or yellow onion *and* cabbage, diced
> ¼-½ cup apple juice (¼ cup if using the dried fruit/soaking water)
> ¼ cup minced parsley
> 1 tablespoon lemon juice or brown rice vinegar

soak choice of dried fruit in ¼ cup water 5-10 minutes
soak arame in cool water 5 minutes, strain and place in a skillet
add carrots, onion, cabbage and juice (and dried fruit/soaking water if using)
cover and bring to a boil, then sauté 5-8 minutes, until the liquid is burned off
transfer to a bowl, toss in parsley and lemon or vinegar

For variation:
- sauté diced (or matchsticks) parsnip, onion and carrot, and snap peas in the juice (or orange juice), add arame near the end. Omit dried fruit.
- sauté mushrooms, onion or leek, and green beans with the arame

What to eat it with:
- noodles and beans or mixed into morning hot cereal (really, try it!)
- rolled in the Curried Tempeh Wrap
- minced in a food processor then mashed with millet and pan-fried as patties with Lemon Coconut Velvet soup
- part of a salad platter with Jade Green, Nutty & Nice (Cultured Salads), and Tangy Beet Side (Vegetables)

For other recipes with arame, see Noodles with Arame & Hemp seeds and Cultured Confetti with Arame

Hijiki Mushroom Sauté

mineral-rich, exotic, hearty . . .

Hijiki or Hiziki cooks up chewy and flavorful. Mixed with fresh or dried shiitake or crimini mushrooms serves as a mineral-packed side dish.

> ½ cup hijiki seaweed
> 4-8 shiitake mushrooms, dried or fresh or other mushroom
> ½ red onion, quarter moon slices, see Glossary under Onions
> 2-3 teaspoons shoyu, optional

soak hijiki in plenty of water, it triples in bulk, for 30-60 minutes
cover shiitake mushrooms with water if dried, 10-15 minutes
drain hijiki, place in a skillet, cover with fresh water, bring to a boil
simmer covered, 15 minutes
slice the fresh or dry mushrooms, add to hijiki with their soaking water
add onions, cover, simmer 10 minutes
turn heat up (add shoyu if desired) and let liquid boil off, 5 or minutes
serve with a scattering of sliced green onion or chopped parsley

For variation:
- add carrots, parsnip, rutabaga, daikon or burdock to hijiki
- after initial simmering of hijiki, add ½ cup apple juice and carrot matchsticks when you add and simmer the onions
- add chopped collard greens or cabbage to the sauté, season with rice vinegar and shoyu, then roll in Phyllo dough, bake until golden
- omit mushrooms, chop and mix into muffins, see Quinoa Muffins

Enjoy as is with grain or noodles, or:
- in a cultured salad, Classic Green Salad, or Potato Salad
- mix into cooked grains and beans, then mash and fry up as patties
- layer it on a platter over raw or steamed chopped greens, shredded carrot, leftover grain pilaf, sprouts and/or cooked beans and drizzle with a dressing (see Layered Salad)
- roll it in a tortilla (flour or corn) with grain, steamed greens and a Creamy Seed Dip, Bean-Naise, or Sesame Dressing

Seaweed Salad

Yield: 4 cups

½ cup arame, soak in cool water 5 minutes, drain and set aside
½ cup wakame seaweed, soak in cool water 5 minutes, drain then chop
3 inch piece kombu seaweed, soaked until soft, then sliced thin
1 celery stalk, sliced in thin diagonals or ½ cucumber cut in ¼ moons
2 cups carrots, large grate or matchstick-cut
2 cups green cabbage, very thinly sliced
1 tablespoon umeboshi vinegar, or use shoyu if desired
¼ cup lemon, lime or orange juice, mix it into the cabbage/carrot
1 cup Golden Tofu, Spicy Tempeh or any cooked beans, optional
2 tablespoons roasted sesame seeds (see Glossary under roasting)

Marinade:
3 tablespoons rice vinegar or other
1 tablespoon barley malt, rice syrup or a few drops stevia, optional
1 tablespoon ginger juice or finely minced ginger, optional
1/3 cup water or stock

place vegetables in a bowl and knead in the vinegar (or shoyu) and lime juice
press 30 minutes, see Cultured Salads for instructions
set the seaweeds in a skillet and add the marinade. If using any vegetables from variation below, add them now or leave them raw, simmer 4 minutes
pour this cooked mixture over the pressed salad, toss
sprinkle with sesame seeds, (and even cilantro, parsley, green or red onion)

For variation:
-   don't press the vegetables, sauté seaweeds in marinade and pour over vegetables, use the umeboshi vinegar or shoyu in with the marinade
-   add ½ cup snap peas or zucchini matchsticks, or corn or peas
-   add Golden Tofu, Spicy Tempeh or cooked garbanzo or adzuki beans
-   set carrot/cabbage in with the sauté and cook a few minutes
-   toss in 2 cups arugula at the end (leave raw or cook it in)

What to eat it with:
-   Creamy Corn Soup, Black Bean Soup or Sweet Rice Balls . . .

Salads Fresh

To health! With raw & fermented foods . . .

Fresh salads are suggested in every healing regime. They are live, enzyme-rich, colorful, provide light, cleansing energy, and crunch! Eating an abundance of vegetables is one of the best things we can do, but not raw all the time. In fact, most of the time I eat quickly steamed or blanched greens and vegetables, which breaks down the cellulose, or fibers that we don't always chew well. Cooking greens and vegetables only a few minutes so they still have their crunch, leaves many nutrients intact as well as unlocking deeper ones. It is a super and necessary way to enjoy vegetables.

Raw vegetables contain natural sugars and enzymes necessary for health. Yet deeper nutrients are only released by cooking as well as thorough chewing. Raw is not everything, neither are enzymes. The most important enzymes are in saliva. When food is chewed well, enzymes and nutrients locked in the deeper fibers, are released. Most of digestion miraculously takes place in the mouth! When dealing with any kind of symptoms, whether it be chronic disease or simple stuff like headaches, allergies, skin problems, indigestion, weight issues, etc. then working with food, especially vegetables, in all forms of cooking, but primarily steamed, blanched, sautéed, cultured . . . is the way to go. The natural sugars are buffered and tough fibers are broken down so deeper nutrients are available.

Most of us do not chew well. Cooking aids in that breakdown process as does fermentation. Check out the section on Cultured Salads, the age-old process of kneading vegetables with a salty substance so they "sweat" or start to release their juices, then pressing them. This breaks down the fiber making it easier to digest.

For more raw vegetable snacks and salads, see also:

-   Seaweed Salad (Sea Vegetables), Pasta Salad (Noodles)
-   Salad Wrap, and Collard Green Wrap
-   Wilted Kale Salad, Steamed Salada, and Potato Salad (Vegetables)
-   Croutons (Miscellaneous) as an accompaniment
-   Kale Chips (Bread, Tortilla, Cracker)

Classic Green Salad

Even the most basic and simple has its own charm and character. I had a beautiful salad in the south of France that I have never been able to copy – a bit of that sensuous and eclectic countryside was infused in it . . .

> 1-2 leaves romaine, green or red leaf lettuce
> handful Mesclun greens and/or sprouts
> 1 leaf Napa cabbage, thinly sliced
> handful arugula or radicchio, thinly sliced or torn
> ½ avocado, diced, optional
> 1 small carrot, grated and 1 green onion, minced
> Quick & Easy Dressing (Salad Dressings)

wash and chop or tear the lettuces into a bowl
add rest of ingredients and drizzle with dressing

Fresh green salad is great simply with a bowl of quinoa or pasta, a side of steamed vegetables or a bowl of Vegetable Soup. Toss with a Creamy Seed Dip and roll in a tortilla with warm rice or grilled tempeh – take it on the go. For variation:
- toss with steamed and diced beets, rutabaga, turnip, or radish
- toss with steamed or raw broccoli or cauliflower florets
- toss with cooked rice or millet
- add cooked garbanzo, adzuki or other bean
- toss with raw or steamed slices of green beans or asparagus
- use a different Salad Dressing: Miso & Fresh Herb or Quick & Easy

Greek 'n' Tangy Cuke 'n' Carrot

Simple I know, yet apropos sitting with vibrant and animated Greeks in Athens before a traditional fried rice dinner, this was perfect.

> 1 cucumber, wash, leave peel on and run a fork down its sides
> 1 carrot, wash, cut in thin diagonals
> 1 lemon (and pinch of salt or umeboshi vinegar, optional)

cut cucumber in large diagonal ¼-inch slices, then in halves
place both on a platter, (sprinkle with salt/vinegar) and a lot of lemon juice

Layered Salad

colorful, diverse, textured . . .

Eating raw and cooked vegetables are important, this salad uses both, the texture and taste are outstanding. I often eat this around 10:30 or 11 as my first meal, sometimes just after a cup of miso soup.

    2 leaves lettuce, or handful Mesclun salad mix
    ½ cup Seaweed Salad, Hijiki Mushroom Sauté or Mystic Arame
    ¾ cup Tangy Beet Side (Vegetables) or ¼ cup grated raw beet
    1 cup cabbage or bok choy, roughly chopped and lightly steamed
    1 small carrot, finely grated
    ½ cup sprouts
    dressing of choice or simply lemon and fresh ground seeds

use a large plate or small oval platter, cut lettuce and lay down first
scatter carrot, then Tangy Beet or grated beet on top of lettuce
arrange steamed cabbage or bok choy, or others, see variation
then seaweed of choice, sprouts, then drizzle with dressing
finish with all or choice of: chopped parsley, cilantro, green onion, nutritional yeast, roasted seeds

Look in the Sea Vegetables section for seaweed suggestions

For variation:
- if no lettuce, use sprouts (see Making Sprouts) or finely grated carrot, beet, cabbage (raw or steamed) as the base
- use just fresh baby mustard greens and arugula leaves, then in-season tomatoes, black olives, sprouts; lemon or vinegar
- layer with thinly sliced tart green apple or bosc pear and beets (lightly steamed), then Juniper Berry Splash (Salad Dressings)
- add cooked beans or soaked nuts or seeds to one of the layers
- sprinkle with nutritional yeast, ground flax, and/or hemp seeds
- sprinkle with steamed lentil sprouts, sliced zucchini or radish
- add steamed cubes of butternut squash and minced cilantro

I'll add leftover pieces of vegetables I have around steamed briefly, beans, and quinoa or millet. Use what you have. Fresh and finely grated burdock root is a refreshing, earthy addition as well, and it aids in cleansing the lymph system.

Salad Raw and Warm

I like the sensation of chewing cool, crisp raw vegetables mixed with quickly steamed or blanched warm greens. It is very satisfying. Experiment with other combinations: steamed cabbage or bok choy, pea or lentil sprouts, green beans or snap peas. See also Layered Salad.

> 2 leaves collard or kale greens, rinsed
> 1-2 cups lettuce leaves, sliced thin or torn
> 1 small carrot, grated (or beet)
> ½ cup red cabbage, minced
> 1 green onion, minced
> 1 cup sprouts
>
> ½ cup Creamy Seed Dip (Spreads, Dips, Salsa), or a Salad Dressing: Sesame Dressing, Fresh Herb Vinaigrette or Quick & Easy Dressing, Light Miso Dressing

prepare a steamer or bring to boil one inch water in a small pot
steam collard/kale leaves whole, 2-3 minutes
cut them down the middle vein, then across the leaves in thin strips
place lettuce in a bowl with steamed greens and rest of ingredients, toss with one of the dressings

A Quick Delight

1/3 cup *each* grated daikon radish and carrot
1 small green onion, minced
a few drops each, lemon juice and umeboshi vinegar

Toss all together. For variation add:
- handful sprouts, chopped steamed (leftover) greens
- cubes of avocado, roasted sunflower or pumpkin seeds
- drizzle any dressing over (Salad Dressings)

Prepare sprouts at home (Miscellaneous), they provide fresh greens and an incredibly rich source of protein, enzymes, chlorophyll, fiber, antioxidants.

Creative Chef Salad

Yield: 1-2 servings

the best of all worlds . . .

1-2 leaves kale, bok choy or collard
1 stalk broccoli, in florets, the stem peeled and diced
1 small beet, cubed small or sliced thin
2 cups sliced or torn lettuce
1 small carrot, grated
½ avocado, cubed, optional
¼ cup roasted pumpkin or sunflower seeds
½ cup red cabbage, shredded
¼ - ½ cucumber, sliced in quarter thins
¼ cup cooked garbanzo or other beans
House Dressing (or other)

prepare a steamer
wash and cut kale/other down its main vein, slice in ½ inch strips
place in steamer with broccoli, steam 2-3 minutes, remove
steam beet until tender, 5 minutes (or grate instead, and have raw)
combine all ingredients in a bowl, toss in House Dressing

Or set the lettuce and cooked greens on a platter, layer or arrange other vegetables and ingredients, drizzle with dressing.

Add one or more of the following:
- 1 minced green onion
- Golden Tofu or Spicy Tempeh
- roasted or soaked almonds, walnuts or pecans (Cook's Notes)
- pan-fried polenta or Magic Millet cubes (Grains)
- goji berries or golden raisins
- Pan-Seared Apple (Breakfast)
- 1-2 tablespoons hemp or chia seeds, or ground flax
- Sauerkraut (Cultured Salads) or homemade pickle (Condiments & Seasonings)
- cut cauliflower and radish, raw or quickly steamed
- nutritional yeast powder
- 1/3 cup Hijiki Mushroom Sauté or Mystic Arame (Sea Vegetables)

Salad Dressings

A simple dressing can be as easy as sprinkling a few drops of umeboshi vinegar or lemon juice and a dash of vegetable steaming liquid or dunking in a bowl of Creamy Seed Dip. Adding seasoning enhances a dish. It doesn't have to be fancy, oily, or salty – in fact, *For the Love of Eating's* dressings are all oil-free.

I use a lot of vegetable steaming liquid (see Cook's Notes and Glossary) as part of the base in dressings, which you should have around if eating steamed vegetables daily . . . a good thing to do. I also use leftover Miso Soup broth, or see the second variation under Soup Stock in Miscellaneous.

Quick and easy seasonings include:

- roasted and ground seeds: sesame, sunflower, pumpkin
- nutritional yeast, umeboshi vinegar, other vinegars
- lemon or lime juice with umeboshi vinegar
- tangerine or grapefruit juice, vinegar and mustard
- ground together seaweed such as nori or dulse with seeds
- minced fresh parsley/cilantro mixed with ground roasted seeds

Use imagination and palette to decipher: if a salad is crunchy with roasted seeds and sweet with Pan-Seared Apple, raisins or grated carrots, perhaps a light and sour dressing, such as Easy Umeboshi or Lemon Mustard will complement it.

Dressings can enhance or drown a dish. Choose carefully, consider the five tastes: bitter, pungent, sour, sweet, and salty:

- watercress, arugula, parsley, citrus rind, or roasted seeds for *bitterness*
- ginger, grated radish or onion, green onion or chives for *pungency*
- citrus juices and vinegars for *sour*
- molasses, maple syrup, stevia, fruit juice, miso, sweet vegetables (carrot, winter squash), dried fruit, apple sauce for *sweet*
- salt, shoyu, umeboshi vinegar or its paste, or miso for *salty*

Also see: Spreads, Dips, Salsa and Sweet Mustard Sauce (Sauces)

Easy Umeboshi

½ teaspoon umeboshi paste or umeboshi vinegar
1-3 tablespoons vegetable steaming liquid (see Glossary) or water

mix together, enjoy over boiled, steamed or
raw vegetables, etc.

Quick & Easy Dressing

Yield: approx. ½ cup

Great on Potato Salad, Classic Green Salad, any grain or pasta salads.

1 tablespoon chia seeds or ground flax seeds
1 clove garlic, pressed, finely grated or minced
1 tablespoon lemon juice
2 teaspoons prepared mustard (I use stone-ground)
1 teaspoon dry dill or 1 tablespoon fresh, minced
1 tablespoon umeboshi vinegar + dash shoyu
¼ cup vegetable steaming liquid or water, or red beet juice*

whisk ingredients together, taste and adjust seasonings

* for **Rouge Vinaigrette**, add red beet juice (see Tangy Beet Side)

For variation:
- mix in half a ripe avocado and 1 teaspoon rice syrup or other
(for Pasta Salad 2)

Fresh Herb Vinaigrette

Yield: approx. 1 cup

> 1 tablespoon chia, or whole or ground flax seeds
> 2-3 teaspoons light or red miso (see Glossary) or shoyu
> ½ cup warm vegetable steaming liquid (see Glossary) or water
> 1½ tablespoons lemon juice or apple cider or rice vinegar
> 1 cup cilantro, roughly chopped, include stems
> ¼ cup fresh dill, basil, arugula or parsley
> 1 tablespoon umeboshi vinegar

purée all in a blender until smooth, it will thicken as it sits

For variation:
- do not blend, use ground flax seeds, less than half the fresh herbs (minced) and stir together with a fork

Creamy Walnut Vinaigrette

Use Fresh Herb Vinaigrette with these changes:
- blend with ¼-½ cup soaked (and roasted) walnuts, if you do not want to blend, then finely mince the walnuts, see Cook's Notes for soaking nuts
- omit chia/flax seeds
- add more liquid as necessary to get desired consistency
- leave herbs out and stir them in after blending

Spring Onion Vinaigrette

Use Fresh Herb Vinaigrette with this change:
- omit herbs, use 1-2 minced green onions or chives

Delicious on salads, pasta, beans, just about anything. Store in a glass jar in the fridge, up to one week.

Thousand Island Dressing

1 cup garnet yam or butternut squash
2 teaspoons shoyu or ¼ teaspoon salt
½ cup sunflower seeds, soaked* see Cook's Notes for soaking
1 tablespoon lemon juice
1 teaspoon mustard powder or 1-2 teaspoons prepared mustard
1 tablespoon apple cider vinegar

steam squash/potato with the shoyu or salt, keep cooking liquid
place all in a blender, and blend adding cooking liquid from the squash to get a thick and smooth consistency, it thickens as it sits

*if no time, soak only 1-2 hours in water with a pinch of salt, or simmer in water for 10 minutes. Either way, discard soaking/cooking water.

For variation: try ½ cup leftover Italian Sauce instead of the cooked sweet potato/squash and mix it with lemon juice and Bean-naise (Condiments).

Creamy Plum Dressing

½ cup almond "milk" (Miscellaneous)
2-3 tablespoons Plum Sauce (Miscellaneous)
2 teaspoons stone-ground mustard

combine ingredients in a jar and shake

Great on Layered Salad, or any raw salad, steamed vegetables, etc.

For variation:
- use apple or pear sauce instead of Plum Sauce
- use any "milk" instead of almond
- blend ingredients with ½ cup cooked beans (white, garbanzo, red, adzuki) and vegetable steaming liquid to desired consistency. Season with umeboshi vinegar if necessary.

Sesame Dressing

Yield: 1½ cups

A thick and creamy dressing that needs a little more than lettuce to hold onto such as Crunchy Cabbage Salad with added grated carrot and raisins, or steamed and/or raw chunks of vegetables, or drizzled over cooked grain or noodles, cucumber slices, etc. and rolled in a tortilla.

> ½ cup sesame seeds*
> ½-1 lemon, juice and pulp (4 tablespoons)
> pinch cayenne, 2 teaspoons shoyu
> 1 tablespoon onion

combine all in a blender or suribachi (see Glossary) and blend with 1 cup water for a thick dressing, add more water and lemon if desired

* soaked, see Cook's Notes for soaking seeds, or simmered in water for 10 minutes. If you do not want to use a blender, finely grind the sesame seeds in a coffee grinder then whisk together with other ingredient.

Papaya Seed Dressing

> ½ cup fresh papaya seeds *and* ½ cup onion
> 1 lemon or orange, juice and pulp
> 3-4 tablespoons rice vinegar or other

blend ingredients until papaya seeds are small black flecks
add water/vegetable steaming liquid as needed to get desired consistency

Delicious with Millet Patties and lettuce in steamed corn tortillas, on potato or pasta salad, on Sweet Potato & Zucchini Tumble.

House Dressing

Yield: 1 cup

Use on Chef Salad, bean salads, steamed vegetables, simply on sliced romaine lettuce and grated carrots.

  ¾ cup warm water or vegetable steaming liquid
  ¼ cup sesame or pumpkin seeds, finely ground
  1 tablespoon lemon juice
  2 teaspoons umeboshi vinegar
  2 teaspoons rice vinegar or apple cider vinegar
  ¼ cup mix of fresh herbs minced: cilantro, basil, dill, parsley*
  1½-2 teaspoons prepared stone-ground or Dijon mustard

whisk all together with a fork in a small bowl
add a pinch of cayenne if desired

* or use 2 teaspoons dry herb: dill, basil, chervil, marjoram, tarragon.

Light Miso Dressing

Yield: almost 1 cup

  1 tablespoon light miso (see miso under Glossary)
  1 tablespoon rice vinegar, apple cider vinegar or lemon juice
  1 tablespoon roasted sesame seeds, whole or ground
  ½ cup water or vegetable steaming liquid
  1 small green onion, finely minced

mix all ingredients together

For variation add:
-   1 teaspoon maple syrup, Plum Sauce (Miscellaneous) or drops of stevia
-   instead of vinegar/lemon use twice as much tangerine/grapefruit juice
-   1 tablespoon finely grated carrot or/and a dash of toasted sesame oil

Toss with sliced Napa cabbage, carrot and daikon matchsticks or buckwheat pasta, vegetables and ginger, or steamed cubes of sweet potato, green beans, and kidney beans.

Ranch Dressing

Yield: 1 cup

Sunflower seeds blend up creamy if you have a good blender and replace the buttermilk and sour cream in traditional Ranch dressing. The lemon adds the tang and herbs take care of the rest. It's great for dipping vegetables in raw or steamed, in Pasta Salad, spread over Golden Tofu or Spicy Tempeh, polenta or Magic Millet, on a burger, with crackers, or sautéed vegetables and pasta.

> ½ cup sunflower seeds, soaked (see Cook's Notes for soaking seeds)
> 2 tablespoons lemon juice
> ¼ teaspoon salt, to taste
> 1 tablespoon *each* parsley and chives/green onion
> ½ teaspoon dry dill or 1½ teaspoons fresh
> ¼ teaspoon dry mustard powder or 1 teaspoon prepared mustard
> 1 small clove garlic or ¼ teaspoon powder, optional

drain seeds and discard soaking water, place in blender
blend soaked seeds with lemon juice and ½ cup fresh water
add rest of ingredients and blend very briefly until just combined
taste and adjust seasonings. Keep refrigerated.

Add jalapeño or cayenne to spice it up and cilantro instead of dill. Great with Polenta & Caramelized Onions (Grains).

Juniper Berry Splash

Yield: ½ cup

> 2 tablespoons juniper berries
> 1 tablespoon flax or chia seed
> ¼ cup lemon or tangerine juice
> vegetable steaming liquid

place all in a blender, blend adding vegetable steaming liquid until smooth
strain and drizzle on grain pilafs, noodles, or steamed vegetables

Nice mixed into House Dressing or Quick 'n' Easy Dressing for fresh salads, cultured salads, on steamed rutabaga, asparagus . . .

Cultured Salads

I learned about pressing or the light pickling of vegetables at the Kushi Institute, a leading center on healing through macrobiotics. We prepared colorful, pressed or fermented – cultured dishes – that were so new to me.

Three factors are needed:
1. salt (or umeboshi vinegar) – draws out the juices from vegetables
2. pressure – breaks down the molecular structure of the vegetable
3. time – short fermentation – pre-digested, vegetable fibers are broken down, nutrients released, chewing and digestion are easier.

A delicious salad is created in its own juices. The salt pulls the juice out so that a salad dressing is not needed. Truly an incredible discovery I think.

Cultured Salads bring an enzyme-rich crunch to the palette. They contain B-vitamins, provide an acid environment in the bowel where friendly bacteria can thrive and overcome non-friendly bacteria. Store-bought pickles, sauerkraut, kimchee are pasteurized, heated to seal them, and over-salted and seasoned. There are brands available in raw form but are expensive to enjoy daily. Check Condiments & Seasoning on how to make homemade pickle. Cultured Salads can be eaten alone, in wraps, mixed into salads, noodles, grain, etc.

For culturing salads:
1) prepare vegetables and place in a bowl
2) add salt or umeboshi vinegar, and knead with hands until vegetables begin to sweat, or get wet, then knead/crunch with hands a bit longer
3) gather all into the middle in a neat pile
4) find a plate that will fit into the bowl without getting caught on its sides (it needs to be ½ inch or so from the sides of bowl), set on top
5) find a weight, such as a heavy clean rock or bricks, a gallon jar of beans or water, etc., set the weight on top of the plate and press
6) let set as long as per recipe, don't worry if it presses longer
7) every time you pass by, press down on the weight, its natural juices will rise up over the vegetables which means the vegetables are breaking down, a great sign that things are working

See troubleshooting in Glossary if it's not working. I often let the salad press much longer, even overnight, it just gets better.

When done, remove weight and plate, toss salad, taste it. If too salty, quickly rinse under water and squeeze out. If dry and didn't seem to get juicy while pressing, it didn't have enough salt. Knead some in and press again.
For another cultured salad see also Seaweed Salad in Sea Vegetables.

Nutty & Nice

Yield: 3 cups

    4 cups napa cabbage, sliced thin
    4-6 red radishes or ½ cup daikon, sliced thin
    1 tablespoon dulse or wakame seaweed, soaked, then chopped
    ¼ scant teaspoon salt
    1 teaspoon chia seeds
    1-2 tablespoons roasted sunflower seeds or hemp seeds
    1 tablespoon lightly roasted sesame seeds
    ¼ cup roasted or raw (soaked) walnuts or pecans
    1 tablespoon currants, dry cranberries or goji berries

toss first three ingredients together and knead in the salt
press 20-30 minutes
mix in one or all of the next five ingredients
garnish with minced green onion and lime or grapefruit.

For variation add:
- minced red pepper and/or carrot
- Pan-Seared Apple (see Breakfast)

Crunchy Cabbage Salad

purple, green, crisp & fresh

    1 packed cup *each:* red cabbage, green cabbage and napa cabbage
    1 cup bok choy, sliced very thin, white stem and greens
    ½ cup snap peas, cut in half on the diagonal
    ½ cup arugula, radicchio or cilantro, roughly chopped
    3 tablespoons apple or tangerine juice

slice all the cabbage very finely, place in a mixing bowl
add rest of ingredients except the juice, knead in a scant ½ teaspoon
salt until vegetables sweat, set a plate and weight on top
press 30-50 minutes, drain excess liquid, toss in juice

For variation: drizzle with Thousand Island Dressing or Sesame Dressing

Delicious rolled in a tortilla with a grain or bean burger and Sunflower
Dream Cheese or other creamy dressing.

Sauerkraut

Yield: 1 quart

The Great Wall of China was built by the digestive strength of sauerkraut more than 2,000 years ago. Then Genghis Khan discovered it, later the Germans, then the Dutch on their sea-faring voyages to prevent scurvy. What a healing miraculous food, and so easy to make at home. Eat a few tablespoons daily with meals to ensure proper digestion and absorption of all nutrients and to provide remarkable friendly bacteria.

One pound cabbage is about 4 cups shredded or sliced thinly.

> 6 cups green cabbage, thinly sliced
> 2-3 teaspoons sea salt, may need more or less

place cabbage in a large bowl, see Cultured Salads for instructions
rub/knead salt into cabbage with your hands until it sweats
set a plate on top*, a weight, and a tea towel (keeps bugs and dust out)
let ferment 4-6 days. Press down often on the weight.
It's best to let the kraut ferment in either a glass or ceramic container.

* place a whole or part of a cabbage leaf on top of the sweated cabbage tucking it in down the sides and then the plate and weight. While fermenting, it needs to stay under its juice at all times – or at least after the initial 8-10 hours.

For variation:
- use part red cabbage with the green cabbage for pink kraut
- add grated beet, carrot, onion, greens, apples, turnip, or burdock
- add juniper berries, lemon, fennel seeds, crushed chiles, dill

Fresh Broccoli Salad

Yield: 4 cups

> 4 cups napa cabbage, thinly sliced
> 2 cups broccoli, chopped very small
> 1½ cups celery, minced (inner lemon-colored stalks are best)
> ½ cup (packed) chopped cilantro + 1 green onion, minced
> 1½ tablespoons umeboshi vinegar, lime or lemon juice

combine vegetables, knead in umeboshi vinegar (cilantro is optional)
press 45 minutes-1 hour. Squeeze in fresh lemon/lime juice if desired

Rainbow Pressed Salad

When I used to private cook, this one was a favorite among clients. Its refreshing, naturally sweet taste and soft crunch satisfied any palette and helped in cravings upon finishing a meal.

    1½ cups red cabbage, thinly shredded or sliced
    1 cup green cabbage, thinly shredded or sliced
    ¾ cup carrots, cut in very thin matchsticks or shredded
    ½ teaspoon salt
    1 red skinned apple, matchsticks
    ½ lemon juice & pulp

knead and crunch vegetables and salt together in a bowl
when they begin to sweat add apple, lemon juice and pulp
place a plate over and a weight on top. Let stand 30-40 minutes
remove plate, toss and enjoy – even better the next day

Pressed & Fresh

I like combination salads of soft and crunchy, warm and cold – the sensation in the mouth is exciting – which in turn aids in the satisfaction of eating and enjoying a meal – a necessary component to keeping it simple and whole . . .

    2 cups napa cabbage, sliced very thin
    ½ cucumber, matchsticks (about 1 cup)
    1 teaspoon dulse seaweed
    2 teaspoons umeboshi vinegar
    handful any lettuce, watercress or arugula
    ¼ cup *each* parsley and mint leaves (optional), both chopped
    1 tablespoon roasted pumpkin seeds, coarsely chopped, optional
    2 tablespoons tangerine (or orange), apple, lemon or lime juice

knead cabbage, cuke, dulse and vinegar
press for 20 minutes, meanwhile wash lettuce and cut thinly
when pressed salad is done, add lettuce, parsley and mint if using
add seeds and juice (and fresh grated orange rind if desired too)

Carrot, Jicama and Pear Salad
sweet-tang, summer magic . . .

1 cup carrot, cut in thin matchsticks
2 cups jicama, cut in matchsticks
2 tablespoons red onion, sliced thin and chopped
1 firm bosc pear (or green apple), cut in matchsticks
lemon or tangerine juice, and parsley

toss ingredients together in a bowl, add ½ teaspoon salt
knead until vegetables sweat
press 20 minutes
add lemon or tangerine juice, garnish with parsley

This works without pressing, but omit the salt, and add a dash umeboshi vinegar instead. If you do not have jicama, use the inside greenish-white leaves of green cabbage, or the white stems of bok choy and add 1 or more tablespoons of apple or pear juice.

Jade Green
dazzling green, crisp . . . a poem

1 tablespoon dulse seaweed (or 1 teaspoon dulse flakes)
2 cups cucumber, sliced in thin half moons*
1 celery, thinly sliced
2 ribs bok choy, thinly sliced on a long diagonal
2 teaspoons umeboshi vinegar
1-2 tablespoons roasted seeds, green onion, parsley or dill

soak dulse in water until soft, a few minutes (don't soak flakes)
chop it and mix it in with the vegetables, add vinegar
knead so the vegetables sweat, press salad for 15-20 minutes
garnish with seeds, green onion or herbs if desired

* see Glossary under onions on how to cut half moons if needed

Squeeze in some lemon juice or brown rice vinegar and then toss with noodles, or roll in a tortilla with Hummus or a Millet Patty.

Cultured Confetti with Arame

¼ cup arame seaweed
1 large carrot *and* 1 small yellow summer squash or zucchini
1½ cups green cabbage *and* ½ cup burdock
3 tablespoons red onion or 1 green onion, minced
¼ cup parsley, chopped
dash apple cider vinegar, rice vinegar or lemon juice
½ cup Sesame Dressing or Bean-Naise

soak arame in cool water until just soft (5-10 minutes) place in a bowl
pulse vegetables in a food processor or grate small (4-5 cups total)
toss with arame, knead in ½ teaspoon salt
press for 30-40 minutes, press down often to get the juices rising
add choice of vinegar or lemon juice and serve with a side of dressing

Cabbage & Carrot

6 cups thinly sliced green and/or napa cabbage
2 cups carrot, matchsticks (the best way) or grated
1-2 teaspoons salt

combine all ingredients in a large bowl
knead with hands until wet, then crunch together more
scrape down sides into a neat pile
place plate and then weight on top
press over night, leave out on kitchen counter
check often, press down on weight, make sure liquid has just barely
risen and covers the vegetables (when you press down on it)

I often add a few tablespoons water if I used green cabbage (not napa) –
if it is a bit tough to get the juices going. My favorite is to leave it pressing
3-5 days. It will be like sweet sauerkraut.

The next day, remove the plate/weight and toss. If you don't want to leave it
overnight, then just press it for several hours. This salad will last a week in the
fridge. Enjoy mixed into other vegetable, grain or noodle dishes. My favorite is
with a bit of Sunflower Dream Cheese or Bean-Naise.

Zucchini Matchstick Salad

    6 cups zucchini* matchsticks
    ½ teaspoon salt
    ¼ cup apple cider vinegar or rice vinegar
    1 tablespoon rice syrup, 2 teaspoons maple syrup, or 5-6 drops stevia

cut zucchini in thin matchsticks and place in a medium bowl
knead the salt in with your hands
boil vinegar and sweetener of choice with ½ cup water, 30 seconds
pour this hot mixture over the zucchini, mix briefly
press 20 minutes, or longer (up to an hour), taste and adjust seasonings,
if more is needed, add a dash of umeboshi vinegar, and/or sweetener

* the striped Italian zucchini works best for this salad

I love this salad rolled in Salad Wrap, Nori Rolls, in Speedy Quesadillas, or if I
didn't get around to eating it in time, I sauté it into a stir-fry with onions, cauliflower and beans. The zucchini is smooth with a soft crunch, really satisfying.

For variation:
    - add thinly sliced red onion, cucumber, arame, and nappa cabbage

Pickled Cucumber Strips

I use this in Nori Rolls, Salad Roll, or wraps of any kind, or tossed into
salads, or simply with other vegetables and seasonings tossed in.

    1 cucumber, trim ends, drag a fork down its sides, cut in thin strips

knead a large pinch of salt into the cucumber, set aside as is, or set a plate
and a light weight on top, 10-15 minutes, or as long as overnight

For variation, add:
    - dash vinegar or lemon juice (or press in thinly sliced lemon w/ rind)
    - a couple drops of stevia or a teaspoon of brown rice syrup
    - chopped parsley, cilantro, fresh basil or any fresh herb

Grains

Whole grains sprout and grow = energy . . .

It is important to soak grains 12-24 hours before cooking. Place the grain in a bowl or pot it will be cooked in, cover with water, add apple cider vinegar (1 tablespoon per 1-2 cups of grain). In the morning, drain, add measured amount of fresh water, a pinch of salt, turn on heat and cook for specified time. Soaking and rinsing for several days will develop sprouts. These processes make the grain more digestible (by initiating the sprouting process), which neutralizes their phytic acid (as does the sourdough method of bread making). Phytic acid and other naturally occurring "toxins" interfere with assimilation and absorption. See Cook's Notes for more on soaking grains.

If no time to soak, then place one cup of grain in a pot (1-2 quart size), cover with water, swish around with a wooden spoon or your hands, gently pour off the top layer of water (excess debris, perhaps shells of the grain and unwanted grain pieces, even stones). Do this first rinse and then any following rinses, pour through a mesh strainer so as not to lose any grains. Rinse until the water is relatively clear. Place the rinsed grain back in the pot. Add the suggested amount of water, bring to a boil, add a pinch of salt, allow to boil a moment, cover, simmer on *very low* for specified time. Place a flame tamer (Glossary) between the pot and burner to make sure the heat stays very low and evenly distributed – this depends on the stove. It should boil, not rapidly, but *very* gently. Leave the lid on, try not to open for the duration of cooking. When done, allow the grain to set, covered, after the heat has been turned off for 5-10 minutes. This relaxes the grain allowing the steam to settle and moisten the bottom of the pot for easier cleaning as well as enjoying the condensed texture of "bottom" grain.

If I forget the amount of time it has been cooking, I will scratch the bottom of the pot with a chopstick and if water bubbles up, it's not done. If I feel stickiness at the bottom, meaning grain is starting to adhere to the bottom of the pot, it is done. If it's been cooking for a long time and there is still water, turn the heat up to let the excess liquid cook off. If the grain sticks to the bottom too much, taste it. Is it too dry? Add a bit of water and let simmer another 10 or so minutes. When ready to serve, scoop with a wooden spoon from the top all the way to the bottom so as to get the full array of texture/energy the grain holds.

This is a basic recipe. Enjoy with Sesame Sprinkle, Salt Brine Pickle, Vegetable Soup (or any soup), sautéed vegetables, in a tortilla, mashed into burgers, blended into a spread, fermented into a yogurt, the ideas are endless.

One cup whole grain yields approximately 2½ cups cooked grain, and lasts 3-5 days in the fridge. Whole grains provide energy, fiber, unprocessed and whole nutrients and a naturally sweet taste.

Use the steaming or boiling water from cooking greens and vegetables to cook your grains, beans, pasta, soups or to blend in sauces, dips, smoothies, etc. The gluten and starch in whole grains is different from refined grains. Organic, unprocessed, whole grain contains the seed, bran, germ, fiber – the whole food with its whole food complexes that work synergistically providing nutrition un-surpassed by any other food. Whole grain will sprout and grow = live energetic food. Processed foods (even whole grain bread), canned, boxed, organic or not is still processed. Give whole foods most of the room in your life.

Chewing grain 50 and even 100 times per mouthful unleashes a deep, natural – very subtle – "sweetness." This essence rejuvenates and heals; it breaks down the fiber, gluten and nutrients rendering a food rich in pure "fuel" to sustain our active bodies and minds throughout the day. It is relaxing and calming. Chewing makes a simple, lightly seasoned meal, satisfying and complete. I generally chew grain well (100 times/mouthful), and other foods, chew well, but do not count like with grain. It's most important to be mindful with grains.

 A note on Quinoa. I believe it is one of the most important grains to soak and not just rinse. After soaking 12-24 hours, drain completely, then simmer in 1 heaping cup fresh water and a tiny pinch of salt for 15 minutes.

If ever using amaranth, I soak it first, as all grains, but being so small I soak it separately and strain with a very fine mesh strainer. See Glossary for wild rice.

1 cup grain	water or stock	cooking time in minutes
Basmati white rice	1½ cups	25
Basmati, brown	1¾-2 cups	40
Barley, whole	4 cups	60-80
Barley, pearled	2 cups	40-50
Buckwheat, kasha	2 cups	15
Couscous	1½ cups	4-5
Millet	2½-3 cups	35-40
Quinoa	1 (heaping) cup	15-20

Simply Brown Rice

Yield: 2½ cups cooked grain

1 cup short grain organic brown rice
1¾ cups water or broth

Place the rice in a pot (1-2 quart size), pour water over the rice, add a couple teaspoons apple cider vinegar and soak overnight, even for one or several hours, but 12-24 is best. After soaking time, drain water. If no time to soak, just rinse rice and use 2 cups water/broth for cooking (see Cook's Notes).

set on stove, add water or broth, bring to a boil
add a pinch of salt, just a few granules
cover and simmer on <u>very low</u> for 50-60 minutes
place a flame tamer (Glossary) between the pot and burner to
make sure the heat stays very low. It should boil *very* gently
try not to open the lid for the duration of cooking
when done, turn flame off, let sit covered 5-10 minutes

Variations simmered in 1¾-2 cups water or stock (Miscellaneous):
½ cup short or long grain brown rice + ½ cup millet
½ cup long grain brown rice + ½ cup short grain brown rice
¾ cup short or long grain brown or (1 cup white rice) + 1/3 cup quinoa
1 cup rice + ¼ cup amaranth, simmer in 2¼ cups stock = my favorite

How to eat it:
- first, take a mouthful of rice and chew it 50 times
- second, take a mouthful, chew it 100 times . . . just try it to see how it feels. Keep moving it back into your mouth and chew

What to eat it with:
- delicious and simple with Sesame Sprinkle and chopped homemade pickle (Condiments & Seasonings), or sauerkraut (Cultured Salads)
- cut a sheet of nori seaweed in four small squares, roll a bit of rice in it, add a spoon of Creamy Seed Dip or Sesame Sprinkle . . .
- make Rice Yogurt (Miscellaneous) with some of it
- Use in burger recipes such as Rice & Carrot Patties or Black Soybean Spice Patties, etc. (see Patties)

Quick Rice Stir-Fry
"cooking 101" starts here . . .

½ cup red or yellow onion, thinly sliced or 2 scallions, sliced
1 stalk broccoli, peel stem and dice, separate florets
handful snap peas, cut in half or leave whole (or other, see variation)
1 tablespoon shoyu or umeboshi vinegar
½ cup Spicy Tempeh, diced, optional
2 cups cooked brown rice (long or short grain or white basmati)*
1 tablespoon green onion or parsley + roasted pumpkin seeds

heat ¼ cup water in a skillet, add onion, broccoli and peas or other
add shoyu or salt toss and stir-fry 2-3 minutes, then cover
cook covered 2-3 minutes more, check and toss a couple of times
add tempeh and rice, do not stir them in just scatter atop vegetables
cover for 30 seconds-1 minute for the rice to warm
toss and transfer to a serving dish or bowls
sprinkle with minced green onion or parsley (or other fresh herb)
and roasted pumpkin seeds

* see Simply Brown Rice for cooking instructions

This is a basic recipe I use several nights a week for a quick meal. Substitute any vegetables such as cauliflower, carrot and green beans, or parsnip, turnip matchsticks and red onion or leek. Instead of rice use cooked grain or noodles, even cubes of polenta, Magic Millet or spaghetti squash. Instead of tempeh use beans, roasted nuts or seeds, or Walnut Cheesy Sprinkle.

For variation add:
- corn, carrot matchsticks, green beans (with or instead of snap peas)
- Golden Tofu or beans instead of tempeh
- spices: cumin, cayenne, ginger, garlic
- herbs: rosemary, basil or cilantro (at end of cooking)
- Sliced beets (see Tangy Beet Side), diced cabbage and black olives
- whatever is in the fridge

Roasted Rice

light, fragrant, delicious . . .

Roasting or browning grain changes the sticky chewiness it naturally has to a lighter texture and nutty taste. It is great for stir-fries and pilafs since the grain separates and tosses well with vegetables, seeds and dried fruits.

> 1 cup grain: brown rice, long or short grain, or ½ millet + ½ rice
> 2¼ cups water or broth

soak the grain overnight (if using millet soak together) see Cook's Notes
place in a dry skillet on medium-high heat
let it get hot and you will hear it crackle as the water burns off
toss often, when crackling stops turn flame down to medium-low
sauté this grain 12-15 minutes, stir frequently! It can burn easily
boil water or broth in a pot with a pinch of salt
when grain is browned and smells roasted, pour it into the hot water
careful, it will immediately boil over, take it off the heat as you do this
cover and simmer 50 minutes. Fluff with a fork when done.

Roasted Sesame Rice with Peas

> 1 cup long grain brown rice
> 2 cups broth/stock
> ½ cup sesame seeds, see Cook's Notes for soaking seeds
> 1 teaspoon cumin seeds or ½ teaspoon cumin powder
> 2 teaspoons fresh turmeric root, minced or ½ teaspoon powder
> 1 cup green peas
> lemon, cut in wedges, fresh parsley and/or green onion, minced

prepare rice as above in Roasted Rice, use broth instead of water
rinse sesame seeds, roast in a dry skillet, 10 minutes, stir often
add cumin seeds, turmeric and ½ teaspoon salt, sauté 5 minutes
stir sesame and spice into the rice, cover, continue to simmer
when the rice has cooked 45 minutes, add peas on top, cover
simmer until rice is done, turn heat up to boil any remaining liquid off
garnish with lemon wedges, parsley or green onion

The spices are optional, it's great just rice, sesame seeds and peas.

Pan-Fried Mochi

Mochi is made from sweet brown rice. It has a natural mild sweet taste and rich heavy texture. It melts like cheese if put between layers of moist foods then heated. It can be pan-fried and added to soups or plain dipped in apple sauce, baked in the oven until puffed, grated into casseroles, or cut in thin strips and placed on a well-greased waffle iron.

> ¼-½ package mochi, plain or flavored
> oil: olive, coconut, or sesame

cut mochi in 1-inch cubes, or smaller if making for soup
wipe a dry skillet *very lightly* with oil, heat on medium-low
fry mochi on all sides until golden, puffed yet soft in the middle

- dip in mixture of heated maple/rice syrup, shoyu and rice vinegar
- nice in Miso Soup, Creamy Onion Soup (or any soup)

Mochi Melts   Yield: 6 melts

Vegetable filled pancakes for a meal or snack, chewy, sweet, and filling. A bit difficult because mochi is sticky, but don't let that stop you from trying them.

> 1 small carrot, matchsticks
> ½ cup onion, diced or thin slices
> 1 cup green beans, cut in 1 inch lengths or shredded cabbage
> shoyu to taste, sesame or coconut oil for lightly greasing pan
> 1¼ cups mochi, roughly grated
> 6 small slices (1"x 1" and thin) cooked polenta, optional

sauté carrot, onion, green beans/cabbage in a skillet in ¼ cup water
add shoyu to taste, cover, simmer 10 minutes then set aside
wipe that skillet out, wipe warmed skillet *very lightly* with oil, arrange ¼ cup of mochi in a 2-inch sized circle, repeat to total 2-3 in the pan
place a few tablespoons vegetable sauté on top, then a piece of polenta
top with 2 tablespoons mochi, cover, cook 2-3 minutes
flip over, sprinkle a bit of water on top of each pancake to soften the mochi, cover and cook a few minutes
gently remove, repeat with rest of ingredients. Enjoy immediately

Nori Rolls (vegetable sushi)   Yield: four rolls

rolled gems, incredible nutrition . . .

1 carrot and/or zucchini
½ cup leftover miso soup, water, or other broth
4 sheets nori seaweed, roasted or raw
3 cups cooked short grain brown rice, basmati white, or millet
1 avocado, sliced, optional
½ cucumber, sliced in thin strips or thinly sliced purple cabbage
2 dill pickles or homemade pickle (Condiments) or sauerkraut
1 recipe Dipping Sauce, optional, see Sauces*

slice carrots (and/or zucchini) lengthwise in long thin slivers or matchsticks
simmer in miso/water/broth covered, 5 minutes, remove and set aside
Use the leftover cooking liquid to make the dipping sauce if making
place 1 sheet nori, shiny side down, indent lines vertical, on a bamboo mat
dampen hands, spread ¾ cup rice evenly, leaving ½ inch border at the top nearest you, and 1 inch at end farthest from you
middle of nori/rice, place carrot/zucchini, cuke/cabbage, avocado, pickle
beginning at the end nearest you, roll up the mat, pressing firmly against the nori to enclose the filling all the while keeping the end of the mat from rolling into the sushi
continue rolling up to the top, wet the end of the exposed nori to seal it
gently squeeze the mat around the sushi roll, remove the mat and set aside seam-side down, repeat with other rolls
cut roll using a sharp knife into 6-8 pieces
arrange cut side down on platter, enjoy with dipping sauce

* if not using a dipping sauce, add a bit of mustard or umeboshi paste (or umeboshi vinegar) at the top end nearest you before rolling up

They store well in the fridge but will sweat and become soggy if the cover of the container is sealed tightly (so leave a corner of the cover loose), or if wrapped in a plastic bag, roll it in a paper towel then in the plastic bag.

(cont'd next page)

For variation add:
- Spicy Tempeh, Golden Tofu, or cooked beans
- peeled broccoli stem, sweet potato or squash: thinly sliced lengthwise and simmered/steamed until almost soft
- nut butter alone or mixed with umeboshi paste or mustard
- umeboshi paste, prepared mustard, wasabi (horseradish)
- sautéed sliced shiitake or other mushrooms
- minced green onion or fresh sprouts, lettuce or arugula greens
- greens raw and/or cooked and chopped
- Sesame Sprinkle or soaked sunflower or pumpkin seeds
- instead of rice try cooked long noodles such as udon or soba
- lay grain on nori sheet, then a large leaf of lettuce, then fillings
- use rice wraps instead of nori, or even a corn or flour tortilla

One of my favorites is to use ½ cup (or less) cooked grain per roll, spread it out on the nori sheet, then add a large amount of vegetables such as: sauerkraut (Cultured Salads), Cultured Confetti Salad, Pickled Cucumber Strips, and/or leftover stir-fry from the night before, etc.

REVERSE SUSHI roll as follows (rice is on outside of nori):
Place half sheet nori on rolling mat, shiny side down. Cover with rice leaving half inch of nori free farthest from you. Sprinkle rice with roasted sesame seeds. Lay a piece of plastic wrap or wax paper (size it the same as the rolling mat) over the rice, then flip whole thing onto rolling mat so plastic wrap is against the mat. A third way down the nori, place fillings horizontally, gently roll up, lightly wet the half inch end of nori and seal. Gently squeeze. You may need to wet your knife each time you cut.

Eating organic is a very important decision to make. It may be more expensive but not when looking at the chemical profile. The amount of nutrients organic food contains doubles that of commercial food. More importantly, organic keeps the chemicals out of the body (as well as the soil and waters). These chemicals create imbalances, cravings, toxicity, weakness and degeneration. The taste of organic is far superior to commercial and local is even better – the less traveling produce is exposed to, the better.

Quinoa or Millet Pilaf

Pilaf is simply a grain browned in oil then cooked in a seasoned broth. I don't always brown the grain but it does add flavor and lightness (see Glossary on how to prepare Quinoa, and Cook's Notes for Soaking Grains).

1-2 cups of liquid is needed: stock, broth, leftover miso soup, or water (1 cup liquid if using quinoa, 2 cups for millet).

> 1 cup quinoa or millet, soaked (if no time, rinsed very well)
> ¼-½ cup almonds, soaked, lightly roasted, then coarsely chopped
> 1 cup parsley, minced
> ½ cup fresh mint, minced, or 1 tablespoon dry mint
> juice of 1 lemon
> ½ apple, diced (green or other firm apple) or Bosc pear

If browning the grain, do it first (see Roasted Rice for instructions)
bring stock to a boil in a medium pot
simmer grain and stock: 15 minutes for quinoa, 30 minutes for millet
roast almonds (or use soaked and not roasted) then coarsely chop
place parsley, mint, lemon and almonds in a mixing bowl
sauté apple (or pear) with ¼ teaspoon salt, 4 minutes
when grain is done, let steam in covered pot off heat, 5 minutes
add apple to parsley mixture, toss all together with the grain

For variation try this alternative:
> 1 cup diced butternut squash, steamed 4 minutes
> ½ cup each: diced zucchini, onion or leek, and cut radish or green beans
> ½ cup cooked garbanzo beans or 2 tablespoons roasted sunflower seeds
leave squash in steamer and sprinkle it with 1 teaspoon umeboshi vinegar
add vegetables to the squash in the steamer, sprinkle with umeboshi vinegar
steam 5-8 more minutes. Toss this into the cooked millet/quinoa
season with lemon, instead of mint use minced green onion, thyme or savory
add beans and/or seeds if desired

Also for variation: use half recipe of Roasted Rice and ½ cup cooked wild rice(see Glossary) instead of quinoa or millet.

Stuffed Squash

Yield: 2 servings

harvest of apple, walnuts, celery & onion . . .

Whichever grain you choose in this recipe is a winner, all nutritious, gluten-free, and interesting. Both buckwheat and quinoa are complete proteins; millet is high in magnesium and is a "heart healthy" grain.

>   1 acorn or delicata squash cut in half, or 2 thick slices of choice
>   ¾ cup walnuts or pecans, soaked (see Cook's Notes for soaking nuts)
>   ½ cup apple, minced, or/and 2-3 dry apricots, chopped
>   1 rib celery, minced
>   2 tablespoons light miso or 1 tablespoon shoyu
>   1 cup cooked millet, buckwheat or quinoa

remove seeds, steam squash cut side down, 15 minutes, or bake (375°) squash in a pan that has a bit of water in it, until medium-soft (20-30 minutes)
rinse nuts (if not soaking), roast in a dry skillet, then finely chop
when squash is done, save steaming/baking liquid
scoop out some of the flesh leaving about ¼ inch in shell
mix scooped-out squash with nuts, apple, celery, miso/shoyu and grain
fill squash, place in a baking dish, add a splash of water to the pan
bake 30 minutes in 375° oven* then brown the tops under a broiler

* if you don't want to bake it, just sauté the ingredients and fill the cooked squash (which is generally what I do).

Prepare sauce (optional):
>   1 small red onion or white part of a leek, minced (¾ cup)
>   1 tablespoon flour (I use rice)
>   fresh basil or thyme, optional and green onion or parsley as garnish

simmer onion/leek in rest of squash steaming liquid (add water to make 1¼ cups) with pinch of salt for 5 minutes
whisk flour into sauce, add the fresh herbs if using
simmer 5 more minutes, stir often
remove herbs, ladle sauce over squash, garnish minced onion/parsley

Magic Millet

Millet is a versatile grain, gluten-free, mildly "sweet," and pleasantly yellow in color. Here it is mashed and pressed into a loaf that has many uses: cut and pan-fried like polenta, or diced and added to stuffing, stir-fries, soups, stews, as "bread" in bread puddings, made into Croutons (Miscellaneous), or as the "bread" for Cinnamon Toast (Breakfast).

     1 cup millet, see Cook's Notes for soaking grains
     3 cups water

boil millet and water together in a medium pot, add a pinch of salt
cover and simmer 30-45 minutes, let sit off heat, covered, 5 minutes
mash with a potato masher like mashed potatoes
scoop into a loaf pan, press down evenly, cover with a tea towel
when cool, remove, cut in squares, dice, or slice and grill, or even toast
(if you did not soak the millet then cooking time may be a little longer)

For variation add ¼ teaspoon salt to the simmering millet and:
- 1½-2 cups diced rutabaga or
- 2-3 cups chopped cauliflower

and mash or pulse the cooked mixture in a food processor. Serve like "mashed potatoes" with Ginger Glaze or Mushroom Sauce.

Sweet Rice Balls

These are chewy, dense, nutritious and can replace a craving for a brownie, at least some of the time. They are a fun way to spend a cold, wintery afternoon. If you have a pressure cooker, use it for this. See Cook's Notes for soaking grains and nuts.

> 1 cup <u>sweet</u> brown rice, soaked if possible
> ½ cup short grain brown rice or millet, soaked
> 1½ cups water
> 1 cup walnuts, soaked and dried if possible
> 2 tablespoons dark barley or red miso

rinse rice (and millet), place in a pressure cooker with the water
bring to a boil, add a pinch of salt, bring to pressure for 45 minutes
(if you are boiling it in a pot, use 2 cups water + pinch salt, simmer 1 hour)
rinse walnuts if no time to soak, then roast and finely chop
mix together walnuts and miso in a small bowl, set aside
mash grain well with a potato masher in the pot, it will be very sticky
wet your hands each time and spoon out a heaping tablespoon of grain
mold into small balls, place on a platter
roll each rice ball in walnut/miso mixture, return to platter

Other toppings or fillings (push hole in rice ball, add filling, cover):
- mashed and seasoned cooked squash or lentils
- make a mixture of 2 tablespoons of *each:* roasted and finely ground rolled oats or ground dried crumbs of cornbread, roasted coconut, date sugar, ½ teaspoon cinnamon – grind all together and roll rice balls in it as soon as you make them. If not, the rice balls will dry a bit and the topping will not stick. If doing it too late, roll the balls in rice syrup or coconut milk first.
- Sweet Bean Sauce in Sauces section

Make a platter of these with a few different toppings.

Polenta *with* Caramelized Onions
sunny yellow and light . . .

1 cup corn grits/polenta*
3¼ cups water + 1 teaspoon rosemary
2 red or yellow onions (2½-3 cups), thin slices**
½ cup apple juice
1 tablespoon shoyu or ¼ teaspoon salt
Creamy Seed Dip, Apple Sauce and/or roasted nuts or seeds

rinse the polenta, place in a pot with water and rosemary
bring to a boil while stirring, then cover and *simmer* for 30 minutes
stir the polenta often. When done, scoop into a pie plate or baking dish
smooth with a rubber spatula, let cool and set
slice onions in half, in half again, then slice *very* thin
simmer onions, juice, shoyu/salt in a skillet, covered 20-30 minutes
stir often, they will brown. If they do not, cook a bit longer, uncovered
cut polenta in squares, quickly pan-fry both sides in well-seasoned cast iron
skillet. This step is optional. It can be enjoyed without frying as well
place on a plate, spoon the onions on top

If making this polenta for grilling or anything else, follow the polenta recipe,
the rosemary is optional, allow to cool and cut in thick slices (see Cinnamon
Toast in Breakfast).

Try spreading Bean-Naise on the polenta, then stack the onions on top.

* I soak polenta as well as all other grains. See Cook's Notes for soaking grains.

** see Glossary under onions for cutting technique

Leftover polenta can be used in Three Bean Salad, Scrambled Tofu (or polenta)
see Breakfast, Croutons, or in thin slabs with Mochi Melts as well as added to
many recipes notated throughout under variations.

Millet-Quinoa Dosas

Yield: 36 dosas

This is a fermented pancake of India (traditionally made with rice and dal) eaten as a snack or main meal, often for breakfast with cooked lentils and a chutney. When steamed they are called Idlis. The key is in the fermentation, the batter needs to puff up, so it is almost doubled, which may take longer in winter. Use brown or white rice instead of millet/quinoa if desired. Dosas keep in the fridge up to 2 weeks, they freeze well.

> 1 cup millet *and* 1 cup quinoa
> 2 cups red or brown lentils
> 1 onion, minced or grated (1½ - 2 cups)
> 1 cup peas or corn, or both
> ½ cup chopped cilantro or parsley, optional
> 1 cup cooked black or pinto beans, or black-eye peas, optional
> 1-2 jalapeño peppers, finely chopped, optional
> dash coconut, sesame, or olive oil for greasing skillet if needed

soak overnight, millet, quinoa and lentils in one large bowl, in plenty of water to cover and 2 tablespoons apple cider vinegar
next day, drain, then blend together in a blender with 3 cups fresh water (total), in batches, until *very* smooth, pour into a bowl
ferment 12-24 hours or until batter is puffed up and foamy*
stir in onion, peas and/or corn, herbs, beans and peppers if using
heat a *lightly* greased skillet, pour in ¼-½ cup batter** like pancakes
cook 3 minutes, flip and cook other side 1-2 minutes
set on a cooling rack while making the rest of the dosas. You do not have to cook them all at once, the batter will keep in the fridge several days.

* the batter will discolor, don't worry, just stir it in.
** or they can be steamed (or poached) and are called Idlis; place in small greased cups, steam 8-10 minutes, gently remove with a butter knife.

What to eat them with other than just plain:
- Classic Green Salad, Spicy Lentils and Apple-Apricot Chutney
- Sunflower Dream Cheese and steamed broccoli (the best), or tomatoes
- nut/seed butter and jam

Quinoa Salad

This salad is the same as the Pasta Salad (Noodles) just using quinoa.

Quinoa is best to soak before using. It contains saponins, or its own natural pesticide, see Soaking Grains in Cook's Notes. If you are unable to soak the quinoa, then rinse it very well.

> 1 cup quinoa, soaked or rinsed very well
> 1-1½ cups water/broth (1 cup if using soaked quinoa, 1½ cups if not)

simmer quinoa and water/broth for 15 minutes
let sit 10 or so minutes before tossing with other ingredients
prepare vegetables as in the recipe for Pasta Salad (see Noodles)
mix quinoa and vegetables gently together when done

See Glossary for more information on Quinoa, and Grains chapter for, A note on quinoa, at the end.

Find the energy and desire
to get back to basics,
in the kitchen,
using your hands,
and your teeth –
chew well –
it is the way to
unlock the hidden
flavors and nutrients.
Saliva is naturally alkaline
and begins the digestive process.
Chew whole grains, 50 times each bite . . .
and then more and more and more

Beans

one of the longest cultivated plants . . .

In any recipe that calls for beans, canned are fine if you don't want to cook your own, but preparing your own is best. One cup dry beans yields approximately 2½-3 cups cooked (1 can is approximately 1½ cups).

To soak: sort and discard odd-looking dry beans/peas, stones and debris. Place in a bowl, cover with water, at least three inches over the beans, add a dash of apple cider vinegar and soak overnight, or at least 12-24 hours. In the morning, drain, choose between:

1) cooking right away: place beans in a large pot. For every cup of *dry* beans, add 2-3 cups of water, bring to a boil, lower the flame so it is still boiling, just not going over the top. Skim the foam and discard. Keep it at a hard boil and skim foam off until there is almost none, it takes 5-10 minutes, then add one inch piece of kombu seaweed, cover, turn flame down to a low simmer, cook 45 minutes-1½ hours, depending on the bean. Or pressure cook 15-45 minutes, see also below.

2) sprouting: see Making Sprouts in Miscellaneous. Beans can be used just sprouted and not cooked. But I cook them after in soups, or briefly steam for stir-fries, salads, etc. I find that the texture of certain raw sprouted beans is a bit chalky for my liking. I also believe that briefly cooking them after sprouting enhances digestion. After soaking beans, drain them in a colander, cover with a damp towel and set on kitchen counter, rinse 2 times/day until sprouts form (takes 1-3 days). Barely cover sprouted beans with water, and follow directions as above for cooking right away. Sprouted beans need less water and time, cook until desired softness, pressure cook 5-10 minutes, or steam 15-20 minutes. It depends on the bean, lentils take minutes compared to garbanzo beans, etc.

More often I do the initial soaking then sprout them before cooking.

If at any time more water is needed, boil it first then add to the cooking beans. If unable, just add the water gently down the *inside side* of the pot. During the length of cooking, stirring is not needed. Just let them gently simmer, keep covered, and let them cook.

The high mineral content of kombu balances the protein of the bean making them easier to digest. Adding half an apple, epasote (a Spanish herb), ginger, turmeric, or fennel to the cooking beans can also help.

It is not necessary to soak lentils, peas, adzuki or mung beans, but I do anyway if time permits. You can also cook lentils and adzuki in their cooking water if desired though generally I use fresh water. Sometimes I add an inch of fresh ginger root and a couple of dried shiitake mushrooms to the beans as they cook. Then, at the end of cooking discard the ginger, slice the mushroom and return to the pot.

I do not add salt or spices to the cooking beans until near the end in the last 15-30 minutes, it prevents them from softening completely. If the beans are not getting soft after an hour of cooking, they may be old, or the simmering heat was too low, and so, fifteen to thirty minutes of pressure cooking may be needed (or just keep cooking them if no pressure cooker is available).

When cooking beans, I soak 3 cups at a time so I have enough to freeze small batches which saves time (and energy) and offers quick additions to meals. They are also better quality than canned beans. If no time to soak overnight, do a quick soak.

Quick soak: bring the beans and plenty of water to cover them to a rolling boil, turn off heat, cover lightly and let soak one hour. Discard water, add fresh water and follow directions as above for cooking right away.

PRESSURE COOKING
I do not pressure cook often, the *energy* produced in the food can be tightening in the body (see Glossary under pressure cooker). Yet beans are an exception, under pressure they cook up soft and quick. Follow the same directions as above, scoop off foam, then cover and wait until pressure is full before turning heat to very low, cook 10-30 minutes (depending on the bean), turn off heat, let sit until pressure releases (or manually release it). See Resources for a book on pressure cooking.

See Spreads, Dips, & Salsa for bean dips (such as Hummus, Lentil Walnut Paté, White Bean Dip, etc.), Noodles with Greens & Beans, Patties, and Index under Tofu and Tempeh for recipes containing them.

Indian Lentils & Greens

1 cup green lentils, rinsed and/or soaked (see Cook's Notes)
1 inch piece kombu seaweed
8-10 crimini mushrooms, quartered or sliced (about 3 cups)
½ teaspoon salt
2-3 cups greens, chopped (collard, bok choy, turnip/radish greens)
1 cup Oat Yogurt (blended smooth), or other

simmer the lentils and kombu in 2½-3 cups water until soft, 1 hour
sauté the mushrooms, salt, 5-8 minutes
when the lentils are soft, strain, remove 1 cup for another use
layer greens, then lentils on top of the mushrooms, simmer 10 minutes
turn off heat and stir in the oat yogurt

For variation: add the seasonings below in the last 5 minutes of cooking:
¼ cup fresh cilantro, chopped
½ teaspoon cumin
pinch of clove *and* cinnamon

If not cooking lentils, use 1 can. Instead of Oat Yogurt, try Savory Rice Cheez Spread without the basil and add 1 teaspoon lemon juice, or use thick coconut milk with lemon juice as well.

Spicy Lentils

1½-2 cups onion, finely diced
¼ cup fresh cilantro, chopped
1 teaspoon cumin + pinch clove and cinnamon
¼ teaspoon *each:* cayenne and coriander

cook lentils as in Indian Lentils, omit mushrooms, yogurt and greens
sauté onion in broth or water (just enough to prevent burning) 5 minutes
add spices to onion, sauté another moment
strain lentils when they are done and stir them into the onion mix, simmer 5 or so minutes. Serve as is or blend half and mix it together. Great with Millet-Quinoa Dosas, rice or noodles.

Black & Tan

real, earthy talented fare . . .

This is a traditional macrobiotic recipe, one of the first I ever had. It is rich, mildly sweet and fulfilling with fresh steamed rice and Skillet Greens. *Black soybeans* are available (canned) at most health food stores (by Eden). You can substitute regular black beans or any other bean in this recipe, but Black Soybeans have a healing quality and a fresh, simple taste (see Glossary).

> 1 cup dry chestnuts*, soak in 2 cups water overnight
> 1 can black soybeans
> 1 inch piece kombu, soaked, then cut in small pieces
> 1 tablespoon molasses, 2-3 tablespoons rice syrup or ¼ cup apple butter
> ¼ teaspoon salt

place the soaked chestnuts with their soaking water in a medium sized pot
add another cup of water, bring to a boil and simmer one hour
add beans and their juice, kombu, molasses or apple butter and salt
cover and simmer 30 minutes more or until the chestnuts are soft
when soft, uncover and let excess liquid boil off, let it bubble and thicken
taste and adjust, may want more sweetener

* if unable to soak the chestnuts overnight, do as long as possible and remove any dark skin that may be lodged in the veins. If using bottled or already cooked chestnuts (about 1½ cups) simmer together with the soybeans, kombu, and salt in enough water for 15 minutes.

By the way, sometimes I find chestnuts to take a long time to cook depending on how old they are, and therefore will pressure cook them to get them soft.

What to eat it with:
- rice or millet, steamed greens, Miso Soup
- mixed into shell or elbow pasta with Rainbow Pressed Salad
- use one cup of it mashed into your favorite brownie or cake recipe!
- Corn Bread, Green Salad, Matchstick-Cut Stir-Fry
- mixed into any soup

"Baked" Beans

A mouthful of these sweet, soft, dense beans is rather pleasing. I do not bake this dish – I don't bake often because baked foods tend to be contracting in the body. *For the Love of Eating* is about healing through digestion, so lighter methods such as steaming, sautéing, braising and blanching are suggested more often. These beans simmered in a cast iron skillet develops a rich sweetness which is so satisfying – and even better the next day.

> 1 onion, chopped or finely diced (1-1½ cups), see Glossary
> ¾-1 cup burdock root, shaved (see Glossary), or small diced
> 2 carrots, diced (1 cup)
> 2 teaspoons barley or red miso
> 1 tablespoon umeboshi vinegar
> 3 cups cooked navy or pinto beans (or a mix)
> 1 tablespoon prepared mustard (stone-ground)
> 1½-2 tablespoons molasses, barley malt, or 1/3 cup apple butter
> 1 teaspoon shoyu, optional

sauté the onion and burdock in a skillet in ½ cup water, 10 minutes
simmer the carrots in a pot in ½ cup water and pinch of salt, 10 minutes
when the carrots are soft, blend until smooth with ½ cup of the onion sauté and the miso and vinegar
then pour it into the onion sauté along with the rest of the ingredients
simmer 10 minutes, let bubble, stir occasionally

For variation:
- use Light Miso or Quick & Easy Dressing (both in Salad Dressings) instead of the carrot sauce and seasonings; for a quick version omit carrot sauce
- try black eye peas, lima beans, and/or pinto beans

What to eat them with:
- steamed or blanched collards, kale, bok choy or cabbage
- rice or Corn Bread and steamed vegetables
- Carrot, Jicama & Pear Salad, Wilted Kale Salad, or Cultured Confetti with Arame, Greek 'n' Tangy Cuke 'n' Carrot

Adzuki Beans & Squash
traditional, nutty, warming

Adzuki beans are a small red bean, high in protein like most beans, yet low in fat and one of the easier beans to digest. This is a winning combination with winter squash. Leave the skin on the squash, it cooks up thick, its texture dense and earthy. Truly a nutrition packed, calming, grounding dish.

> 1 cup adzuki beans, soak in 3 cups water overnight
> 1 inch piece kombu seaweed
> 2 cups winter squash, diced (kabocha or butternut)

strain most of the water out of the beans, place in a pot
add 2 cups fresh water to cover, and kombu
bring to a boil, simmer 20-30 minutes
place the squash gently on top, do not stir in
add a pinch of salt (or up to ¼ teaspoon), or 2 teaspoons umeboshi vinegar
cover and simmer another 20 minutes until soft, toss gently and serve

Enjoy with lightly steamed vegetables and Creamy Seed Dip (made with pumpkin seeds), Nori Rolls and a cultured salad.

Variations:
- leftovers can be mashed with cooked grain and vegetables and pan-fried into patties or used in Sweet Adzuki bean topping under Sweet Rice Balls (Grains)
- rolled into tortillas with avocado and sauerkraut
- use any bean such as lentil, mung, lima, navy (last two may need a bit more simmering before adding the squash)
- use Japanese sweet potato or other, rutabaga, Jerusalem artichoke or parsnip in place of or along with the squash
- pour cooked mixture into a casserole dish, make Corn Bread batter and dollop on top, bake, enjoy with Ranch Dressing, Tofu Sour Cream, or Creamy Seed Dip and steamed vegetables
- add sliced leeks to the beans just before placing the squash on top.

Three Bean Salad

It's so good that you'll have to stop yourself from eating too much because even if beans are cooked right and chewed well, we all know what happens when we eat too many of them. Scoop this into crisp romaine or Boston/butter lettuce leaves and compliment with a cultured salad.

1½ cups cooked adzuki beans or 1 can
1½ cups cooked black beans or 1 can
2 cups cubed polenta*
1 cup green beans, cut or snap stem end off
1 cup red (or yellow) onion, chopped, see Glossary under Onion
1 tablespoon shoyu
2 teaspoons stone-ground mustard
1/3 cup liquid from the adzuki beans if possible or other
3 dates, chopped or ¼ cup apple sauce
1 tablespoon light miso
1 tablespoon minced green onion

If cooking beans use 1 cup dried of each and follow the directions in Beans.

drain beans and save 1/3 cup liquid of the adzuki beans
set the beans and polenta in a bowl
steam the green beans 10 minutes, then cut in 1 inch pieces
combine onions, shoyu, mustard, dates if using and bean liquid in a small saucepan, simmer until onion is just soft, 3-4 minutes
mix in apple sauce if using, and pour this and the green beans in with the beans/polenta and toss gently, sprinkle the green onion on top

* see Polenta with Caramelized Onions to make polenta

For variation:
-   instead of green beans use peas, snap peas cut in half, pea sprouts, garbanzo or any other cooked bean
-   toss in minced parsley and black olives
-   add Pan-Seared Apple

Pinto Bean Zambullida

Zambullida is Spanish for dip or dive as in the verb, but I couldn't resist. Simmered with squash, mochi, and onion, then seasoned with cumin and lemon, it's simple, it's satisfying, it's a meal . . . but really it's a dip.

> 1 cup winter squash, grated (medium or large grate)
> ½ onion, chopped
> ½ cup mochi, diced
> 2 cups cooked pinto beans
> 1 cup cooked rice
> 1 teaspoon cumin
> 2 teaspoons umeboshi vinegar
> ½ cup salsa, optional
> 2 tablespoons parsley and 1 green onion, chopped
> fresh lemon or lime, 1 avocado, diced (optional)

sauté squash and onion in 1 cup water in a skillet, 5 minutes
add mochi, beans and rice, do not stir, just scatter on top
sprinkle with cumin and umeboshi vinegar
cover, simmer 5 minutes more until mochi is almost melted, gently stir
add a bit of salsa on top
sprinkle the parsley/green onion and squirt of lemon on top + avocado
serve as is in the hot skillet, just place on a hot pad on the table

Delicious with Seed Crackers or rolled in steamed corn tortillas.

Variations:
-   for a simpler version of a similar dip, see Skillet Bean Dip
-   use any cooked bean: black, black-eyed peas, lentil, navy, kidney
-   add chopped cilantro, fresh lime, bell pepper or jalapeño
-   add fresh basil, ripe summer tomatoes and cucumber at the end
-   bake this with grated mochi, crumbled tofu or Tofu Sour Cream, chopped greens until melted; top with a chopped mixture of arugula greens, lime/lemon, cucumber, onion, black olives
-   simmer the onion, beans, rice and spices for a quick dip
-   mix in Carrot Ketchup for an eclectic Sloppy Joe

Split Pea, Pinto & Black

simple, rich, filling, creative . . .

In one of my many lifetimes working in a health food store, I would often get bags of beans or grain that were mistakenly mixed together and left on the staff table. Experimenting with creative combinations such as this one, gave me ideas for exciting, new dishes.

> 1 cup *each* pinto beans and black beans
> ½ cup split peas
> 2 inch piece kombu seaweed

soak beans and peas overnight in separate bowls
drain the soaked beans/peas, place in pressure cooker with 8 cups water
bring to a boil for 10 minutes, scoop off foam, add the kombu
cover and bring to pressure for 30 minutes
when done, allow pressure to release naturally, uncover, test for softness
cool completely, store in fridge or freeze in batches

If not pressure cooking, then simply boil the beans/peas, stir on occasion, watch the water, it may need more. They cook up creamy and rich, and are great in Red Chili Spaghetti, Warm & Sassy Bean Chili. Enjoy plain with a little seasoning of choice, minced green onion and hot rice, millet, noodles, in any soup, with tortillas, or use in recipe below.

Quick Beans

> 1 onion, cut in half, in quarters, then thinly sliced across the grain
> 1 zucchini, cut in matchsticks
> salt or umeboshi vinegar to taste
> 2 cups cooked red beans or other
> ½ teaspoon *each:* cumin and chili powder

sauté onion and zucchini in ¼ cup water and salt/vinegar to taste
after 5-8 minutes, add beans and spices
enjoy as is or pulse in food processor for great refried beans

Warm & Sassy Bean Chili

Ever since I was a kid, the absolute treat on a winter day of skiing was to go to the half-way house at Thunder chairlift in Jackson Hole for a bowl of hot chili. It was from a can, which we never had at home, as well as having meat in it, which we didn't eat . . . .but it was better than anything. This fills its place completely!

  ¼ cup beet, diced
  1 cup butternut squash or other, diced (if no squash use carrot)
  1-2 cloves garlic, roughly chopped
  1 red or yellow onion, diced (1-1½ cups), see Glossary under onions
  2-3 teaspoons shoyu or ¼ teaspoon salt, or to taste
  4 cups cooked pinto and black beans*
  1 tablespoon chili powder
  1 teaspoon green chili powder, optional
  ½ teaspoon cumin powder
  2-3 teaspoons umeboshi vinegar

simmer beet and squash in water to cover until soft
pour into a blender, add garlic, and blend until very creamy
simmer onions, shoyu or salt and ¼ cup water in a medium pot
after 5 minutes of simmering, pour in beet/squash sauce
add beans, spices, and seasonings, simmer 5 minutes
garnish with nutritional yeast, green onion OR minced green onion mixed with finely ground roasted pumpkin seeds (see Pumpkin Parmesan in Condiments.

* see Split Pea, Pinto & Black in Beans. Or use one can of each, or bean of choice (adzuki, pinto, white, or/and black).

For variation:
-   add diced bell pepper or/and zucchini, celery, or fresh fennel to the simmering onions

Blackened Tofu

Cajun, lime, garlic & cilantro

1# firm tofu, cut in ¼ inch strips then in small pieces
2 tablespoons shoyu
3 tablespoons Cajun spice (or its alternate), see Miscellaneous
1 orange and 1 lime, juices only
1 tablespoon apple cider vinegar or rice vinegar
6-8 cloves garlic, chopped
½ cup fresh cilantro, chopped, optional
1 onion, chopped
2 ribs celery, diced
1 red pepper diced or small zucchini sliced in thin quarter moons

place tofu in a skillet, cover with water, cook on high 4 minutes
drain excess liquid and add the shoyu, sauté 8 minutes
add Cajun spice, citrus juices, vinegar and garlic
add cilantro, onion, celery, and green pepper or zucchini
sauté 5-8 more minutes adding water/broth if needed
Best on a bed of white basmati rice.

Jerk Tofu

For a different kick, try this with a few changes. Use ingredients above, but
omit citrus juices and vinegar and use this spice mix (instead of the Cajun):

1 tablespoon allspice, pinch cinnamon
as much hot pepper (habanera, jalapeño) as you can take
1 teaspoon thyme, ¼ teaspoon sage
1 large bunch green onions, minced
½ cup apple juice

combine these spices, garlic, green onions, shoyu and juice
stir this into the tofu after initial water sauté, cook a few minutes, then
add the vegetables, and cook until just soft

I often freeze the tofu first (great texture), thaw, squeeze out, and use as above.

Patties

Once a week I make patties from leftovers or fresh made grain and/or beans. They are easy to make, so satisfying combining a chewy, dense texture, fabulous flavor and everyone likes them.

They freeze well and can be popped into a toaster to re-heat. We love them with Carrot Ketchup that I make and freeze in small batches to have on hand, with or without mustard, Bean-naise or Sun Dried Tomato Mayo, or Sunflower Dream Cheese. They are great for morning snacks (sort of like a mid-morning muffin, see Morning Mashers).

Cut patties in slices, lay in a tortilla with diced onion, finely grated mochi and cooked winter squash or grated carrot, fold tortilla and heat in a skillet with a dash of water. Add sliced avocado and lettuce, a dollop of Sunflower Dream Cheese, Hummus or drizzle of Salad Dressing.

I use coconut, sesame or olive oil to grease a pan. I do it usually once, and then perhaps again when half of the patties are done. I know certain oils withstand higher temperatures, but I don't think it's good to heat any oil. I keep very little oil in the house, usually one or two varieties in the fridge since I use it rarely. Keep its use to a minimum. Cast iron skillets need very little oil and cook patties (and just about everything), beautifully.

If patties aren't working, see Glossary under Troubleshooting.

For the Love of Eating is a journey towards independence and self-healing. Most of us say we eat well, but do we? Do we know that salting food (and not cooking the salt in), eating meat, cheese and bread in excess (everyday), drinking liquids with meals, craving fruit or sweets after a meal, eating standing up or on "the run," eating canned, frozen, boxed, prepared foods, drinking soy, rice or nut milks endlessly to satisfy the need for milk, or soy hotdogs and processed soy "meats" and "cheeses" lead to the degenerative conditions that plague our society. Whether it be cancer, depression, sore joints or dandruff – we create our conditions.

Millet Patties

Yield: 13-15 patties

From a light snack to a hearty meal, these are great alone or in a tortilla with Mustard, Carrot Ketchup, lettuce, onion, etc. Try to soak millet before using, see soaking grains (Cook's Notes).

> 1 cup millet, rinsed, placed in a pot with 3 cups water
> 1 cup onion, minced and 1 rib celery, finely diced
> 1 large or 2 medium carrots, grated
> 2 tablespoons flax seeds
> 3-6 tablespoons sesame <u>or</u> sunflower seeds, raw or roasted
> ¼ teaspoon cayenne pepper or 2 teaspoons pepper flakes
> 1 tablespoon dulse flakes, optional
> ½ teaspoon *each* thyme, sage, cumin OR 1 teaspoon *each* basil, dill

bring the millet to a boil, add a pinch of salt, cover, simmer 35 minutes*
sauté onion, celery and carrot in a skillet in ¾ cup water + 1 teaspoon salt
grind flax and sesame/sunflower seeds *finely* in a coffee grinder
add seeds and seasonings to vegetables, toss, set aside in a bowl
when millet is done, mash with a potato masher in the pot
stir the vegetable/spice mixture into the millet, cover
heat a cast iron skillet on medium heat, wipe it very lightly with oil if needed
have a small bowl of water next to you and wet your hands in it, then
scoop ½ cup of the millet mixture, roll into a ball
flatten, place in skillet, wet your hands each time, it makes a smooth patty
Or use an ice-cream scoop, dip in water each time, and flatten patty
pan-fry until golden, 5-10 minutes each side. I oil the skillet once during cooking, and sometimes again half-way through if needed

* may add 1 teaspoon minced fresh turmeric or rosemary to the cooking millet.

For variation, use the millet mixture as:
- a stuffing for baked onions or squash (before frying the millet mixture)
- as "meatballs" on pasta (mold into balls and pan-fry like the patties) or "falafel" type balls with a Creamy Seed Dip or Sunflower Dream Cheese
- see Millet Log Appetizers (Snacks, Wraps, Sandwich)

Rice & Adzuki Bean Patties
Yield: 15 patties

strong, nutty, and perfectly combined . . .

I love any combination of grain, beans or seeds and minced vegetables molded into a patty and pan-fried, smothered in Sunflower Dream Cheese or Carrot Ketchup and eaten just like that still standing at the counter.

> 1 cup cooked rice
> 2 cups cooked adzuki beans, drained from any liquid
> 2 cups broccoli (peeled stems and florets)
> 2 leaves of kale, collards, or other
> 2 teaspoons chili powder + 1 tablespoon shoyu
> ½ onion, grated (about ½ cup)

pulse onions, greens and broccoli in a food processor until minced
add rice and pulse, then beans and pulse. Transfer to a mixing bowl
season with chili powder and shoyu
form into patties, pan fry both sides until just browned on medium low
allow to cool and air on cooling racks

These are a bit mushy, and better warm, not hot, even without the seasonings. Place in a tortilla with grated carrots or beet, lettuce, and Creamy Seed Dip. Experiment with seasonings, a dash of basil or oregano.

This is a loose recipe with room to experiment. Mashing together any grain and beans with ground seeds or nuts, a bit of flour or cornmeal and seasonings, and then pan-frying or baking is an easy and creative way to use up leftovers. Try mashing in cooked squash or sweet potato, whole sunflower seeds, or sautéed mushrooms or leeks.

What to eat them with:
- see Speedy Quesadillas
- dice and toss into curly or elbow pasta
- stone-ground mustard and Carrot Ketchup or Bean-Naise
- in a corn tortilla with avocado and sliced red onion
- with a thick slab of salted in-season, local tomatoes
- Wilted Kale Salad and Creamy Corn Soup

Black Bean Patties

Yield: 16 patties

seeds, squash, and cornmeal crisp

2 cups cooked black beans
1½ cups cooked grain (rice, millet, buckwheat)
¼ cup roasted walnuts or sunflower seeds, ground to a fine meal
1 cup sweet potato or winter squash, diced and steamed until soft
6 green onions, minced Or ¾ cup onion, minced or grated
2 tablespoons arrowroot starch
cornmeal

combine all ingredients in a large bowl and mash well
form into patties (if they seem wet, add more arrowroot powder)
place some cornmeal on a plate
coat both sides of patty
pan fry until golden, approximately 8 minutes per side

For variation:
-   use any beans, homemade or canned
-   any grain, just keep in mind that some grains mash and combine better than others. If using quinoa, more of a binding ingredient may be necessary, so increase the ground seeds and arrowroot
-   anything leftover: grated or finely chopped carrot, radish, broccoli, green beans . . . just sauté or steam until soft first
-   spices can be added such as fresh cilantro or dill, and either all or one of (½ teaspoon amount) cumin, pepper, dry mustard, basil

What to eat them with:
-   avocado, red onion and cucumber tossed in lemon
-   stone-ground mustard and Carrot Ketchup
-   Classic Green Salad with Sesame Dressing
-   Crunchy Cabbage Salad, Fresh Broccoli Salad

Rice & Carrot Patties
nori, black pepper & sunflower seeds

It is rare that I use black pepper, a spice that is somewhat irritating to the liver and can be overly stimulating, even though it contains piperine, an alkaloid shown to increase the bioavailability of nutrients in food. But it adds flavor, as well as enhancing these simple patties in to a gourmet treat.

> 2 cups cooked short grain brown rice
> 1 cup finely shredded carrot
> ½ cup roasted sunflower or pumpkin seeds, *finely ground*
> salt and black pepper to taste
> 1 sheet roasted nori, tor n or cut into small pieces

combine all ingredients in a bowl, knead with hands
add a very small amount of water, a tablespoon at a time, keep it just moist
squeeze this "batter" through your fingers until blended
form into small thin patties
pan fry both sides until golden

What to eat them with:
- stone-ground mustard, Carrot Ketchup or Bean-Naise
- bread with mustard, Seared Zucchini & Onion
- Creamy Seed Dip and Easy Steamed Vegetables
- Hummus and Classic Green Salad
- Noodle Soup, Adzuki or Black Bean Soup
- Tangy Beet Side and Jade Green
- Sweet Winter Squash or any steamed vegetables such as Green Bean Vinaigrette, Nourishing Root Braise . . .

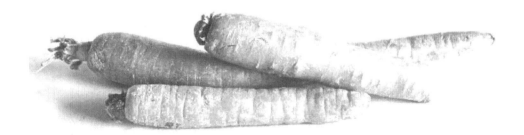

Black *Soy*Bean Spice Patties   Yield: 14 patties
purple cabbage, chili & garlic

This is my favorite burger. Maybe because it gets a good amount of red cabbage into me, but more likely because lathered in Sun Dried Tomato Mayonnaise or Avo Mayo . . . they are delicious . . . as anything would be!

> 3 cups red cabbage, very finely minced in a food processor*
> ½ teaspoon salt
> 1 can black *soy*beans, drained
> 1 cup cooked rice or millet
> 1 heaping teaspoon garlic powder or 4-6 garlic cloves, chopped
> 1-2 teaspoons chili flakes or ½ teaspoon cayenne powder, to taste
> 3 tablespoons flour, I use rice flour

sauté the red cabbage in a skillet with the salt and ½ cup water, 5 minutes
pulse beans and grain in a processor until well combined (like hummus)
add the beans, rice, garlic and cayenne to the cabbage, sauté a moment
mix in flour, let sit a few moments off heat
rinse the pan you just used for the cabbage (or use a clean one), wipe it very lightly with oil and pan fry each side until just browned

* after mincing, the cabbage will measure 2 heaping cups

I have made this recipe with quinoa instead of rice, and it does not bind into a burger, but it makes an interesting and creative hamburger-like filling/stuffing to be used in chili, stuffed peppers, onions or squash. I pan-fried it anyway and rolled the broken pieces in corn tortillas.

For variation:
-   use any cooked beans
-   instead of red cabbage, use green, or a combination of other finely minced vegetables such as leek, parsnip, green beans, sweet potato
-   use cooked polenta instead of rice
-   add more spice, garlic, cumin, and minced cilantro

Quinoa & Portobello Patties   Yield: 13-15 patties

classy, rich protein, and tasty . . .

1 cup quinoa, see soaking grains in Cook's Notes
1 heaping cup water or broth/stock
1½ cups onion, chopped
2 Portobello mushrooms, diced (include stem), 2-3 cups
2 tablespoons shoyu
1/3 cup sunflower seeds, sun-dried or roasted, *very* finely ground*
¼ cup flour (I use rice) or arrowroot powder (or half and half)

If unable to soak quinoa overnight or at least for a few hours, then rinse very well, place in a pot with water/stock

bring quinoa to a boil, add a pinch of salt, cover and simmer 15 minutes
sauté onion, mushroom and shoyu, covered, 5 minutes
pulse in a food processor, add quinoa and pulse a few more times
place in bowl, add the ground seeds and flour and/or arrowroot
pan-fry each side on lightly greased skillet 4-5 minutes until browned

If using already cooked quinoa, you'll need 2½-3 cups, and if dry from sitting in the fridge, steam first to get it soft and moist. When I form patties, I scoop with an ice cream scoop and flatten with damp hands. See troubleshooting in Glossary if having trouble with the patties.

What to eat them with:
- a Cultured Salad or sauerkraut and stone-ground mustard
- Classic Green Salad, Creamy Broccoli Soup
- Green Bean or Artichoke Vinaigrette (Vegetables)
- Savory Cauliflower & Broccoli
- Easy Steamed Vegetables or steamed greens

* see Soaking seeds in Cook's Notes, and roasting in Glossary

See note on quinoa in Grains (near the end) for cooking it, and Glossary for more information on quinoa. See soaking seeds in Cook's Notes for sunflower seeds. I soak them, then let them dry or lightly dry roast them.

Noodles

"Life is a combination of magic and pasta . . ."
Federico Fellini

I love to hike in the mountains. I've been doing it all my life. It gets me away from civilization – people, cars, noise, my cluttered studio. I can remember what life is really all about. After a long hard hike, a cold swim in a mountain lake, a simple lunch of carrots and Nori Rolls, I drive home and make noodles. It is one of the most satisfying meals I can think of. It nourishes me on every level, and can be prepared quickly since I am usually starving after a day in the high altitudes.

Noodles are primarily flour and water, and some with the addition made with eggs, but not necessarily, sometimes potato and vegetables. Just about every culture has a classic type and recipe. I use only whole grain varieties such as the Japanese Soba and Udon (which contain wheat, though soba is made with just buckwheat, or buckwheat and wheat, read the label if sensitive to gluten), as well as those made from only organic brown rice, or corn and quinoa. Avoid white flour, it is an extremely degenerative and toxic substance. Whole wheat noodles are fine, and though I am not intolerant to wheat, I find them heavy and don't use them.

When I am hungry and don't want to chew a lot, and just want to eat, I often make noodles – cold or warm, in soup or mixed with sauce, or tossed in a salad. I know there are raw varieties made with summer squash, and that is fine, but there is nothing like the real thing.

When I studied and worked at the Kushi Institute, I learned the benefits of Japanese noodles. They are processed differently, both in ingredient and method. Soba is made with buckwheat flour, which contains protein and rutin, a necessary bioflavonoid and powerful antioxidant. Udon is made from wheat or spelt, and when combined with broth it is called dashi, an excellent cold/flu buster (see Noodle Soup).

Also see in Condiments & Seasoning the recipe, Shoyu Pickle with Rutabaga & Carrot, in the blurb following the title, you'll find a quick and tasty noodle dish.

Cilantro Walnut Pesto with Noodles

Yield: 1½ cups
> ¾ cup walnuts* or pine nuts, roasted, see Roasting in Glossary
> 2 teaspoons umeboshi vinegar
> 1 bunch cilantro or basil, 4 cups loosely packed
> ½ cup parsley or arugula, optional
> 2 tablespoons onion or 1 green onion, roughly chopped
> 1 large garlic clove, chopped
> 1 tablespoon white miso
> 4-6 tablespoons water/broth
> noodles of choice, cooked

blend walnuts and vinegar until smooth in a food processor
add rest of ingredients, except water/broth
while it blends add small amounts of water or broth
omit miso if desired and use salt
If it turns out chunky, transfer to a blender for a creamier pesto.
toss with your favorite pasta

I always use cilantro because it is my favorite. Using a mix with basil and parsley, even the soft tops of fresh fennel is nice too.

* or sunflower, pumpkin, or sesame seeds, soaked and roasted (see Cook's Notes for soaking nuts and seeds), or simmer the seeds in water for 10 minutes before blending with other ingredients (if using seeds, you may want to use a blender instead of a food processor to get it smooth).

Using no nuts (or seeds), it can be a very light pesto, my favorite kind actually. If doing this, give it a little substance with a handful of steamed collard or kale greens (see Greens Pesto in Sauces).

For variation:
- see Greens Pesto in Sauces
- use all basil or all arugula instead of cilantro and parsley

Red Chili Spaghetti

I had cooked up a batch of pinto and black beans, and they were really soft and needed to be mixed into something. This is a really quick meal if you have the Red Chili Sauce made. However, a cup of salsa or Italian Sauce will do. Just taste and adjust any seasonings.

   1# spaghetti pasta, cooked and set aside
   1½ cups pinto/black beans*, well cooked
   1 cup Red Chili Sauce
   1-2 green onions or ¼ red onion, minced
   1 clove garlic, minced, optional
   salt or umeboshi vinegar to taste

warm the beans with the chili sauce, onion, garlic and salt/vinegar
toss into the pasta so it is well covered

* see the Beans section for cooking beans, or use one or both, ½ can of each.

"mi espíritu canta,
sus golpes del corazón,
el'amor se encuentra
por todas partes,

mi espíritu canta,
sus golpes del corazon
el'amor es la confianza
la confianza el'amor,
el'amor"

my spirit sings
your heart beats
love is all around
love is found

my spirit sings
your heart beats
love is trust
trust is love
love

Noodles Quick & Easy

1   noodles of choice, cooked
Sesame Sprinkle and/or umeboshi vinegar to taste
ground flax seeds
1-2 tablespoons Salt Brine Pickle or other, chopped
Mix together . . . it's quick and tasty for a fast meal

2   **Garlicky Noodles**
1-3 cloves garlic, minced or finely grated/pressed
umeboshi vinegar to taste
minced green onion, cilantro, parsley, or fresh basil, optional
noodles of choice, cooked
2 cups cut broccoli, steamed 2-4 minutes (or peas, corn, squash)
Whisk together first 3 ingredients in a bowl, add pasta and broccoli.

3   noodles of choice lathered in "Beefy" Lentil Sauce (see Sauces)

4   cooked noodles of choice, cover with Walnut Cheesy
Sprinkle, Easy Steamed Vegetables (just steam some collards or
kale), and a cultured salad . . . toss all together.

5   cooked noodles of choice, toss with nutritional yeast, umeboshi
vinegar, Salt Brine Pickle (chopped), Simply Squash, cooked beans.

6   mince 1 red onion (or yellow), sauté in ¼ cup water and a teaspoon
of umeboshi vinegar (or ¼ teaspoon salt), cover and cook, stirring
often, 15-20 minutes. Place leftover cold and cooked noodles on
top, cover and let steam until warmed. Toss and enjoy plain, or with
Sesame Sprinkle, Walnut Cheesy Sprinkle, or Mac 'n' Cheez Sauce

Noodles *with* Greens & Beans
buckwheat, garlic, and sesame . . .

Soba is a delicious, whole grain noodle made in the Japanese tradition. It often contains mostly buckwheat flour and some wheat, though there are brands made with 100% buckwheat. They cook quickly and have an earthy, delicate taste. I do not specify how much to cook since the recipe is for approximately two healthy servings, you decide on the amount of noodles needed. And use a different noodle if desired, or eat this dish without them and add more greens!

> 2 small zucchini, large grate or matchsticks, 1½-2 cups
> 2-4 cups collards, kale, bok choy, or arugula, chopped
> 4 cloves garlic, sliced thin, or fresh ginger and fresh turmeric
> 1 cup cooked garbanzo or adzuki beans (or other)
> cayenne to taste, or 1-2 teaspoons jalapeño pepper, chopped
> Soba pasta, cooked
> Sesame Sprinkle, or just roasted sesame seeds (see Cook's Notes
> for soaking seeds and Sesame Sprinkle for roasting them)

heat 4 tablespoons water in a skillet and add the first 3 ingredients
sauté on high, 1 minute, toss often
add beans, jalapeño, then the noodles on top
cover, cook for 1-2 minutes. Do not stir, let it steam layered
toss, enjoy with a generous amount of Sesame Sprinkle

The beauty with recipes like this is that they are very versatile. Change the kind of noodles, beans and vegetables, and a whole new dish is ready, quick and easy to sauté after a long day. This contains greens, protein and starch, a full and complemented meal. Add a quick cultured or raw salad, or steamed Sweet Winter Squash, Easy Steamed Vegetables, or Daikon Medallions for a relaxing side dish.

For variation:
- instead of zucchini use green beans, quartered Brussels Sprouts, parsnip or rutabaga and cook a bit longer, at least 5 minutes.
- other beans such as navy, pinto, black eye, or lima

Noodles *with* Mushrooms & Greens

I like to eat greens as often as possible. They are the one food I believe to be the most important to consume, everyday, and they go well with anything. If you don't have kale, use bok choy, napa cabbage, mustard greens, collards, etc.

Yield: 2-4 servings

> 1 bunch kale, washed and chopped (4 packed cups)
> 1/3 cup leftover Miso Soup or broth/stock* or water
> ½ cup onion, green onions or leek, chopped, see onion in Glossary
> 3-4 cups crimini mushrooms or other, sliced (I like a lot)
> 4 cloves garlic, minced, optional
> ½# noodles, cooked (bowties, penne, spaghetti or any of choice)
> ¼ cup roasted sunflower seeds, pine nuts or walnuts, chopped

knead ¼ teaspoon salt into kale or other greens a few moments
heat the soup/broth/water and pour it over the kale, mix and set aside
sauté onion, mushrooms (and garlic) in a ¼ cup water** 5 minutes
when tender add kale mixture, cover and steam 3-4 minutes
add the sauté to the noodles or plate the noodles and place a serving of the sauté on each, garnish with seeds or nuts

* if you have no soup/broth, use 1/3 cup water with 1 teaspoon barley/red miso mixed in, or if using water, add 1 tablespoon shoyu to the onion/mushrooms.

** or use cooking water from the noodles, and if the sauté starts to scorch, add dashes of water, broth or cooking water from the noodles as well.

If the noodles are cold, place on top of the sauté at the end and cover to steam.

For variation:
- instead of kneading greens with salt, omit broth and sauté shoyu to taste with the mushrooms, onions etc. then add the greens
- add beans, Golden Tofu or Spicy Tempeh at the end of the sauté
- use 1 cup of cilantro as part of the greens mixture
- use cubes of polenta or Magic Millet instead of or with the noodles
- add a bunch of cut dandelion greens to the kale

Noodles & Winter Squash
pumpkin seeds & dulse

I use winter squash such as kabocha, butternut, or hokkaido in this recipe since they are rich and sweet when cooked. Any noodles will work or replace with cubed polenta or Magic Millet (Grains).

>   Angel Hair or Rice Vermicelli pasta
>   2 cups winter squash, diced
>   ½ cup roasted pumpkin seeds (see Roasting in Glossary)
>   umeboshi vinegar to taste
>   1 tablespoon dulse (soaked and chopped) or cut nori
>   chopped parsley, green onion or chives, or any fresh herb

boil water for pasta, add squash to boiling water
cook until tender, 10 or so minutes, remove with slotted spoon, set aside
add pasta to this squash water and cook
when pasta is done, drain, place in a large bowl
toss with vinegar, dulse or nori and seeds, then squash
garnish with parsley, green onion or chives, or fresh herbs

If using nori, fold in half, and then again and again until it is in a layered small square, and with scissors, cut into very small pieces. Or, grind in a coffee grinder.

For variation add:
-   sliced black olives, cooked beans
-   different roasted seeds or nuts

What to eat it with:
-   Jade Green cultured salad or any Cultured Salad
-   Wilted Kale Salad, or steamed greens of any kind
-   Classic Green Salad
-   Hummus with crisp romaine leaves
-   Vegetable Soup

Pasta Salad

Yield: 2 servings

many seasonings, layered taste . . .

½ pound pasta: spiral, elbow, pagoda, shell, penne, etc.
½ cup water/broth or vegetable steaming liquid
½ cup *each:* peas and corn
1 rib celery, finely diced, optional
½ red onion or 2-3 green onions, minced, about ½ cup
1-2 carrots, grated, approximately 1 packed cup
1-2 teaspoons umeboshi vinegar, to taste
2-3 tablespoons ground seeds: flax, sesame, sunflower, pumpkin

cook pasta of choice, set aside
warm water/broth/vegetable steaming liquid in a skillet and
sauté the peas, corn, half the celery, onion, half the grated carrots, and umeboshi vinegar for 1 minute, then lay the pasta on top
cover and let warm through another moment, scoop into serving bowls
toss with the other halves of raw vegetables and ground seeds

For variation:
-   leave the celery and carrot raw, or cook it all
-   toss in roasted seeds, chopped nuts, beans, or Golden Tofu
-   add chopped olives, cubes of cooked sweet potato or winter squash
-   use different vegetables, both raw and cooked, or garbanzo beans
-   leave the umeboshi vinegar out, use Ranch Dressing, Sesame Dressing, or House Dressing

Pasta Salad 2

Combine in a bowl: ½ cup grated carrot, 1 celery rib diced, ½ cup chopped black olives, ½ cup sauerkraut (hold in hand, run under water and squeeze to rinse it) chopped, ½ cup cooked white beans or other, 2-3 cups cooked noodles of choice, Quick & Easy Dressing with the avocado and sweetener whisked in.

Mac 'n' Cheez

Yield: 3-3½ cups cheez

sauce

mellow butternut squash & mochi

Here is an all-time favorite with a holistic twist. The combination of orange-colored, dense squash and textured mochi is remarkable, I think, to that of a conventional cheese sauce. It can be used in many other dishes although best with noodles. Try half the recipe in Nachos. The sauce freezes well.

3 cups butternut squash, diced
½ teaspoon salt
½ cup onion, chopped
3/4 cup plain mochi, diced
2 tablespoons sesame or sunflower seeds or tahini, optional
1 tablespoon umeboshi vinegar
1 teaspoon apple cider vinegar or rice vinegar

cook any kind of noodles, penne, curly, or elbow work best
meanwhile prepare the sauce:
simmer squash, salt, and onion in 1½ cups water, 12 minutes
add mochi, seeds/tahini if using, vinegars, simmer 5-8 minutes
blend until creamy in a blender, pour back into pot or directly onto pasta

If the sauce is too thin for your liking (*it will thicken* a little as it cools), mix 1 tablespoon arrowroot or 2 teaspoons kuzu into 2 tablespoons cool water and add to the simmering sauce, stir quickly until thickened.

For variation:
- add green chile, red or yellow peppers, corn, garlic
- add cubed and fried tofu or tempeh, white beans or other
- add cayenne, chili powder, nutritional yeast
- mix noodles with crumbled Tempeh Sausage or Spicy Tempeh into the sauce, pack into a baking pan, add finely diced or grated zucchini or collard greens, sprinkle with paprika and Corn Bread crumbs (if you have some), cover and bake at 375° for 30 minutes.
- like fondue – dip with roasted or steamed chunks of vegetables, cubes of Golden Tofu, Croutons, Magic Millet, olives, etc.

Bell Pepper Sauce (on Pasta)   Yield: 3 cups
pumpkin seed & mellow miso

Many years ago I attended a cooking class taught by Brother Ron Pickarski. He introduced me to elegant, tasty, and sophisticated recipes. I bought his book, Eco-Cuisine, and continue to learn from his expertise. I wrote him and asked if I could use a very changed rendition of his Yellow Pepper Sauce I created using his idea. He wrote back a very nice letter saying, yes as well as " . . . Nutrition is as much about friendships and happiness as it is about consuming nutrient dense foods . . . " It is isn't it?

> ½-1 red or yellow onion, chopped (1 cup)
> ¼ teaspoon salt
> ½ cup corn
> 2 red or yellow peppers, roasted and diced* (about 2 cups)
> 1 rounded tablespoon flour, from rice or other
> ¼ cup pumpkin seeds, soaked** or 2 tablespoons tahini
> garnish: minced green onion, lemon, Walnut Cheesy Sprinkle

combine in a skillet the onion, salt and corn
add 1 cup of water, simmer 10 minutes covered
add rest of ingredients + ¾ cup water, sauté 4 minutes, stir often
let bubble and heat a few moments stirring, then blend all until smooth
prepare and enjoy with your favorite pasta or/and vegetables
garnish with the green onion, fresh lemon and/or Walnut Cheesy Sprinkle

* roast the peppers in an oven or over a gas burner then place in a paper bag to sweat, then peel as much skin off as possible, remove seeds and dice.

** see Cook's Notes for Soaking Seeds and Nuts. Instead of seeds use cashews or almonds. If no time to soak, rinse them well.

For variation:
- use broth or soup stock, even leftover Miso Soup instead of water
- instead of peppers use zucchini, broccoli or green beans

Noodles *with* Arame & Hemp Seeds
tangy red cabbage & fresh basil

1 cup red cabbage, sliced thin
6 red radishes, sliced in thin half moons
1 tablespoon *each:* apple cider vinegar and umeboshi vinegar
½ cup arame, soaked in cold water 2 minutes, drain, set aside
2 green onions, sliced on the diagonal very thin
½ pound noodles cooked, set aside: bowties, curly, shell, or other
¼ cup hemp seeds
¼ cup fresh basil, roughly chopped (don't replace dried for this)

sauté cabbage, radish and vinegars in ½ cup water, 5 minutes
add arame and half the onions, cook another minute
set noodles and hemp seeds in a bowl, add the vegetable sauté
toss in the rest of the green onions and fresh basil

For variation:
- instead of the basil use any fresh herb: cilantro, parsley, savory
- add fresh, in-season cherry tomatoes in late summer
- crumbled Tofu Cheese, Spicy Tempeh
- instead of umeboshi vinegar, use shoyu or ¼ teaspoon salt
- omit the sweetener and use citrus or apple juice instead

. . . like anything, we are creatures of habit,
bound by shame, controlled by love, battered
by our need to know, create, believe, to feel . . .
. . . whole food is a mirror to our own image,
it keeps the mind calm, blood clean,
it provides what we require
to do the things we want to do . . .

Burrito, Quesadilla, Fajita

Just like I love noodles, I love anything wrapped in a tortilla – satisfying and fulfilling. Millet or rice with Crunchy Cabbage Salad and sautéed onions rolled in a warmed corn tortilla works well. Speedy Quesadillas (this section) are a few different combinations for quick dishes. Many flavors and textures can be included: leftovers from cultured salad, stir-fries, beans to finely grated mochi, Sunflower Dream Cheese, avocado, grated raw vegetables, chopped greens (raw or cooked), cucumber or lettuce, can be wrapped and heated (in steamed tortillas, see Cook's Notes) or eaten as is.

Often for lunch I set up my steamer, place turnip or rutabaga matchsticks in it, steam 1 minute, add a spoonful of cooked rice or millet, a dash of umeboshi vinegar and 3-4 corn tortillas, let steam another moment, and then lay tortillas on a plate, and the grain mixture on top. If I haven't used umeboshi vinegar I'll use Sesame Sprinkle or Sunflower Dream Cheese, then roll up the corn tortillas and enjoy. Cultured Salad or sauerkraut, or chopped homemade pickle (which I always have on hand), a few beans if I have them steamed with the rice is a nice addition.

The process of cooking is just as, if not more important, than the actual eating. Sometimes the gathering, prepping and preparing of a meal satisfies our soul, palette and mind that help reduce over-eating, squelches anxiety and fill places otherwise inhabited by stress, tightness and a feeling of being rushed.

Do not underestimate the power of cooking. Let it infuse you with its color, rhythm and creativity. Let the experience of whatever you create in the kitchen fill every cell of your being. And let your tongue truly taste the food. When we chew well, 50 times minimum per mouthful, we not only taste the food to the fullest, but that chewing activity fulfills a deep craving – that pit, or emptiness – many of us experience where the need for something to satiate after is a constant vicious cycle. Chew. Especially when whole grains are part of the meal.

mochi in block and grated

Hot Mesa Burrito

squash, carrot, mochi & music

I never thought of having a burrito for breakfast until living in New Mexico where a warm tortilla is wrapped around rice, eggs, cheese, sausage, chile or beans. It's a great way to take something on the go. Below is *For the Love of Eating's* version of this traditional Southwestern fare, enjoy as is or with Green Chile Sauce (Sauces).

> ½# firm tofu, crumbled*
> 1 cup squash, or red or Japanese sweet potato, diced
> ½ teaspoon turmeric powder
> ½ onion, diced
> 1 carrot or/and red bell pepper, diced
> 1 tablespoon umeboshi vinegar or salt to taste
> ½ cup mochi, grated small, optional
> 1-2 teaspoons jalapeño pepper or ¼ teaspoon cayenne pepper
> 2 flour tortillas (see Bread, Tortilla, Cracker to make your own)

simmer tofu in water to cover for 4 minutes, then drain off excess liquid
steam (in a steamer pot) squash/potatoes or a combination, 8-10 minutes
add turmeric to the tofu and sauté until golden in a few spots
then add onion, carrot/pepper, vinegar/salt and a few dashes of water, cover
sauté a few minutes then add the cayenne/jalapeño and mochi if using
cook until melted and most of liquid is gone
set potatoes aside in a bowl
fresh basil or cilantro is a nice addition, add it now if desired
place half tofu (or beans*) and half vegetable filling in each tortilla
roll up (gather sides in), place seam side down in a dry or lightly oiled skillet, cover and heat on low until warmed through

* instead of tofu use cooked grain, beans, diced polenta or Magic Millet

For variation add:
- cooked lentils, pinto, or black beans and some rice or millet
- steamed and chopped collards/kale or any greens
- Barbeque Sauce or smoked paprika to the onions

Warm Hearth Quesadilla

Yield: serves 2

avocado, mochi, jalapeño & chili spice

½ cup onion, finely diced, see Glossary on how-to cut
1 teaspoon umeboshi vinegar
¼ cup *each* carrot and daikon, finely grated
1 teaspoon fresh turmeric, minced or ¼ teaspoon powder
½ cup grated peeled broccoli stem or zucchini, optional
1-2 teaspoons jalapeño, minced or 1/8 teaspoon cayenne, or to taste
½ teaspoon chili powder
½ cup grated mochi *finely* grated (see Glossary under mochi)
2 flour tortillas (for homemade see Bread, Tortilla, Cracker)
2 tablespoons cilantro or 1-2 green onions, minced
½ avocado

simmer onion in ½ cup water and umeboshi vinegar covered in a
skillet for 4 minutes
add carrot, daikon, turmeric and broccoli or zucchini if using
sauté on high 5 minutes, or until liquid is almost gone
sprinkle jalapeño/cayenne and chili pwd. (all are optional) then mochi
on top, do not stir it in, turn heat to very low, cover, meanwhile,
heat another skillet, warm a tortilla on one side
flip over, scoop half of the filling into the warmed tortilla, fold in half
place quesadilla so the curved edge matches the curved edge of the skillet
repeat, two tortillas fit in the skillet, cover and warm, then flip over
slice the avocado and serve with the cilantro or green onion on top, or
place inside. Cut in wedges

See Troubleshooting in Glossary if having trouble cooking them.

This is delicious and quick when plain, or hearty with Black or Adzuki Bean
Soup and Tofu Sour Cream, Ranch Dressing, or Sunflower Dream Cheese.

For variation:
- add ½ cup cooked beans to sauté before adding mochi, once this filling
  is in the tortilla, add some cooked grain, then flip and heat. Or omit the
  mochi and mash in cooked squash.

Speedy Quesadillas

For all quesadillas spread or mash ingredients onto a full corn tortilla (then set another full one on top) or half a flour one and then fold over. For cooking: heat a skillet, lightly wipe it with oil and add 2 tablespoons of water. Set the quesadilla(s) in the hot steamy pan, heat both sides adding dashes of water as needed. Keep temperature low so it warms/cooks gently, 5-10 minutes/side.

1 Cooked millet with steamed/cooked squash or grated carrot, minced green onion or other. When done, add lettuce, cut in wedges, enjoy with steamed vegetables and Creamy Seed Dip made with pumpkin seeds.

2 Cooked rice/millet (¼ cup), minced green onion, ¼ cup hummus or Sunflower Dream Cheese. When plated add lettuce/cultured salad.

3 Cooked grain or steamed sweet potato/squash, chopped homemade pickle, cultured salad or sauerkraut, Sesame Sprinkle/roasted seeds or spread with Creamy Seed Dip/Sunflower Dream Cheese/Ranch Dressing.

4 Mash cooked beans (½ cup) with cooked rice/millet or finely grated mochi, and steamed/cooked squash/sweet potato. Season lightly with umeboshi vinegar or shoyu and if desired, pinches of: chili powder, cumin, nutritional yeast, minced cilantro or parsley and green onion. When plated add avocado, lettuce, leftover cooked greens or cultured salad if desired.

5 Pinto beans (or other) with cooked rice/millet, grated zucchini, season with umeboshi vinegar, a pinch of cumin and garlic powder. Spread Cashew Cream Cheese on one side, lay filling on other. Cook, when plated add minced chives.

6 Spread Sunflower Dream Cheese, finely grated mochi, and Zucchini Matchstick Salad between two corn tortillas and steam both sides.

See Troubleshooting (Glossary) if having trouble cooking quesadillas. For variation: add to any of above when plated: avocado, tomato in season, minced onion, leftover cooked/chopped greens, cultured salad, lettuce, arugula . . .

Tempeh Fajitas

Yield: 4 servings

peppers, onions, tempeh & tortilla

A Tex-Mex traditional made with flank steak originally, here, tempeh takes the main role and plays it well. If not fond of peppers, use zucchini, patty pan squash, or peeled and sliced stems of broccoli.

1 package tempeh, cut in ¼ inch strips, then in half
1 package firm tofu, freeze overnight, thaw and squeeze out water*
1 red pepper (or orange or yellow)
3 tablespoons shoyu, or to taste
2 teaspoons apple cider vinegar or balsamic or other
2 red or yellow onions, half moon slices, see Glossary on how-to cut
1-2 zucchini or patty pan squash, cut in thick wedges
1 package corn or flour tortillas
handful cilantro and/or green onion, minced
lemon or lime wedges
Bell Pepper Sauce or Lime Marinade (Sauces), optional

place the tempeh in a skillet, cover with water
simmer until water is burned off, approximately 15-20 minutes
*tofu is optional, if using, cut like tempeh, set in a separate skillet and cover with water, simmer 4 minutes, drain excess water, season with shoyu, sauté until just browned, set aside
cut pepper in half, remove seeds and inner fleshy ribs, cut in long spears
season tempeh liberally with shoyu and vinegar, sauté until browned
add onions, peppers, zucchini to tempeh, and ½ cup water
cover and simmer on high 5-8 minutes, stir/toss a few times
cook until almost all liquid is gone
place tortillas on top of tempeh/vegetables to heat them
leave tortillas whole or cut in large wedges, set on the platter
transfer fajita mixture to middle of platter, sprinkle with cilantro or green onion, and lemon or lime or serve with Lime Marinade (Sauces) on the side

Bell Pepper Sauce with this dish is great too.

Spreads, Dips, Salsa

. . . and hummus, guacamole, "sour cream", "paté" . . .

Creamy foods are essential: we love ice cream, yogurt, sour cream, nut butters, anything smooth and spreadable. Why? It relaxes and satisfies us. We were brought up on milk, in one form or another. Once we leave the toddler age, milk is no longer necessary, as every animal stops "nursing" at a very young age. But this desire does not end. And so a good blender is essential in the kitchen. I lasted for decades on used blenders from yard sales, old osterizers, etc. The time came to purchase a real heavy-duty machine after tasting a nut milk shake at a raw food café that was out of this world. I bought a Blendtec. A Vitamix is similar, both incredible, expensive I know, but worth it. They make Sunflower Dream Cheese like cream cheese and it grinds fresh flour!

Dips and spreads can be made from vegetables, seeds, nuts and beans, blended into quick and satisfying high protein, fiber-rich, easy to eat, simple meals with cut vegetables, tortillas, or Seed Crackers. Seeds add richness without needing to use oil, as well as protein, potassium, B-vitamins, iron, calcium and other minerals. Seeds, grains and beans are best soaked, sprouted, roasted, or simmered before consuming. It breaks down toxins and acids that inhibit proper digestion. See Cook's Notes for information on soaking and roasting in Glossary for roasting seeds and nuts.

Also: Pinto Bean Zambullida, Creamy Greens, Bean-Naise for other dips and spreads.

I was a head cook at the Kushi Institute in Massachusetts, at dude ranches in Wyoming and a back country resort in the Canadian Rockies. I prepared backpacking meals for adolescents through elder hostel in an outdoor school. I have taught whole food cooking classes (and still do) and have cooked in cafés and health food stores across the western United States, Canada and Hawaii. And my experience has taught me, without a doubt, that food can heal — but we have to be diligent in the commitment. What we eat directly affects our health, energy, and mood.

Sunflower Dream Cheese

Yield: 3 cups

1 cup sunflower seeds, soaked* (see Soaking Seeds in Cook's Notes)
2 green onions, roughly chopped (use less for a less oniony taste)
1 clove garlic and 1 teaspoon salt
1 lemon, juice and pulp
small handful fresh cilantro or/and parsley, optional

drain seeds, place in a blender with rest of ingredients
blend with 1-1½ cups fresh water (depends on blender) until very creamy
add small amounts of water *if* needed to get blender going
transfer to a glass or ceramic container, good like this *or* culture it as follows,
cover lightly, it needs to breathe, set on counter 12-24 hours. This step goes beyond sprouting, it aids the digestibility of seeds; enzyme-rich, live food.

It will brown on top and liquid will gather on the bottom, just stir the cheese and refrigerate, up to a week.
* instead of soaking, simmer the seeds in water to cover for 10 minutes, drain and follow recipe, makes a very creamy dip, more than soaking.

Cashew Cream Cheese, use 1½-2 cups soaked cashews in place of sunflower seeds. Blend with 1 tablespoon *each* red miso and nutritional yeast, ½ teaspoon salt, and ½-¾ cup Rye Tonic (or water with a dash of lemon juice). Ferment as above, but longer, 2-3 days, depends on temperature of house.

Quick Avocado Dip (guacamole)

¼ cup onion or 1 green onion, minced, see how to cut in Glossary
2-3 teaspoons umeboshi vinegar *and* jalapeno or serrano pepper
1-2 avocados, halved, pitted, diced
1-2 tablespoons lemon or lime, juice and pulp
1 clove garlic, minced and ¼ cup cilantro, both are optional
pound together onion, vinegar and pepper (or cayenne to taste)
place avocado in a bowl, stir in rest of ingredients, taste and adjust
For variation see Avo Mayo, as well as:
- leftover Calming Onions blended with an avocado and seasoned
- leftover Tempeh Fajita filling pulsed (food processor) with avocado
- process with warmed peas and artichoke hearts instead of avocado

Piñata Bean Dip

Yield: about 2 quarts

This is a colorful and tasty combination that will last several days in the fridge, and gets better as it marinates. Enjoy with Seed Crackers, wrapped in warm tortillas, tossed into rice, or piled on a piece of Corn Bread or polenta. If using canned beans, drain liquid and discard.

> 1 cup cooked chickpeas
> 2 cups cooked black beans
> 1 cup cooked red beans
> 1 can black olives, chopped
> 1 can or cup of corn
> 1-2 avocados, diced, optional
> 1-2 tomatoes, chopped, optional
> 3-4 green onions, minced, see Glossary on how-to cut
> 1 small red onion, minced
> ½-1 cup cilantro, chopped
> 1 teaspoon salt or 1-2 tablespoons umeboshi vinegar (or to taste)
> 1-2 tablespoons cumin
> 1 each red and green jalapeño peppers, minced (or cayenne to taste)
> 1 cup lime juice + its pulp

combine all ingredients in a large bowl

If using frozen corn: steam or blanch it. If using fresh off the cob: steam 30 seconds before adding.

The avocado tends to get a bit mushy as does the tomato if using, so if you plan to make ahead, add those just before serving.

What to eat it with:
- as above as well as Rice Flatbread, mixed into any soup
- layered on any of the suggested tortillas, Corn Bread, flat bread or dosa with a dollop of Savory Rice Cheez Spread
- cooked grain, pasta, vegetable stir-fry
- Millet-Quinoa Dosas

White Bean Dip
with umeboshi plum & fresh thyme

Yield: 2½ cups

1½-2 cups onion, diced
1 tablespoon light miso or ¼ teaspoon salt
1 tablespoon umeboshi paste or umeboshi vinegar
tablespoon fresh thyme or 1 teaspoon dry1
2 cups cooked white beans, drain off all liquid
garnish: minced green onion or parsley, or sun-dried tomato

sauté onion, miso or salt and vinegar 10 minutes covered, stir often
near end of cooking, you may need to add 1-2 tablespoons of water if it is getting too dry, stir it in and cover/sauté. If using sun-dried tomatoes add to the onions, or re-constitute, chop, and add with beans while blending
place beans in a food processor
add thyme to the cooking onions in the last minute
transfer onion mixture to beans in processor and pulse/blend until blended, leave a bit chunky
garnish with onion, parsley or tomatoes (or all)

A simple dip to go with others (Hummus or Sunflower Dream Cheese) with crudités, bread, Seed Crackers or wedges of Rice Flat Bread.

For variation, try this alternative:
    2-4 leaves kale, collards, bok choy, or other, steamed or blanched
    juice of half lemon
    handful fresh basil or 2 teaspoons dried
    2 tablespoons onion or 1 green onion, minced
    1 tablespoon umeboshi vinegar or to taste
    1 teaspoon light or red miso

chop greens and place in a food processor with all other ingredients
blend until desired consistency. Taste and adjust seasonings.

get healthy to the core and live simply

Lentil Walnut Paté

I have always loved chopped liver, I know that may sound strange, but there is something about the texture and taste that absolutely resonated with me. This is amazingly similar as is the green bean version below.

> 1 cup green lentils, soaked (see Soaking Beans in Cook's Notes) or 2 cans
> 1 inch piece kombu
> 1 cup walnuts, rinsed or soaked, see Cook's Notes
> 1 small leek (or 5-6 scallions)
> 1 tablespoon umeboshi vinegar, optional*
> 2-4 teaspoons light miso, optional

drain lentils (if soaked), place in a pot and add 3 cups water, bring to a boil
remove foam, add kombu, simmer 40 minutes or until soft, check the water
dry roast walnuts in a skillet, stir often, 10-15 minutes*
cut leek in half and wash out well, get in between the layers, then dice
when walnuts are done, set aside, quickly wipe out that skillet
sauté leek in that pan in a dash of water, ¼-½ teaspoon salt, 4 or so minutes
blend walnuts until nut-butter-like in a food processor, leave them in it
when lentils are soft, drain (save the liquid), set aside ½ cup lentils
blend rest of lentils with walnuts in food processor
add small amounts of cooking liquid to get it creamy, but not too loose
add seasonings, taste and adjust, pulse in cooked leeks
transfer to a bowl, garnish with minced parsley

Delicious with chips, crackers, bread, steamed or raw vegetables, in a tortilla with cucumbers or lettuce, or with grain and a cultured salad.

* or roast in a 325° oven, 20-25 minutes, do more and freeze for later use

Green Bean Paté   Yield: 1½ cups
Sauté 2 cups chopped onion in ½ cup water and ½ teaspoon salt for 10 minutes covered, stir often. Roast ½ cup already soaked pumpkin seeds (see Cook's Notes), cool and grind well in a coffee grinder. Steam 2 cups (½#) green beans 8-10 minutes, then roughly chop. Blend all ingredients in a food processor with 2 tablespoons lemon juice (or more).

Savory Rice Cheez Spread

> 1 cup cooked brown rice, short or long grain
> 2-3 tablespoons cashews or other seed or nut, soaked
> 1 teaspoon umeboshi vinegar (or to taste)
> ½ teaspoon apple cider or rice vinegar
> ¼-1 teaspoon dry basil

simmer rice in ¼ cup + 2 tablespoons water in a small pot, 5 minutes
blend until very creamy while adding rest of ingredients
work it with a rubber spatula, gently, try not to add any more water
transfer to a bowl or container, it will thicken a little as it cools

The flavor is like a cheese spread. Scoop into a nice bowl, line with crackers, dark bread slices, cucumbers, red pepper spears, thin carrot rounds.

This savory spread can be used:
- in a tortilla or crêpe with steamed broccoli and mushrooms
- as "sour cream" or "ricotta" in lasagna, enchiladas, etc.
- baked into rolls, stuffed into manicotti pasta
- as a white sauce for pizza, as a base for a dip
- in Cucumber Sandwiches (see Snacks, Wraps, Sandwich)

Sweet Rice Spread

Follow directions as above, use the vinegars, omit the basil, blend in a couple of dates or re-constituted dried apricots or raisins, or/and a few drops of stevia or a few teaspoons of maple syrup, or just use it plain with jam or cinnamon.

This sweet spread can be used:
- in crêpes with fresh fruit or fruit compote
- flavored and then used as a frosting on cupcakes or cakes
- a dollop atop fruit cobbler, puddings, pies
- spread on toast with jam or for Cinnamon Toast (Breakfast)

Hummus

Yield: 3 cups

Hummus is an incredible bean dip. I make it without oil or tahini, which makes it easier to digest, and less heavy. Below is my favorite way to prepare it blended with fresh parsley and spring onion.

> 3 cups cooked garbanzo beans (chickpeas), or 2 cans
> 3-4 tablespoons lemon juice and pulp, or 2 tablespoons vinegar
> ½ cup parsley, washed, chopped, stems included
> 1-2 green onions, washed, roughly-cut, roots included
> ½ teaspoon cayenne pepper and/or cumin powder, optional
> 1-2 cloves garlic, minced, optional
> ½ cup or more of warmed bean cooking liquid, water or broth

For seasoning choose one of the following:
> 1 tablespoon umeboshi vinegar, to taste
> 1 tablespoon shoyu, or to taste
> ½ teaspoon Roasted Salt (see Miscellaneous), or to taste

blend all ingredients in a food processor (or a good blender)
add liquid from cooking beans, or water or broth to get it smooth
taste and adjust seasonings, add more lemon or vinegar, salt, etc. if needed

Parsley helps digest beans and gives it a beautiful green color as does the green onion. I don't always have parsley on hand, so I leave it out, or substitute fresh cilantro, chopped arugula, or young mustard greens.

For variation:
- sauté 1 diced onion or leek in a dash of water and 1 teaspoon salt for 5 minutes, omit the other salty seasonings, and fold or blend in

What to eat it with:
- raw carrots, celery, firm leaves of lettuce
- steamed corn tortillas, rolled in flour tortillas with lettuce
- Seed Crackers, Rice Flat Bread, Corn Bread, noodles . . .

Creamy Seed Dip

Yield: 1½ cups

seeds: versatile, delicious, nutritious . . .

Seeds. A miracle food. If you put them in water, they'll grow. Seeds are high in so many nutrients, just include them in your daily fare. If you don't chew well, then blend into dips such as this one. Try to always soak or simmer seeds in water to break down and eliminate the enzyme inhibitors and toxic substances (phytates and certain polyphenols). Keeps 3-5 days refrigerated. See Soaking Seeds in Cook's Notes.

> 1 cup sunflower, pumpkin or sesame seeds, soaked or not*
> 2 green onions and/or ½ cup parsley, fresh dill, or cilantro
> 1 tablespoon *each* umeboshi vinegar and rice vinegar**
> ½-¾ cup water, broth, or vegetable steaming water

place seeds in a small pot with 1½ cups of water
simmer 10 minutes* then strain
blend with rest of ingredients until creamy, may need more liquid

This is also a thick and delicious dressing for salads, grains, pasta, raw or steamed vegetables, with grains or beans wrapped in tortillas. My favorite is to prepare a bowl of raw and steamed vegetables and just dunk them.

* if seeds have been soaked (see soaking seeds in Cook's Notes), they do not have to be simmered, but I often simmer instead of soaking for this recipe because they blend up so creamy.
** instead of umeboshi vinegar and rice vinegar, use rice vinegar (or apple cider vinegar) and 1 tablespoon light miso.

What to eat it with:
-   on vegetable salads, with Millet Patties or other (Patties)
-   in a tortilla or collard green wrap with a patty and other fillings such as shredded carrot, Sliced beets, cultured salad, etc.
-   as a dip for raw and steamed vegetables, croutons, bread, crackers
-   baked into casseroles, mixed into beans or use in Creamy Greens recipe instead of Tofu Sour Cream (Vegetables)

(cont'd next page)

For variation:
-   after making the dip, cover lightly and let stand on kitchen counter 12-24 hours to ferment for a seed "cheese"
-   add fresh garlic and lemon juice
-   use walnuts, cashews or macadamia nuts instead of seeds

If made with sunflower seeds, it can be used:
-   to make Thousand Island Dressing (nice for a pasta salad) or a Ranch dressing, see Salad Dressings for the actual recipe
-   like a sour cream with enchiladas, nachos, etc.

Tofu Sour Cream   Yield: approximately 1 cup

Use in place of regular sour cream, although, more often I use Creamy Seed Dip or Ranch Dressing.

½# firm tofu, cut in cubes
1 tablespoon rice vinegar or apple cider vinegar
1 tablespoon umeboshi vinegar
2-4 tablespoons broth/stock/leftover miso soup or water
1 green onion, minced

boil tofu in water 4 minutes, drain
blend it with the vinegars, stock/water and onion until creamy
fold in green onion after blending if you don't want to blend it

Tofu is an un-fermented soy product, one I do not advocate often. But there is a sprouted tofu by Wildwood Organics so I indulge occasionally. Tempeh, on the other hand, is fermented. Fermented soy products such as tempeh, miso, shoyu, and natto tend to be easier to digest because the tough proteins and naturally occurring acids innate to the soybean are broken down. Tempeh has a meaty, dense texture and can be heavily seasoned to fit any palette.

Tofu "Cheese"

Tofu is an un-fermented soy bean curd. This process of covering it in miso, a fermented and enzyme-rich paste, breaks down the components in tofu that are difficult to digest. Store in the fridge 7-10 days.

> ½ or 1 pound firm tofu
> 6-12 tablespoons dark barley or red miso, more if needed

let the tofu sit on a tilted plate for several hours, even overnight with a weight on top to get as much water out as possible, a very important step
spread miso on all sides, even the bottom, an 1/8 inch thick
set on a plate and let sit on a quiet part of your counter for 4-6 days
after, scrape miso off, store in a container in the fridge and use it in sauces and dips or bean dishes

This is the "cheese." It will be colored light brown/tan and have the consistency of a medium-soft cheese. It can be used:
- crumbled on top of pizza, sautéed in any dishes or bean soups
- rolled in tortillas with rice, lettuce, and shredded carrots
- anything cheese or cottage cheese is used in, but it does not melt
- sliced in sandwiches, tossed into noodles with Italian Sauce

Savory "Cheese" Ball

> ½# tofu cheese
> 1 teaspoon savory
> 1 small firm apple, grated large
> 2 green onions, chopped
> 1 teaspoon wet mustard or ½ teaspoon dry mustard powder
> ½ cup walnuts (see soaking nuts in Cook's Notes)

cut tofu cheese in cubes and place in a food processor with the rest of the ingredients – *except* walnuts
pulse to consistency of ricotta cheese
roast nuts (see Roasting in Glossary), then coarsely chop
roll tofu in nuts and roll into a ball

Set on a serving platter with crackers, bread, celery and other vegetables.

Skillet Bean Dip

2 cups cooked pinto, white or black beans
2 cups winter squash, Japanese sweet potato or other, grated
1 small red onion and/or 1 cup daikon, finely diced
3 green onions, chopped
½ cup parsley, chopped (or cilantro)
2 teaspoons ground cumin, ½ lemon

heat 1 cup of water in a skillet, add onion and 1 teaspoon salt
add grated squash/other, daikon if using, cover and simmer 15 minutes
when soft, add beans and cumin, stir delicately, don't mush the beans
cook until warmed through and most of the water is gone
stir in the parsley and green onions (save 1 tablespoon of each for garnish)
transfer to a serving bowl, squeeze fresh lemon over dip and garnish
with minced parsley and onion, sliced black olives are great too

Tomato Salsa

When the real deal is desired, and Roots Salsa won't do, here it is. I enjoy
tomatoes in season only, when they are beautifully plump, juicy and tasty.
Get them at farmer's markets where they are grown close to home.

3-4 roma tomatoes, diced
¼ red onion, minced, see Glossary on how-to cut
1-2 cloves garlic, pressed and minced
¼ cup cilantro, chopped
½ teaspoon *each* cumin and oregano
½ lime, juice & pulp, or more to taste
½ teaspoon salt, to taste
½-1 jalapeño pepper, minced or cayenne powder to taste

combine ingredients in a bowl, mix gently, taste and adjust seasonings
add corn nibs, green onion, green chile, cooked pinto or black beans
keep refrigerated up to 3 days, it gets better as it marinates

Roots Salsa

daikon, carrot, umeboshi & love . . .

I created this while working at the Kushi Institute in Becket, Massachusetts. It accompanied a macrobiotic Spanish meal to provide a zesty salsa-like taste, without of course, tomatoes. It's a great way to enjoy daikon. Use it like salsa for dipping or rolling in a tortilla with beans and rice.

3-4 cups onion, finely diced, see Glossary on how-to cut
½ teaspoon salt
2-3 carrots, minced finely in a food processor (1½ cups)
1 large daikon, also minced finely in a food processor
½ cup chopped fresh cilantro
1 small jalapeño minced OR ¼ - ½ teaspoon cayenne pepper
2 tablespoons umeboshi vinegar
½ teaspoon cumin
1 tablespoon arrowroot powder mixed into 2 tablespoons water

sauté onion and salt in ¼ cup water or broth in a large skillet
place carrot and daikon, just spread evenly on top, do not stir in
add 1½ cups of water/broth, gently, so it barely rises up to the vegetables
cover and simmer 15 minutes
stir in cilantro, pepper, cumin and vinegar, simmer a few minutes more
add arrowroot mixture and stir in while bubbling until smooth and thickened. Taste and adjust seasonings.

Take off heat, place in serving bowl, allow to cool.

For variation:
-   add cooked pinto or black beans
-   use minced sweet potato or winter squash in place of carrots
-   add sun-dried tomatoes

Harvest Salsa

I can eat this with a spoon – it's rich, earthy taste and texture is outstanding. It goes with anything from simple grain or pasta to polenta, stuffed into onions or squash, mixed with Corn Bread and wild rice for a creative stuffing . . . or simply with Seed Crackers or steamed corn tortillas.

> 2 cups winter squash, finely diced
> 1 red (or yellow) onion, minced, see Glossary on how-to cut
> 1 parsnip, finely diced
> 1 small golden beet or rutabaga, finely diced
> ½ cup daikon, finely grated
> 4 cloves garlic, minced, optional
> 1 red or yellow bell pepper, diced
> ¼ cup parsley or green onion, minced
> 1/3 cup pumpkin seeds or pecans, lightly roasted, roughly chopped

simmer first 4 vegetables in 1 cup broth/water and pinch salt for 15 minutes covered, stir often, add water/broth if needed to keep from sticking
add daikon, garlic, pepper and sauté another few minutes uncovered
transfer to a serving bowl, garnish with parsley or green onion, seeds/nuts

Becoming aware of our condition: not being able to relax, stressed too often, unable to lose or gain weight, indecisive, forgetful, irritable, sluggish, too cold or warm, too sweaty or dry, or if diagnosed with a disease . . . we often turn to sweets, alcohol, drugs, processed food, excess protein and dairy, etc., which causes our bodies to become overloaded over time.

For the Love of Eating is about preparing whole food simply to help the body relax and soften, internally. This allows pathways to open enabling a constant release of toxins thus helping the body to become balanced. Once the body is brought into balance by following *For the Love of Eating,* we can learn to adapt to our situation regardless of changes in weather or mood, and maintain a sustained energy.

Snacks, Wraps, Sandwich

and nachos, popcorn, crunchy nuts and seeds . . .

It helps having really good quality quickies now, to squelch any cravings that may get out of hand. Snacks, Wraps & Sandwich are favorites that of course take a bit of time to prepare, but once used to it, and adept at thinking ahead, fast become best friends. When I need something now, warmed Millet-Quinoa Dosa's lathered with Sunflower Dream Cheese and lettuce works wonders while making steamed vegetables or something else.

Once a week I make different dishes: a dip (hummus, Sunflower Dream Cheese, White Bean Dip, etc.), grain, beans and a cultured salad. I always have Rye Tonic going and make a bread with the sprouted berries. I'll make patties and/or quesadillas toward the end of the week to use up grain and beans. I warm up grain in the mornings and have it with Salt Brine Pickle and possibly Matchstick Cut-Stir-fry (made with carrots only). Steamed greens/cabbage for a snack, Nori Rolls for lunch and dinner, Noodle Soup with Easy Vegetable Stir-fry. Leftover beans are added to a soup or blended into a dip, and some put in the freezer . . . and so my week goes, easily creating diverse and tasty food.

Other ideas:
- Pinto Bean Zambullida (Beans) is a great dip as a snack
- Millet Patties and any grain and bean patty (Patties)
- Speedy Quesadilla's, Sweet Rice Balls, Quinoa Muffins
- Savory "Cheese" Ball, Mochi Melts, Nori Rolls
- Millet-Quinoa Dosa's with Sunflower Dream Cheese
- see Spreads, Dips, Salsa section for more ideas
- Greek 'n' Tangy Cuke 'n' Carrot, raw daikon cut in sticks or rounds
- Kale Chips, Nori Crackers, Seed Crackers with Sunflower Dream Cheese
- carrots (raw or steamed), celery, cucumber, radish with Creamy Seed Dip, Sunflower Dream Cheese, Hummus, or Lentil Walnut Paté
- Crunchy Nuts & Seeds, dry fruit, a carrot, a cup of tea
- Smoothies, Green Drink, Ginger-Mint Lassi, Rye Tonic cut with tea
- Almond Butter on Sprouted Sourdough Bread (with fresh garlic!)
- Rice Flatbread with any spread or dip, apple sauce, or plain
- Corn Bread plain or with jam, or other topping
- Easy Steamed Vegetables, Skillet Greens, steamed greens and cabbage

Millet Wraps

Just the sound of the word, wrap, is fun. Anything wrapped in a tortilla, or a raw or steamed collard green or napa cabbage, tightly shut is like an unopened present, waiting in anticipation for my mouth to find out what is inside.

    corn or flour tortillas, rice papers (Glossary) or large green leaves
    2 Millet Patties (see Patties)
    ¼ cup Creamy Seed Dip made with pumpkin seeds
    sliced cucumbers or Pickled Cucumber Strips, sprouts or lettuce

Decide what you are using: tortilla, bread or bun, rice paper, or collard greens, then layer on it at end nearest you:

Millet Patty, dip or Sunflower Dream Cheese, cucumber, sprouts or lettuce

If rolling in a tortilla or a green leaf, add cultured salad or shredded carrots, Sliced beets (see Tangy Beet Side), and cabbage with the sprouts and lettuce, slice patties in 1" lengths and roll it up.

Additional fillings include:
- sauerkraut, Spicy Tempeh or Golden Tofu
- sautéed or steamed vegetables, avocado slices
- homemade or dill pickles, chopped or sliced
- salsa (see Spreads, Dips, Salsa), or store-bought
- beans or any bean/grain burger
- see Savory Rice Cheez Spread for ideas
- Matchstick-Cut Stir-Fry
- leftovers from any of the recipes from Sea Vegetables

Instead of tortillas or rice paper, try Rice Flat Bread or pita bread – any bread – but you won't be able to roll it up. An easy spread is simply sesame tahini mixed with any miso (or Vegetable Jam under recipes at roannelewis.com), spread on bread or tortilla, and brave it with some raw thinly sliced garlic, then roll it up with a grain/patty/burger and veggies or cultured salad.

Rice Wraps *with* Tofu & Arame   Yield: 4-6 wraps

½ cup arame, soak in water to cover 5-10 minutes, drain, set aside
1 cup leek or onion, chopped
1 tablespoon *each:* shoyu and apple cider or rice vinegar
4-6 whole napa cabbage or bok choy leaves
½# tofu, tempeh, or a few slices of polenta
4-6 rice papers (see Glossary)
1-2 cups cooked angel hair pasta, or rice noodles, optional
1 cup carrot or zucchini, grated or leftover cultured salad, or sauerkraut

simmer arame, leek/onion, shoyu and vinegar in ½ cup water, 10 minutes
lay the napa or bok choy over above sauté at the end, cover and let steam
cut tofu/tempeh in ¼ inch strips, simmer in 1 cup water 5 minutes
drain liquid, leave in pan, sauté tofu/tempeh/polenta in any remaining liquid
from arame sauté. If there is none, just lightly brown both sides in a skillet
run 2 rice papers at a time under water, separate and set on counter to soften
lay a steamed leaf on the paper, leave one inch free at the far end to seal
add part of the arame/onion mix, noodles if using, carrots or other (rinse
and squeeze out sauerkraut if using), and lastly tofu/tempeh/polenta
roll up folding the sides in if possible, or leave ingredients jutting out the ends
lay seam-side down, allow to rest several moments to seal, repeat with others

Serve as is on a platter, cut in half on the diagonal, or enjoy with Creamy Seed
Dip (Spreads, Dips, Salsa), Dipping Sauce, Ginger Glaze, even Barbeque Sauce.

For variation:
- place a steamed corn tortilla on top of the re-constituted rice paper,
  then the other fillings, and roll up – gives it a nice texture
- use Curried Tempeh (Wrap) or Spicy Tempeh
- try almond butter (1 tablespoon) or other mixed with umeboshi plum
  paste (½-1 teaspoon) instead of tofu/tempeh
- carrot and zucchini matchsticks simmered/steamed instead of raw
- use cooked grain: millet, rice, quinoa instead of noodles
- instead of noodles or grated carrot/zucchini, use Zucchini Matchstick
  Salad

Golden Tofu

It is important to cook tofu (and tempeh) before eating. It aids in its digestion, cuts the fat, and seasonings can be added for a more tasty and satisfying dish. This is quick, and can be eaten as is, or with noodles, grain dishes, burritos, salads, wraps or stir-fries. See Glossary for different types of tofu.

> 1# firm tofu, cut in cubes
> 2 tablespoons shoyu, or salt to taste

simmer tofu in water to cover, 4 minutes
pour off any remaining liquid, drizzle with shoyu or salt, simmer
gently scrape and flip over, and again allowing the sides to lightly brown

For variation:
- drizzle with 1-2 tablespoons lemon juice after tofu is cooked
- sprinkle with minced green onion or chives
- mix with grated carrot, sauerkraut and Sesame Dressing
- roll in a tortilla with grain and/or chopped lettuce, Seared Zucchini & Onion, and Sunflower Dream Cheese

Breaded Tofu

> ½# firm tofu, cut in ½ inch strips
> 1 tablespoon *each*: shoyu and vinegar + 1 teaspoon molasses
> 2 tablespoons flour + 1 tablespoon cornmeal or ground rolled oats
> 1 tablespoon each: arrowroot powder and nutritional yeast

simmer tofu in water 4 minutes, then place between two plates and gently squeeze as much water out of tofu, then place tofu in a shallow baking dish
combine liquid ingredients and drizzle over tofu, turning to coat
marinate at least 5 minutes both wider sides and as long as overnight
coat tofu with mixture of flour, cornmeal (or oats), arrowroot and yeast
pan-fry each side until just browning

Enjoy with lemon or/and mustard and see variations under Golden Tofu.

Cucumber Sandwiches

These are a hearty version of a cucumber tea sandwich. I don't like to peel
the cucumber or cut the crust off the bread . . .

    8-12 thin slices bread*
    1 batch Savory Rice Cheez Spread (Spreads, Dips, Salsa section)
    1 cucumber

cut ends off the cucumber, run a fork down its sides
slice it in half, then thinly slice so you have long u-shaped pieces
spread rice spread thickly onto very thin pieces of bread
place cucumber, u-shape end matches u-shape end of bread
arrange on a platter and chill

* thinly sliced store-bought bread, the dark European rye found in the cooler
section of most health food stores works well. Or make your own Sour Millet
Bread (Bread, Tortilla, Cracker section).

More ideas for tea sandwiches, spread on thin bread:
- Hummus with a thin slice of sautéed zucchini
- Lentil Walnut Paté, sliced black olives, and minced parsley
- Curried Tempeh (Wrap) on one fresh crisp lettuce leaf
- tahini mixed with red miso and sautéed onions & mushrooms
- Tofu Cheese, finely grated carrot and Quick & Easy Dressing
- Savory Rice Cheez Spread, slices of avocado, salt and black pepper
- Almond Butter with thin slices banana, sprinkled with ground raw
  cacao or cinnamon
- Sunflower Dream Cheese with fresh lettuce

Prepare different kinds, cut in squares or triangles, arrange on a large platter.

Many of the fillings mentioned can be found in this section as well as Spreads,
Dips, Salsa.

Tempeh Sandwich

1 slab Spicy Tempeh (below)
2 slices of bread (see Bread, Tortilla, Cracker to make your own)
mustard and/or Bean-Naise
Seared Zucchini & Onion or lettuce/sprouts and sauerkraut

toast or steam bread
spread both slices with mustard, Bean-Naise or other
lay tempeh on bread, add vegetables of choice
cover with other piece of bread and press down, cut in half and enjoy

For variation:
- finely grated mochi melted on Spicy Tempeh near end of cooking
- thinly sliced red onion and steamed broccoli
- thinly sliced pickle or sauerkraut

Spicy Tempeh

1 package tempeh (8 ounce), cut in 4 thin squares
2 teaspoons chili powder + pinch cayenne, or to taste
1 teaspoon garlic powder
1 teaspoon umeboshi vinegar

cut tempeh in half and then each half cut lengthwise to result in 4 thin rectangular slabs, slit each one
simmer tempeh in 1½ cups water in a covered skillet 15 minutes
sprinkle rest of ingredients on top of tempeh, leave uncovered and turn heat up slightly, cook until liquid burns off (10 minutes), flip once
add a dash of water at end to soften spices and remove from pan
cool and store in a container in the fridge, keeps several days

Use in Tempeh Sandwich or cube and toss into noodles, grain or vegetables, Split Pea Soup, Creative Chef Salad or other salads, in Speedy Quesadillas.

For variation:
- add 2 chopped green onions with rest of ingredients when cooking
- omit spices and cook tempeh plain with umeboshi vinegar or shoyu

Salad Wrap

2-4 rice papers (see Glossary) or flour tortillas (2), optional *
2-6 leaves lettuce, red, green, or romaine (depending on size)
small handful arugula or spinach
2-4 leaves napa cabbage or collard greens
¼-½ cup hummus (regular or black, see Spread, Dips, Salsa)
½ cup Sliced beets (see Tangy Beet Side), grated daikon or carrot
2-4 tablespoons sauerkraut or chopped homemade pickle, optional
1-2 tablespoons lime or lemon juice

prepare rice papers (I often wet 2 for one wrap), or flour tortillas
lay lettuce and other greens, leave an inch clear at far end to seal wrap shut
add hummus, grated vegetables and sauerkraut/pickle if using
drizzle with citrus juice
roll up gently, let sit a few moments to relax and seal

* if using flour tortillas, quickly steam or warm them so they roll easier, stick a toothpick in after finishing rolling them up to hold together. If not, use large collard greens or try napa cabbage leaves or green part of bok choy:

    cut collard leaves on either side of the middle vein and remove stem
    overlap them on a bamboo mat, add rest of ingredients, leave room at end, and tightly roll, removing bamboo mat as you go

Eat immediately. Or, take it on-the-go as is. Watch it, it's messy . . .

For variation:
- drizzle with House Dressing, Fresh Herb, or Quick & Easy Dressing
- add Matchstick-Cut Stir-Fry, Mystic Arame, Hijiki Mushroom Saute
- add leftover cultured salad of any kind instead of pickle/sauerkraut
- add soaked and chopped nuts/seeds, or nut butter (see Cook's Notes for soaking seeds and nuts)
- quickly blanch leaves before rolling
- add thinly sliced snap peas, green beans, or sprouts
- add minced fresh turmeric or ginger, a dash of cayenne
- use Bean-Naise, Lentil Walnut Paté, Creamy Seed Dip, or Sunflower Dream Cheese instead of hummus (see Spreads, Dips, Salsa)

Curried Tempeh Wrap
quinoa, lemon & cucumber

This is a rendition of a chicken salad I used to make cooking in a bustling café in Petaluma, California. It is also in the Ashland Whole Food Cookbook I wrote with my Mom, though I have changed it just a little. Place in a tortilla or on bread with sprouts or lettuce and Seared Zucchini & Onion (Vegetables). It's out of this world.

> 1 package tempeh, diced small
> 1 cup cooked quinoa or millet
> ½ cup mayonnaise*
> 2-3 tablespoons lemon or lime juice
> 2 tablespoons shoyu
> 1 tablespoon curry powder
> 1 green onion or chives, minced, see Glossary on how-to cut
> 1-2 tablespoons minced fresh parsley
> ½ cup peas, optional
> ½ cup diced cucumber, optional

steam tempeh for 20 minutes, add grain in last 2 minutes
combine mayonnaise, citrus juice, shoyu and curry powder
place onion, parsley, peas and cucumber (if using) in a medium bowl
add cooked tempeh and grain to the vegetables and stir in curry dressing
taste, you may want a bit more lemon juice or curry

* Bean-Naise, Avo Mayo, or if you buy it try Follow Your Heart Vegenaise

I like this so much I have eaten it for breakfast. It's a great lunch or snack on crisp lettuce. You can substitute tofu (steam it like the tempeh for half as long), Magic Millet or polenta cubes (no need to steam) if desired, or add them to the tempeh mixture.

What to eat it with:
- Mystic Arame, Tangy Beet Side, or Salad Raw & Warm
- steamed and raw vegetables
- Calming Onions and steamed greens

Nachos
beans, olives, onion & rice

4-6 cups corn chips or soft corn tortillas cut in small triangles
1 cup cooked rice
½ onion, diced, see Glossary on how-to cut
1 cup *finely* grated mochi* OR ½ recipe Mac 'n' Cheez sauce (Noodles)
½ cup black olives, chopped, optional
1 cup cooked beans (black, pinto, white)
1 cup salsa, Roots Salsa, or Harvest salsa
1 avocado, optional

spread the chips or cut tortillas evenly on a flat baking sheet
mix together rice, onions, mochi if using, olives and beans, scatter this over the chips/tortillas. If not using mochi, dot with Mac 'n' Cheez Sauce
spoon salsa, and any other chopped vegetable: peppers, zucchini, etc.
cover loosely with tinfoil wrap or an oven-safe cover
warm thoroughly in an oven (375 degrees) until mochi is melted, then uncover a few moments under a broiler

For variation add:
- avocado, black olives, cilantro, lime; or side it with Quick Avocado Dip
- side it with Tofu Sour Cream, Creamy Seed Dip or if not using grated mochi, a dollop of Rice Cheez, or Mac 'n' Cheez sauce
- instead of mochi or Mac 'n' Cheez sauce, use Cashew Cream Cheese (see Spreads, Dip, Salsa just below the Sunflower Dream Cheese recipe)

* the zester macrophage is a very fine grater, and best if using mochi in this recipe. After the chips/tortillas are set on pan, then layer rice/onions, then the grated mochi, then beans/salsa; the mochi needs to be between layers of cooked foods and/or wet foods to melt sufficiently, otherwise it will remain dry in its grated form. In the directions above I state to mix the rice/onion/beans and mochi together and scatter on tortillas. Layering in-between or mixing them together then scattering atop tortillas/chips both work.

Crunchy Nuts & Seeds

Thanks to Nourishing Traditions for their information on preparing nuts and seeds, and grains and beans for proper digestion and assimilation.

2 cups almonds, walnuts, pecans OR pumpkin, sunflower seeds

choose one of the nuts or seeds, place in a bowl, cover with water
add 1 teaspoon sea salt, swish around, let stand 7 hours or overnight
next day, drain, let sit in a mesh strainer several hours to dry
spread on a cookie sheet, naturally dry or roast by one of these methods:
1) out in the sun until dry and crispy
2) in a very low oven (150°)
3) in a dehydrator
4) on a flame tamer atop a wood stove or burner, stir often

Stores well in fridge or freezer. These nuts/seeds are now ready to eat, they are much more digestible and a great snack whole with dry fruit, or blended and mixed with seasonings.

Almond or Sunflower Butter

3 cups almonds or sunflower seeds, soaked, see Cook's Notes
¼ cup melted extra virgin coconut oil (or other)
½ teaspoon Roasted Salt (Miscellaneous), or un-roasted, optional

After soaking nuts/seeds, let them thoroughly dry in a dehydrator, in the sun, a very low oven, or pan-roast (see Glossary under roasting), also see above recipe for Crunchy Nuts & Seeds for method, then,
blend the nuts or seeds dry in a Blendtec-type blender until flour-like
stir them up, add the oil and salt, and blend until smooth

For variation: I rarely make this now, and instead, I prepare nuts/seeds as above through soaking/drying, and store them in the freezer. When nut/seed butter is needed, I'll grind a few tablespoons in a coffee grinder, transfer to a small bowl and mix with a bit of mashed dates, cooked sweet potato or squash. It's a great sandwich spread and is less fatty!

Popcorn

½ cup popcorn
extra virgin coconut, olive, flax or hemp oil if desired
shoyu, umeboshi vinegar, or very fine salt (see Roasted Salt)
nori
toasted sesame seeds
nutritional yeast

air pop the popcorn, or pop it in a pot over the stove but you have to use oil
drizzle it with melted coconut oil or other, or no oil
sprinkle with shoyu or umeboshi vinegar (best if put in a spray bottle)
or sprinkle with finely ground Roasted Salt (see Miscellaneous)
grind nori and roasted sesame seeds in a coffee grinder and add to popcorn
add nutritional yeast if desired

Millet Log Appetizers

1 recipe Millet Patties (Patties)
1 cup soaked and roasted sesame seeds* (black or tan)

Follow recipe for Millet Patties. Instead of patties though, shape into bite-sized logs or balls (I use a small ice cream scoop) and,
roll the logs/balls in whole or ground, sesame seeds
place on a baking sheet, bake in 400° oven, 20 minutes, until golden on bottom.

* see Cook's Notes for soaking seeds, and Glossary for roasting them

Arrange on a platter with Sweet Mustard Sauce (Sauces).

For variation:
-   use minced walnuts or other seed or nut instead of sesame seeds
-   roll in spices such as curry, paprika,

Bread, Tortilla, Cracker

"Poetry is an act of peace. Peace goes into the making of a poet as flour goes into the making of bread."
Pablo Neruda

What is it about bread? We all love it. It is satisfying, filling and just so good. I've always loved the dense dark rye types and chewy sourdough. The breads in this chapter are far from conventional. Keep an open mind when trying them. They are not spongy or soft, in fact, more often they are crumbly, sour, and dense but they're better for you this way.

About snacks and good things to eat . . . make kale chips and Seed Crackers (in this section). They are worth the effort. The Seed Crackers are delicious dipped in Quick Avocado Dip, Creamy Seed Dip or Sunflower Dream Cheese. When I sit down to these foods, I purse my lips and raise my eyes in absolute delight and joy. To prepare and eat such natural, tasty good food is heavenly.

What is a "whole" food? A food that has nothing added and nothing taken away. We are responsible for the choices we make in what we eat and therefore how our bodies and minds are affected. Disease is almost always the result of an overly acidic condition in the blood, which prefers to be slightly alkaline. This is rarely the scenario. The foods we eat such as excess protein, processed, salted, sugared stimulants and the unending assault of electronic gadgets, pressure of time and money, having to make a living create "acid" in the body.

I ferment flour (like soaking grain) in recipes that call for it. It aids in the digestibility, and is less mucous producing (no matter what quality the flour is, it all forms excess that is difficult for the body to eliminate). It is not necessary to do this step for sourdough since that method already sours it. And, you don't have to ferment the flour to make these recipes, but if you do, keep extra in the fridge or freezer. See fermented flour in Glossary.

See Millet-Quinoa Dosas (Grains) for a great bread-like pancake.

Corn Bread

An easy bread to go along with soup, beans, stir-fries or just plain. The batter can be spooned onto vegetable/grain/bean/potato combinations and stewed, or cut in cubes after cooked with wild rice and sautéed vegetables.

> 2 cups cornmeal (fermented if you can, see Glossary)*
> ½ cup rice or oat flour (or other), see fermented flour in Glossary
> 1 teaspoon baking soda
> 3 tablespoons ground flax seed or other ground seed or nut
> 1 cup applesauce*
> 1 teaspoon lemon juice or apple cider vinegar
> 1¼-1½ cups water, or Potato Water, or "milk" (Miscellaneous)
> cinnamon for dusting the top, optional

combine first 4 ingredients and then the wet ingredients separately
add wet mix to dry, mix briefly until just combined
pour into an oiled 9-inch cast iron skillet, smooth out, dust with cinnamon
place on burner on high until warmed, then simmer on *very* low for 35-40 minutes with a flame tamer (see Glossary) so it cooks even and won't burn the bottom; test for done-ness with a toothpick. Let cool a bit before cutting, or steam it (which is what I do most often), see steaming "baked" goods in Cook's Notes, it turns out really moist!

* or squash/sweet potato puree (see Miscellaneous), mashed beans, leftover blended soup, or mashed bananas. I often dust the top with cinnamon. If you have no applesauce/sweet potato puree, use all nut or grain milk to equal 2 cups liquid, and omit the 1¼ cups water.

For variation add:
-   ½ cup molasses and reduce water by ½ cup + dash vanilla extract
-   chopped green chiles and/or corn (½ cup each)
-   raisins, goji berries, chopped dry apricots, cocoa/carob chips
-   1 cup grated carrots, squash or zucchini, dust top with cinnamon
-   2 teaspoons orange rind, substitute orange juice for half the liquid

If it gets old, crumble, let dry, and grind in a food processor, store in freezer – great "bread" crumbs (see Sweet Rice Balls in Grains).

Tortilla (chapati)   8-10 medium sized tortillas

When I lived in Nepal, I loved to watch my hajur aama (grandmother) make chapatis – a fascinating ritual. She would put them directly on the fire and they would puff up. It works well on a gas burner but not on an electric stove. The delicacy of a homemade tortilla is special. I use spelt flour (see Glossary for info.), since I have not discovered a way to simply make a gluten-free version without refined flours and strange fillers.

> 2 cups whole grain spelt flour
> 1 cup warm water

make a well in center of flour, dribble water in while stirring
combine for a soft, pliable dough, adding more or less water as needed
knead with your hands for a few minutes, cover with a damp towel
let rest as long as you have, up to 30 minutes, if no time, don't worry
cut dough into 8-10 pieces, cover what you are not rolling or it will dry
sprinkle counter with flour, roll the tortilla to 1/8 inch thickness
heat a small skillet on a burner, place tortilla in skillet
roll out another one, flip the tortilla in the pan, keep rolling and cooking
store cooked tortillas in a damp towel on a plate

If you have a gas/propane burner, put the cooked tortilla right on the flame and, with a potholder, press down on the sides. It will puff up or it may puff up without pressing down on it. It may not puff up no matter what, don't worry, just stack and try with another.

If you don't have a flame, just cook tortillas on both sides so they freckle with brown spots. Try pressing down on the sides with a potholder, it may puff up in spots.

If they seem dry after cooking, set a damp cloth over or around the stack and place in a plastic bag. They will steam until ready to eat. Like any tortilla, they freeze well or last for days, refrigerated. They can be steamed or pan-heated to re-heat.

Roll anything into them:
- leftover stir-fry, pilaf, vegetables, grains, beans, tofu, tempeh, noodles – see Quesadilla recipe – and drizzle with a dressing
- steamed greens, leftover salad, shredded carrot, Creamy Seed Dip

(cont'd next page)

- hummus, Lentil Walnut Paté, Curried Tempeh Wrap, etc.
- spoon on seed dressings, Ranch Dressing, pesto, Bean Naise, Sunflower Dream Cheese, etc.
- cut in triangles for dipping

In Nepal, a version of this is called Alu Roti, where cooked or leftover potato, onion and spice is kneaded into the dough, then cooked as above. Dip into Spicy Lentils, Creamy Greens, or any creamy soup for a satisfying meal.

Rice Flat Bread

I had this up in a mountain village of Nepal, thick and chewy with spots of black char, smelling and tasting of that high altitude air, with its smoky and foreign warmth. And then I came across a similar recipe in a favorite book by Holly Davis, "Nourish." Upon writing her and discovering a like-minded soul, I asked if she wouldn't mind I use a recipe I have that is similar to hers. She didn't mind at all. And so, here are rustic rounds to be enjoyed with Hummus, Spicy Lentils, Lentil Walnut Paté, Sunflower Dream Cheese, Harvest Salsa, Creamy Greens, or just with soup – even as little pizza's with toppings.

> 3 cups cooked brown rice, short grain is best
> ¼ cup roasted pinon nuts, walnuts, or pumpkin seeds, chopped
> ½ cup finely grated carrot or zucchini
> ½ cup cubed Japanese sweet potatoes, steamed until just soft

knead the rice with wet hands so it becomes sticky, a few moments
fold in nuts/seeds, grated vegetable and potato
season with salt and other herbs or spices* if desired, but not necessary
heat a skillet on a medium flame, wipe lightly with oil
snowball the mixture in wet hands, in ¼ cup amounts, flatten to 1/8 inch
place in skillet, press down with metal spatula
pan-fry both sides until dried and slightly golden

* minced fresh herbs such as cilantro, parsley or dill (or dried), or spices such as cumin, chili flakes, oregano.

Sour Millet Bread

a dense, chewy, nutritious bread

2 cups cooked millet
2 cups cornmeal or millet flour, or a combination
1 teaspoon miso, dark is best but any will work

place grain and flour in a bowl, mix until crumbly, or pulse in a food processor
dissolve miso in 1 cup warm water, stir into above mixture
stir until a soft, slightly wet, dough forms
scoop into a greased skillet, a stainless steel/or glass bowl, or bread pan
cover loosely with a plastic bag, poke a small hole in it
let stand 12-24 hours until a sweet sour smell and has settled and risen

After fermenting, if in a skillet place on a burner on very low with a flame tamer (see Glossary), cover, cook 45 minutes.

If in a bowl or bread pan (it will only cover about 1/3 of the pan with batter, if more of a bread is desired, do 1½ times the recipe), very gently remove plastic bag and place in a steamer, see Cook's Notes for Steaming "baked" goods. Steam 45 minutes-1 hour.

Allow to cool completely. Slice thin.

Alternate: sometimes I do not use miso. Instead, I'll leave the cooked grain out on the counter long enough to sour, several days and up to a week, then mix in the flours and warm water or Rye Tonic to get a soft dough, allow to ferment as above. OR, if you do not want to let it ferment, mix in 1 teaspoon *each* baking soda and apple cider vinegar, and cook as above.

Try other cooked grains such as rice or rice and millet to replace the cooked millet. And other flours to replace the cornmeal or millet flour such as rye flour (and caraway seeds to make a rye bread + 1-2 tablespoons blackstrap molasses to the water/miso mixture).

Sprinkle seeds on top before cooking if desired. Try this bread for the Cucumber Sandwich recipe (Snacks, Wraps, Sandwich).

Sprouted Sourdough Bread

1½-2 cups grain sprouts from making Rye Tonic*
1½ cups Rye Tonic, see Beverages & Smoothies
1½-2 cups millet flour, brown rice flour or rye flour
1½-2 cups barley flour, brown rice flour or rye flour

blend the Rye Tonic and the grain sprouts briefly, keep it coarse
place in a bowl, stir in the flour, form a sticky, firm dough
knead dough 1 minute with a wet hand (5 minutes if using rye flour),
when kneading: dip hand quickly in water, shake water off, knead, dip in
water again, shake water off, knead
transfer to a greased 9" skillet or large bread pan
cover with a loose plastic bag, make sure there is room for it to rise and set
in a warm place to ferment, 10-12 hours. It will almost double. Once risen,
treat *very gently* when removing plastic and moving to cook

* if you do not have Rye Tonic use 1½ cups water instead, make grain sprouts
(see Making Sprouts in Miscellaneous) and add 1 teaspoon dark miso to the
dough.

If in a *skillet*, cover, set on medium heat until warmed, set a flame tamer (see
Glossary) between skillet and burner, turn very low for 40 minutes. The top
will be firm and dry when done.

If *steaming*, the pan does not need to be greased before placing dough in it. See
Cook's Notes under Steaming "baked" goods, and steam 45 minutes-1 hour.
Boil extra water and check once, add more if needed to complete steaming.
Cool 20 minutes before removing from pan.

I never bake bread, but if it is the method you want to do, grease the pan before
putting the dough in. Set a pan of water on the bottom rack of the oven, set
bread on middle rack, bake 375° for 15 minutes, reduce to 325° for 35 minutes.
The top should be dry when tapped. Let cool slightly before removing from
pan.

For variation add to the dough:
- chopped nuts, dry fruits, seeds, mashed banana, herbs or spices
- one cup leftover hot cereal: oats, millet or barley, even if it has apples
  or squash cooked into it, extra flour may be needed depending on
  consistency of cooked cereal.

This Pizza
unique – it's an experience . . .

I often steam dishes instead of using the oven: the energy is lighter, it provides moisture, and is much easier on digestion, versus baking, which is contracting and drying on the internal organs.

> 1 pizza crust, next page
> 1 cup Italian Sauce or Pesto Sauce (or ½ & ½)
> 1½-2 cups mochi, *finely* grated, on a macrophage if possible (Glossary)
> 1 tablespoon nutritional yeast, optional
> toppings: onions, mushrooms, zucchini, artichoke hearts, olives, etc.

prepare crust or use store-bought, and place on a round pizza pan
steam crust 10 minutes see * below, or if baking, use a 375° oven
spread the sauce on crust to almost the ends, use more if needed
distribute the mochi evenly, then nutritional yeast if using
layer the toppings** on top, completely covering the mochi*
bake at 375°, or steam in a very large steamer such as a wok, see * below, as well as, Steaming "baked" goods in Cook's Notes.

Mochi needs moisture to melt and needs to be between layers, such as sauce and toppings, otherwise it will dry out – unless steaming it!

* I always steam the pizza. If choosing to steam it: prepare the crust, place it in the hot steamer (such as a wok), cover and steam 10 minutes; frequently wipe the inside of the steamer top to clear condensation (every 5 or so minutes). As you prepare the sauce, toppings, and grate mochi, let the crust just sit in the steamer with the heat turned off, and wipe the top condensation occasionally until ready to move on.
** if steaming the pizza, prepare toppings in this way: mince onion, slice mushroom and zucchini and place in a skillet, season lightly with salt if desired, cover and cook on medium heat 5-8 minutes. They will just lightly steam/cook. When done, add them on top of mochi, make sure to completely cover mochi, add other toppings if using such as artichoke hearts, etc. Cover steamer and let steam 10-15 more minutes. Place pizza on a low burner or warm top of a wood stove to dry and crisp up the bottom a minute or two.

Quick Pizza Crust

    1 cup cornmeal
    1 cup cooked rice, millet or quinoa
    ¼ scant teaspoon baking soda
    1 tablespoon olive oil and ½ teaspoon guar/xantham gum, optional*
    1 teaspoon apple cider vinegar
    ¾ cup lukewarm water or Potato Water (Miscellaneous)

stir together first 4 lines of ingredients in a food processor and pulse
transfer to a bowl, add the vinegar and water, and stir briefly
form a wet dough, cover with plastic and let rest while preparing a pan
wet pan with water (or oil), dust with flour or cornmeal and/or sesame seeds
place dough in middle of pan, lay piece of plastic on top
press with hands to form an even thin crust, remove plastic, poke with a fork
bake in 375° oven OR steam in a large steamer (wok) for a 10 minute
pre-cook (see Steaming "Baked" Goods in Cook's Notes), then follow
directions for This Pizza

* guar/xantham gum makes the crust less crumbly, so you are able to pick
it up with your hands and eat

If not making crust for This Pizza, try:
- spreading crust with Creamy Greens and sautéed vegetables
- with Pesto, thinly sliced steamed winter squash, chopped red pepper
- chopped olives and herbs, minced garlic, and press into dough before
  cooking – like focaccia

For variation, **Rice Crust Pizza Dough**:
    1 cup rice flour _and_ ¾ cup cooked rice
    ¼ teaspoon baking soda
    1 tablespoon _each:_ garlic, onion, fresh parsley, all optional
    1 teaspoon apple cider vinegar in ¼ cup warm water/Potato Water

combine first 3 lines of ingredients in a food processor, pulse briefly
add the vinegar/water, stir until just combined into a soft dough
press onto a prepared pizza pan and follow directions above
Also see Rice Flat Bread (this section) for simple mini pizza crusts.

Garlic Bread

1 onion, minced, about 2 cups
1 head garlic, peeled, then grated or minced, + more if desired
¼-½ cup stock or water + ½ teaspoon salt
1 loaf of bread, sliced (Sour Millet Bread or Sprouted Sourdough)

sauté onion, garlic, stock or water, and salt for 20 minutes
stir often but keep covered, cook until very soft, then mash or blend
add stock/water if needed, fresh herbs and more fresh garlic if desired
spread thinly on both sides of bread slices, cover loaf with foil
place in a dry skillet on stove-top, cover, heat on very low, 30-40 minutes,
turn once, OR place in oven at a high temperature (400°), check often

Add if desired, ¼ cup parsley or cilantro and/or ½ cup minced walnuts.

Alternate: thin slices of warmed/toasted Sour Millet Bread with avocado,
minced *fresh* garlic and a sprinkle of salt.

Croutons

These croutons are fun to munch on while cooking something else. Use any
bread (Sprouted Sourdough Bread is my favorite), cornbread, cubed Magic
Millet or polenta. Magic Millet is our source of "bread" most of the time and
is a meal with a cultured salad, soup or Creamy Greens.

5-6 cups any of the above choices, diced large
1 tablespoon olive or melted coconut oil, optional
2 cloves garlic, minced or finely grated
¼ teaspoon salt or 1 tablespoon umeboshi vinegar
¼ cup water or broth
pinch crushed rosemary, basil, and/or other herb

place cubed choice of bread, millet, polenta, etc. in a bowl
whisk together rest of the ingredients and pour over cubes
gently toss, set on baking sheet or in a skillet
bake in 300° oven until just beginning to brown, or sauté
in skillet on medium heat until just starting to brown and dry

Kale Chips

This is my rendition of these incredibly delectable crunchy satisfying "chips." We easily eat the whole batch in a day. Try it with cabbage or zucchini too.

>   juice of ½ lemon (2 tablespoons)
>   1 cup pumpkin seeds, soaked overnight (see Cook's Notes)
>   ¼-½ teaspoon salt to taste
>   3 tablespoons nutritional yeast
>   handful cilantro or parsley (and cayenne or jalapeño, optional)
>   ½ cup water
>   2 large bunches curly kale (12 or more cups), or cabbage or zucchini

drain seeds, blend with other ingredients *except kale*
wash kale, pat dry, remove most of the stems, tear in small pieces
mix pumpkin seed mixture into kale, coating it evenly
spread onto parchment paper sheets (see Resources) and dehydrate overnight OR place on a cookie sheet in an oven, low temperature, 150° and up to 325°, for several hours, up to 12 hours, until crispy dry. Check often.

Nori Cracker

>   nori seaweed, 2 sheets cut in 9 squares per sheet
>   ½ cup sunflower or pumpkin seeds, soaked, see Cook's Notes
>   1 large carrot, diced and steamed until just soft
>   1 tablespoon lemon juice, sea salt to taste
>   1-3 cloves garlic + 1 teaspoon fresh turmeric or 1/8 teaspoon dry

blend all ingredients, *except* nori, add water to get blender going
spread filling over each nori piece, or place a small dollop in middle
dehydrate or set in a low oven (150°) or higher (325°) until crisp

Seed Crackers

¼ cup *each:* pumpkin and sunflower seeds (sunseeds), optional
3 tablespoons sesame seeds, optional
2 cups flax seeds, preferably golden, but either + ¼ cup more
¾ cup onion, peeled, diced or minced if not using a food processor

soak sunseeds, pumpkin and/or sesame if using together, see Cook's Notes
under soaking seeds, (these crackers can be made without soaking the seeds)
next day, soak 2 cups flax seeds in 3 cups water + ½ teaspoon salt, 1 hour
drain sun/pumpkin seeds and place half of them into a food processor
grind the ¼ cup flax seeds in a coffee grinder, add them with the seasoning
(below) to the seeds in the food processor. If not using the pumpkin/sun seeds
etc. just mix together the soaked flax with the ground and other ingredients
add onion and pulse all until just blended, then place in a large bowl
stir in the soaked whole soaked flax, mix well
cover baking sheets with parchment paper, spread mix thinly with spatula
place in a low oven (150° or higher, just check them), on a woodstove (with a
flame tamer) or near it, or a food dehydrator, let them dry until you can peel
the paper off, 4 or so hours, dry again without paper until crisp, 8-12 more
hours depending on which method you use. Break them up, keeps for weeks

Seasoning
2 tablespoons nutritional yeast
1 tablespoon dulse, optional
1 tablespoon dill, optional
or other herb/spice

Cracker variation*
2½ cups flax seeds
1½ cup carrots
1 cup onion
2 tablespoons dulse or nori

* grind carrots and onions in a food processor until pulp-like, follow directions
for Seed Crackers above, mixing the carrot/onion and dulse/nori in at the end.

For variation:
- replace part or all flax with chia seeds, but don't do the Cracker variation with vegetable pulp, it prevents chia from becoming crunchy. Or,
  juice carrots, celery (apple), and use juice to soak seeds instead of water
- change seasonings such as: ½ cup finely minced cilantro or arugula,
  2 teaspoons red or light miso, and lemon juice

Sauces

bitter   pungent   sour   sweet   salty

It is our responsibility to cleanse our palette, re-train our taste buds and get back to what nature intended: the simple taste and outstanding nutrition whole foods has to offer . . . and sauces help.

A plain dish, even uninteresting, can be awakened by adding a simple sauce.

Food has to taste good, even brown rice, steamed daikon, or pan-fried polenta. As we work at changing what we eat, our taste buds will change to accept and enjoy un-adultered whole foods. And as we learn to slow down and chew more, we will feel nourished by our food, and the need for more seasoning, flavoring, and over-eating will lessen. None-the-less, sauces are great. They complement, richen, and diversify
meals.

In general, there are five tastes:

bitter / pungent / sour / sweet / salty

When a meal has a taste of each category, such as Skillet Greens for bitter; Ginger Glaze with Millet Patties or ginger juice in the Easy Rice Stir-Fry for pungent; Rainbow Pressed Salad for sour; Daikon Medallions (not seemingly *sweet* but as far as our internal organs are concerned, it is the sweet they love and recognize) or Sweet Winter Squash for sweet; and Creamy Celery Soup for salty . . . then our multi-dimensional body, spirit, and mind are fulfilled, at least the moment of chewing and tasting. So let us continue this ecstasy and chew each bite more (50 times *minimum* when whole grains are on the fork, or chopstick), and get even more out of the hidden and available nutrition latent within the fibers of the food.

Sauces can liven up anything. Learn a few so they can be prepared easily. I use a lot of vegetable steaming liquid as the base. I always have it around because I eat steamed vegetables daily. I try to have extra Italian Sauce and the Cheez sauce from Mac 'n' Cheez (Noodles) in my freezer. They are quick and easy for tasty meals.

See also:
-   Apple Sauce, to make your own (Breakfast)
-   Creamy Seed Dip and Salad Dressings
-   Plum Sauce in Miscellaneous
-   Salad Dressings for more thoughts on the five tastes

Dipping Sauce
salty, pungent, perfectly poised . . .

This is for dipping Nori Rolls (vegetable sushi, see Grains). It is an all-purpose sauce that can be drizzled on any grain or pasta salad, over noodles, with steamed vegetables or vegetable wraps. Leftovers can be incorporated into soup as part of its flavoring.

½-1 inch piece fresh ginger root
1 green onion, minced, see Glossary on how-to cut
3/4 cup water, miso soup or other broth
2-3 tablespoons shoyu
1-2 teaspoons stone-ground mustard
1 teaspoon mirin or rice vinegar, optional

If you've made Nori Rolls with mustard and umeboshi paste, and simmered the carrots with shoyu (and barley malt, molasses or apple juice), there is not much need for a dipping sauce. But if not, and want a little extra zing, whip this together. The more ginger, the spicier.

grate ginger on a small grater, squeeze juice into a bowl, run a little water over pulp, squeeze again, discard pulp or use in another dish
place minced scallion in bowl with ginger juice
combine rest of ingredients in a small saucepan and simmer 10 seconds
pour hot mixture over ginger and scallion

I often do not make ginger juice, and just very finely grate ginger into the bowl with the scallions, and pour the warmed mixture over it. It just depends on how much you like ginger. I really love it. And when grating ginger, do it on a macrophage zester grater, they are the best for getting it so small, it just blends in beautifully.

get healthy to the core and live simply

Sweet Mustard Sauce

Yield: heaping ½ cup

A sweet and piquant sauce for dipping Millet Patties when made as appetizers. Add finely ground flax, sunflower, sesame or pumpkin seeds and lemon, and it can be a salad dressing.

>   ¼ cup brown rice syrup, barley malt, or other liquid sweetener
>   ¼ cup stone-ground mustard, or other
>   1 tablespoon lightly roasted mustard seeds, optional
>   2 tablespoons shoyu

combine ingredients in a small saucepan and simmer 3-4 minutes
add small amounts of water for desired consistency
tranfer to a serving bowl, garnish with minced parsley or green onion

Ginger Glaze

Yield: 1¼ cups

A simple glaze for grains, noodles, steamed vegetables, Millet Patties or baked into casseroles.

>   1 cup water or broth
>   1-inch piece of ginger root, peeled, grated or sliced thin and minced
>   1-2 cloves garlic, minced, optional
>   2 tablespoons shoyu
>   1 tablespoon arrowroot powder mixed into ¼ cup cool water

simmer water/broth and shoyu in a small saucepan 5 minutes
add ginger and garlic if using, to the simmering liquid, cook 1 minute
whisk in arrowroot/water mixture, keep whisking on high heat until thickened and the cloudiness is gone, stir the whole time, about 30 seconds
taste and adjust seasonings if needed, add a dash more shoyu and/or ginger, or for a thicker glaze, cook in a bit more arrowroot diluted in water

Variation: simmer thinly sliced mushrooms in the water/broth/shoyu/salt and continue as above. Green peas or finely grated parsnip (allow to simmer in the broth a few minutes as well) are a nice addition too.

Lime Marinade

It's the best with the Tempeh Fajita recipe in Burrito, Quesadilla, Fajita.

> juice from 2-3 limes
> 1 tablespoon shoyu
> 2 tablespoons apple juice
> 1 tablespoon cilantro, chopped
> 1 clove garlic, minced + pinch cumin and cayenne

whisk together briefly in a small bowl

For variation:
- simmer the tempeh in this marinade after the initial 15 minutes of cooking the tempeh in water (see Tempeh Fajita recipe)
- instead of tempeh, mix it into cooked beans and/or polenta cubes with minced green onion and chopped celery

Lemon Sauce

Delicious with artichokes, green beans, broccoli, cauliflower – just about any vegetable dipped into it.

> 1½ cups water or stock
> 3 tablespoons flour (I use rice or millet flour)
> ½ teaspoon salt
> 1 green onion, minced, see Glossary on how-to cut
> ½ lemon, juice only (3-4 tablespoons)
> 1 clove garlic, minced, optional

whisk together water, flour, and salt, bring to a boil while stirring
simmer covered 10 minutes, stir often
add onion, lemon and garlic (if using), stir together well
transfer to a bowl . . . it will thicken as it cools. Add more water if desired.

Mushroom Sauce

Almost like canned mushroom soup, thick and rich over polenta, pasta, vegetables. Also see Ginger Glaze variation for another mushroom sauce.

> 2 cups mushrooms (shiitake fresh or dried, Portobello, crimini)
> ½ cup onion, minced, see Glossary on how-to cut
> 2-4 garlic cloves, minced, optional
> ½ teaspoon salt
> 2 cups "milk" or broth or water
> 2 tablespoons rice or barley flour

soak mushrooms in water to cover if using dried, otherwise,
slice mushrooms, use more than one variety if desired
sauté mushrooms with the onion, garlic (if using), and salt, 5 minutes
add liquid, use mushroom soaking water if available (as part of measurement)
cover and simmer 5 minutes
whisk in flour, stir while it bubbles on low heat 5 minutes more

"Beefy" Lentil Sauce   2-3 servings

> 1 cup cooked lentils, somewhat drained
> 1 tablespoon shoyu, tamari, or umeboshi vinegar
> 1-3 cloves garlic, roughly chopped
> ¼ teaspoon chili powder, or to taste
> 1 green onion, minced
> dash lime, optional

place all but the green onion and lime in a blender
blend until very smooth, add hot broth or lentil water as needed
keep it thick, transfer to a saucepan, add green onion, simmer 5 minutes
stir in lime if using, mix into pasta of any kind

Sweet Bean Sauce

This is one of the toppings for Sweet Rice Balls (Grains) – a sticky, chewy, sweet sensuous mouthful . . . also a creative "frosting" or filling for a cake.

> 2 cups cooked adzuki or black beans, strained
> ½ cup apple butter or ¼ cup rice syrup or other
> 1 tablespoon light miso or ¼ teaspoon salt
> 1 cup chestnuts, cooked (see Glossary), optional – but worth it!

simmer all ingredients together for 10-15 minutes
mash or blend in a food processor, set aside to cool, it will thicken.
For Sweet Rice Balls, indent the balls and place this sauce as filling inside the ball then hide it with more rice; use as a spread for polenta or Corn Bread squares, in morning hot cereal, or in Barbeque Sauce below.

Barbeque Sauce

> 1 recipe Sweet Bean Sauce*
> 1 tablespoon stone-ground mustard
> 1 tablespoon red miso or shoyu
> ¼ cup apple cider vinegar
> ¼ cup onion, minced, see Glossary on how-to cut
> 3 garlic cloves, minced, optional
> 1 tablespoon molasses (black strap or regular)**
> cayenne and/or smoked paprika to taste, optional

simmer all ingredients, 5 minutes, stir often

* if not making Sweet Bean Sauce, replace it with one of the following and taste and adjust extra seasonings if needed:
- 1 large can black, adzuki or red beans
- 1 cup Italian Sauce
- 2 cups carrots and winter squash chopped, then simmered in ¾ cup water or broth until soft. Blend until smooth.
** optional if using the Sweet Bean Sauce

Italian Sauce

Yield: 3 cups

For the Love of Eating's version of tomato sauce for pasta, lasagna, pizza, etc.
I do not advocate the use of tomatoes very often.

> 1½ cups carrots, diced
> 1½ cups kabocha or butternut squash, diced
> 1 cup onion, diced, see Glossary on how-to cut
> 2-4 tablespoons diced red beet – gives it a "tomato" color
> 2 tablespoons umeboshi vinegar
> 2 teaspoons barley or red miso
> 2 cloves garlic, optional
> 1 tablespoon *each* basil, oregano*, even more may be needed

simmer first four ingredients in 1¼ cups water/stock, covered 10 minutes
add vinegar and miso and simmer 5 more minutes
blend vegetables and cooking liquid with the garlic (if using) until smooth
pour back into the pot, add the herbs

It is finished and ready to use, but to make it even smoother, or if it is a little too loose, bring sauce to a gentle boil on medium heat. In a small cup mix 2 teaspoons arrowroot powder or kuzu and 2 tablespoons cool water, pour into sauce while it simmers. Whisk until thickened and smooth.

* if using for This Pizza (Bread, Tortilla, Cracker), double up on the herbs.

This is an all-purpose sauce, the base is carrot/squash, but anything can be tried. I've used carrot and peeled broccoli stems.

For variation:
- sauté mushrooms and onions, add to sauce (see water-sauté in glossary)
- add crumbled Golden Tofu or Spicy Tempeh
- add any diced and sautéed vegetables

Recipes needing this sauce include: Red Chili Sauce, Thousand Island Dressing, This Pizza, Barbeque Sauce.

Bean Gravy

1½-2 cups bean liquid from making any kind of beans
3 tablespoons shoyu, or 1 teaspoon salt
2 tablespoons flour, I use rice, oat or millet flour
1 clove garlic minced + pinch cayenne, cumin, and chili powder
½ cup *each* onion and celery (or zucchini), minced

combine ingredients in a small pot, whisk together on medium heat
stir often as it comes to a boil, then cover and simmer 10-15 minutes
add water as needed to thin the sauce

Green Chile Sauce

1 cup onion, minced + (2 cloves garlic minced, optional)
1 teaspoon toasted sesame or tahini, optional
2-3 tablespoons flour (rice, barley, oat or corn)
2 cups green chiles peeled, seeded and diced
½ teaspoon salt
2 cups water, leftover Miso Soup or other stock/broth*

sauté onion (and garlic) in ¼ cup water and oil (if using), 5 minutes
stir in the flour, it will thicken, add the chiles and salt
whisk in the water/soup (*or mix 1 tablespoon dark or light miso in)
cover and simmer, gently bubbling, stir occasionally, 10 minutes

The sauce should be thick enough to bind chiles and onions together,
if not, whisk in 1 more tablespoon of flour, simmer 5 more minutes.

Sauce can be refrigerated for three days, freezes well.

For variation:
-   use zucchini, celery or bok choy and onion instead of the green chile
-   after making sauce with onion/garlic, then blend with an avocado,
    artichoke hearts, cooked green beans or broccoli stems (peel/cook)

Red Chili Sauce

Yield: 1½-2 cups

Red Chili Sauce can be used for enchiladas, burritos, nachos, tofu or tempeh, Red Chili Spaghetti, mixed into beans, etc. It freezes well. If you do not have or do not want to make Italian Sauce, just simmer 1 cup diced carrots and/or squash in water to cover until soft (10-15 minutes), add the rest of the ingredients and blend well.

> ½ recipe Italian Sauce
> 2 whole cloves, ground, or large pinch clove powder
> 1 garlic clove, minced
> pinch cumin (and oregano if desired)
> 1 tablespoon red chile or chili powder*

place Italian Sauce in a small pot
add rest of ingredients and simmer 1-2 minutes
stir or whisk often as it cooks, add oregano if using
taste and adjust seasonings, adding a bit of cayenne and umeboshi vinegar

If not using red chile powder, add cayenne to taste. Whisking in stock or water may be needed to thin to desired consistency.

* chile powder is ground, powdered chiles (from chipotle, habanero, ancho, etc.), that comes in a mild and hot version. Chili powder is a combination of *chile* powder and spices such as cumin, garlic, oregano, etc. If just using chile powder in this recipe, make sure it is not too hot, otherwise reduce the amount.

Nightshade vegetables: tomato, eggplant, sweet and hot peppers, potato (to name only a few), appear infrequently in *For the Love of Eating* because they tend to deposit too much acid in the body, take calcium from the bones, tissues and blood, compounding arthritic type problems and inflammation. Best to eat these foods in-season, late-summer, and local. See roannelewis.com for more information.

Greens Pesto

This is not just for noodles. Try it on potato salad, steamed vegetables, steamed or baked potatoes, with Seed Crackers. Also see Cilantro-Walnut Pesto.

> 3-4 leaves of collards, kale or bok choy greens
> 1 bunch cilantro or a mix of basil, cilantro, arugula, and parsley*
> 1 green onion and 1 clove garlic
> 1 tablespoon *each:* light miso *and* umeboshi vinegar
> ¼-½ cup broth, stock or water

blanch or steam the greens (not the fresh herbs), 1-3 minutes
place them and the rest of the ingredients in a blender, blend until smooth
add the broth/stock/water slowly, just to get the blender going
taste and adjust seasonings, serve immediately

* concerning cilantro mainly, the stems are soft enough to use. I wash the whole bunch (snip off ragged stem ends) then place in blender. Parsley and basil stems can be too tough, though it depends. Bite into them. If they can be chewed easily, they can be blended up smooth. Clean the root ends of green onion and add to blender as well.

For variation:
-   instead of the greens and herbs, use 1-2 bunches of fresh arugula either all raw or steam/blanch for only a moment part of the bunch. Blend with other ingredients as above
-   peel, dice and steam broccoli stems as part of the steamed greens base
-    water sauté 1 chopped leek (white and green parts) with the umeboshi vinegar and miso, 5 minutes, and blend in. Omit green onion and garlic
-   blend in ½ cup cooked winter squash for a milder tasting pesto. This is a nice spread with mustard and beans rolled in a tortilla

Cranberry Sauce

I eat this with a spoon. The tart and mild sweetness complements foods such as pilaf, Stuffed Squash, Corn Bread, morning hot cereals, Oat Yogurt . . .

> 1 package organic cranberries
> 1 cup apple sauce (see Breakfast to make your own)*
> 1 tablespoon lemon juice
> ¼ teaspoon *each*: cloves *and* ginger powder

place all ingredients in a food processor and blend until chunky smooth
chill until ready to enjoy. It freezes well

* if buying apple sauce, apple-raspberry or pear works too. If using just apple sauce add ¼ cup red raspberries for variation.

Alternate: I just made this but with pears that I cored and diced, and simmered with pitted Italian plums and a splash of apple juice until soft. I then processed them with fresh cranberries. Very nice.

Condiments & Seasonings

When eating whole grains, vegetables, beans, seeds, and other whole foods, and if cooking and preparing meals for a family with different nutritional needs and tastes, condiments and seasonings are crucial.

They not only enhance the taste of a dish and bring in diversity, but add incredible nutrition. I rely on Sesame Sprinkle, Pumpkin "Parmesan" and Walnut Cheesy Sprinkle weekly to provide added minerals and protein to meals. Getting nutrition from many different sources is key to sustaining energy and maintenance with a whole foods diet.

Take the time once every couple of weeks to prepare condiments such as homemade pickle and Sesame Sp rinkle, store in the fridge (pickle and Sprinkle) and freezer (extra prepared seeds for Sprinkle) to have on hand.

Homemade pickles are a fermented or cultured food, easy to make, essential to health. They are full of naturally occurring enzymes that aid digestion, strengthen appetite, and nourish the intestines by supporting friendly bacteria as a result of the lactic acid formed in the fermentation process. Have a few slices with every dish of grain.

There are plenty of recipes with meat, cheese, eggs, sugar, tomatoes, peppers, cream, white flour, yeast, butter, etc. in the world . . . but this is a different book. Its purpose is to have great food using alternative ingredients, getting more vegetables, whole grains, nuts, seeds, beans, and seaweeds into our diet, to provide our body with an abundance of natural minerals, vitamins and nutrients from the food we eat. *For the Love of Eating* means caring for your core, digestion, the root of health. If food is not prepared or chewed properly, then it cannot be digested, assimilated, and absorbed properly.

Sesame Sprinkle

A delicious high mineral, rich protein condiment; strengthens the nervous system, helpful in neutralizing an acidic condition in the blood. I put this on everything from pasta, grain, salads, cooked vegetables . . .

 2 cups sesame seeds, soaked (Cook's Notes for Soaking Seeds)
 1 teaspoon salt*

soak sesame seeds for 8 hours or overnight
next day, drain, leave in mesh strainer several hours even overnight
place seeds and salt in skillet, roast over high heat to get pan heated
reduce heat to *very low*, stir often and let roast until done
seeds will begin to pop and give off a nutty fragrance, 15-30 minutes
check if they are done by one or all of these methods:
-   scoop some seeds up with a metal spoon, if they fall off easily, they are done, otherwise they will stick to the spoon, meaning they still have moisture in them and need to be roasted longer
-   or pinch and crush a few seeds between your thumb and forefinger, if they crush easily, they are done
-   or pop a few in your mouth, crunch down . . . do they taste and pop like they are nicely roasted?

When the seeds are done, transfer to a bowl and let cool completely. Store in a glass jar in fridge or in the freezer. When ready to use, place 1-2 tablespoons in a coffee grinder (or grind by hand in a suribachi or mortar and pestle) alone or with 1-2 tablespoons flax seed (and some nutritional yeast and nori if desired), and grind. These prepared seeds will last months in the fridge, grind fresh as needed.

* or use 3 teaspoons ume-shiso powder (see Glossary) instead of the salt. And cook it in at the end of roasting the seeds, in the last few minutes.

Traditionally, it is Gomashio and prepared a little differently. First the salt is dry roasted in a skillet, then finely ground in a suribachi. Then the seeds are roasted, placed over the ground salt and ground together.

Seasoned Sprinkle

½ cup sesame or/and sunflower seeds, soaked, see Cook's Notes
½ cup pumpkin seeds, soaked, see Cook's Notes
1 sheet nori, ground or 1 tablespoon dulse flakes, ground (or both)
1-3 tablespoons flax seeds, optional, do not soak or roast
2-4 tablespoons hemp seeds
large pinch cinnamon
1 tablespoon nutritional yeast
¼ teaspoon acerola cherry powder or vitamin c crystals

strain seeds, roast each separately in a dry skillet, tossing/stirring often for 10 minutes or so, until golden and smelling nutty (see Roasting in Glossary)
set aside to cool (leave flax raw), then grind in coffee grinder or blender
grind hemp seeds with flax, cinnamon and yeast, or leave hemp whole
combine all and store in a glass jar in fridge up to two weeks, longer in freezer
The flax is optional because it is best used within 24 hours when ground. If using flax, store in freezer. Or freshly grind flax just before using. Delicious on hot cereal (kids love it), grain or pasta salads, cooked vegetables.

Pumpkin Seed "Parmesan"

Sprinkle this mix over Garlicky Noodles or the Creamy Greens and it's pretty close to the real thing. When you have been away from the taste of parmesan for so long like I have, and you really don't want to be eating dairy, then this is a winner as well as the Walnut Cheesy Sprinkle.

1 cup pumpkin seeds, soaked (Cook's Notes under Soaking Seeds)
3 tablespoons nutritional yeast
¼ teaspoon sea salt

soak seeds, if no time, rinse them, then roast in a skillet until lightly roasted, 10-15 minutes (see roasting in Glossary), or in a 325° oven, 15-25 minutes
roast salt in another skillet on medium heat, shaking often 5-10 minutes
grind all together in two batches in a coffee grinder until sand-like
store in a glass jar in refrigerator, up to 2 weeks, or freeze longer

Walnut Cheesy Sprinkle

Suddenly it seemed many seasonings came on the health food market to substitute parmesan cheese. Walnut Cheesy Sprinkle is similar to Pumpkin Parmesan, but richer and spicier . . . store in a glass jar in the fridge, 2 weeks.

    3 cups walnuts, soaked (see soaking nuts in Cook's Notes)
    5 tablespoons nutritional yeast
    1 tablespoon paprika
    1 teaspoon onion powder and 2 teaspoons garlic powder
    ½ teaspoon Himalayan salt, roasted if you can (see Miscellaneous)

After soaking walnuts, drain, and let dry completely in the sun, in a very low oven or in a skillet on a low flame. If no time, use them raw without soaking . . . **place** sun-dried (or oven roasted), or raw walnuts in a food processor
add rest of ingredients, blend until consistency of rough cornmeal

It's the best on noodles of any kind, white basmati rice, steamed vegetables or stir-fry, salads . . . just about anything.

Until one is committed, there is hesitancy,
a chance to draw back, always ineffectiveness.
Concerning all acts of initiative and creation, there
is one elementary truth, the ignorance of which kills countless
ideas and splendid plans. But the moment one definitely commits
oneself, then Providence moves too. All sorts of things occur to help
one that never would have otherwise occurred. A whole stream of
events issues forth from the decision, raising in one's favor all
manner of unforeseen incidents and meetings and material
assistance, which no man could have dreamt would have
come his way. Whatever you can do, or dream you can do,
begin it. Boldness has genius, power, and magic in it.
Begin it now.   Goethe

Salt Brine Pickle

Homemade pickles are delicious, easy to make and can be stored in the fridge for several weeks, even longer depending on the pickle and amount of salt used. They add crunch in a satisfying salty/juicy taste. I often munch a small handful after a meal to help with sweet cravings. They are an integral part of a whole food diet (or any diet!), providing enzymes and beneficial bacteria. Commercial pickles, even organic ones, are pasteurized and no longer contain enzymes, or at least those of poor quality and quantity.

> 1 cup water
> 2 teaspoons salt
> 1 inch piece kombu, quickly rinsed
> 1-3 broccoli stalks, peel tough skin off, slice thin
> 1 carrot, sliced very thin
> ½ turnip, sliced very thin

boil water and salt together until dissolved, 30 seconds-1 minute
add a cold ½ cup of water, set aside, and let cool *completely*
prepare a clean jar, approximately 24 ounce
place kombu seaweed into the jar first
then vegetables, pack tight, use more if needed
when salt water is cool, pour over vegetables, <u>cover</u> them, if not add water
place a piece of cabbage leaf over vegetables, tucking it in, if you have one, if not, just make sure vegetables are covered with brine
cover jar lightly with cheesecloth, it needs to breathe
set on counter for 4-5 days, depending on how warm it is, if very warm only 2 days is needed, cooler temperatures = longer, even up to a week

Have a few slices of this pickle with meals, rinse first under water to remove excess salt. Cover and keep in fridge. May use the brine again to make another batch along with fresh cooked salt water (½ a batch). Experiment with other vegetable combinations. And then a 3rd time, use almost all fresh salt water and a bit of the old brine to top off vegetables after the new salt water has been added. Use this oldest salt brine to soak grains and beans instead of apple cider vinegar (see soaking grains in Cook's Notes).

Sweet 'n' Sour Pickle

I use a 20-24 ounce glass jar (glass jars from store bought pickles, sauerkraut, etc.). Any size jar will work, adjust the amount of vegetables and liquid used. Pickles last for months in the fridge. They are so healthy, providing natural bacteria that our intestines need. Give them a quick rinse, then eat with rest of meal.

> 2-4 broccoli stalks, peeled, thinly sliced in large diagonal slices
> ½ cup daikon or radish, thinly sliced
> ¼ red onion, thinly sliced
> ¼ cup shoyu
> ½ cup apple juice
> ¼ cup apple cider vinegar

place vegetables in a clean glass jar, pack tightly, use more if needed
mix together shoyu, ½ cup water, juice and vinegar
pour mixture over vegetables, add additional water to cover
cover lightly with lid or a cheesecloth/tea towel
set overnight or several days

Umeboshi Pickle

> 1 cup red radishes, cut in spears or sliced in rounds
> 1 cup cauliflower florets
> 2-3 tablespoons umeboshi vinegar

mix radish and cauliflower together in a clean jar
combine vinegar in ¾ cup water in a bowl, then pour over vegetables
add more water if needed to cover vegetables
cover lightly with top or cheesecloth
set on counter and allow to ferment for several days

It turns a beautiful rosy pink.

Shoyu Pickle with Rutabaga & Carrot

This is a favorite. Rutabaga has a distinct flavor and is best as a pickle I think. Toss into noodles with roasted sesame seeds, garbanzo beans, and ground nori seaweed. As in all my pickle recipes, I use a 20-24 ounce jar, though any size will work, just adjust the amount of vegetables and liquid.

> 1 rutabaga, cut in matchsticks, about 1 cup
> 1 medium carrot, cut in matchsticks
> 1 inch piece kombu, rinsed
> ¼ cup shoyu

mix rutabaga and carrot together in a bowl
prepare a 20 ounce or so sized glass jar, set the kombu on the bottom
pack vegetables tightly
combine shoyu in a 2-cup measuring cup, and add 1 cup water
pour over vegetables, add more water if needed to cover
loosely set lid on top, allow to ferment 3-5 days

Quick Pickle Relish
' . . . take keen or zestful pleasure in . . . '

Well, that is what the dictionary says. Relish can be made with any vegetable, homemade pickle, olives, even fruit. Enjoy with Tempeh Sandwiches, beans, grain, or salad, mixed into mustard and Bean-naise then used as a dip for roasted potatoes. Store in fridge, use within 2 weeks.

> 1 large dill pickle, chopped very small
> ¼- ½ cup homemade pickle, or use all dill pickle, minced
> ¼ cup red onion, minced
> 2 teaspoons stone-ground mustard
> 1 teaspoon molasses, rice syrup, or barley malt, optional
> 1 teaspoon shoyu

combine all ingredients in a small bowl, taste and adjust

Carrot Ketchup

2 cups carrots, diced
1 cup onion, diced
¼ cup red beet, diced (for color)
1 teaspoon salt
½ cup water

simmer all ingredients, 15 minutes
blend until very smooth, store in glass container, refrigerate when cool

This is good stuff. We love it on any bean/grain burger (as well as with a touch of mustard or Bean-naise). It is nutritious too, so don't skimp, lay it on thick! It freezes well.

The earth wears in the summer
her golden fleece of sun
warms the sprouts and leaves
so we may eat from this delicate
palate, savior the pungent
burst and lively quench of thirst . . .

Prepared Mustard   Yield: almost 2 cups

1 tablespoon salt or 3 tablespoons shoyu or red or light miso
¾ cup yellow mustard seeds, soaked 8-12 hours (see Cook's Notes)
¼ cup brown mustard seeds (soaked, as above)
¾ cup apple cider vinegar, brown rice vinegar, or a combination
1 tablespoon mirin and barley malt, or rice syrup, all optional

roast the salt for 8 minutes in a dry skillet if using, if not see *
add the mustard seeds with the roasting salt, only for a few moments
blend all ingredients until desired consistency
add mirin (see Glossary) and others if using for a sweet bite and water or sauerkraut/pickle juice if needed to get the blender going, taste and adjust

* if using shoyu or miso, blend it in with the seeds and vinegar
It gets better as it sits in the fridge, give it a few days before using.

Bean-Naise

A mayonnaise made from beans, thick and tasty, and works well spread on bread with Seared Zucchini & Onion or polenta then covered with Caramelized Onions, on any slice of bread or burger, or simply as a dip for celery, carrots, romaine lettuce and Seed Crackers.

> 1½-2 cups cooked white beans*, drained (save liquid)
> 1 tablespoon lemon juice
> 2 teaspoons apple cider vinegar or rice vinegar
> ½ teaspoon salt
> ½ teaspoon dry mustard
> 1/3-½ cup liquid from beans, stock or water

combine all ingredients in a blender and blend until very smooth
store in refrigerator up to a week

* great northern, navy, cannellini

For variation:
-   use garbanzo beans instead of white
-   add fresh garlic and/or green onion or chives
-   add roasted red peppers or sun-dried tomatoes

Sun-Dried Tomato Mayonnaise

This could not be simpler or more delicious. It goes well on any grain or bean burger.

> 4-6 sun-dried tomatoes
> ½ cup Bean-Naise, Avo Mayo, or other*

soak tomatoes in water overnight or until soft
If they are packed in oil, just set them on a counter and
chop tomatoes very finely, mince or blend into a paste
mix together tomatoes with mayonnaise

* Follow Your Heart brand Vegenaise, the purple label made with grapeseed oil is quite wonderful if buying mayonnaise.

Avo Mayo

1 cup cooked brown rice (long or short grain)
scant ½ teaspoon salt
½ avocado, diced in the half shell
1 tablespoon lemon juice
¼ teaspoon dry mustard
2 garlic cloves, chopped

simmer the rice in 1 cup water with the salt, 10 minutes
transfer to a blender, add rest of ingredients and blend until very creamy

Use like a hollandaise sauce as well, just add more lemon.

For variation:
- add fresh herbs and/or prepared mustard
- dice the avocado, omit salt, season with umeboshi vinegar

Apple Chutney

An East Indian sweet 'n' spicy condiment often served with curries. Enjoy with pilaf, beans, even morning hot cereal, stuffed into squash or onions and baked with other grains, nuts or seeds.

2 green apples, diced
1 onion, diced
4-8 garlic cloves, roughly chopped
1 teaspoon salt
1 cup apple juice
½ lemon
1 tablespoon chili flakes or ¼ t cayenne
¼ cup apple cider vinegar

sauté apple, onion, garlic and salt in the apple juice, 10 minutes
add rest of ingredients, simmer 20-30 minutes on very low, covered
stir often, add water or more juice if needed, keep it thick and bubbling
allow to cool, store in glass jar in fridge for several weeks

get healthy to the core and live simply

Breakfast

dark leafy greens as part of every morning meal . . .

Miso soup is better than coffee as the first food to reach the stomach. Quickly steamed or blanched vegetables, especially greens like collards, kale, mustard, cabbage and bok choy have uplifting and cleansing energy, rich in chlorophyll, they gently open and awaken the body to prepare for the day. The soft crunch they offer release tension and ease cravings. See Easy Steamed Vegetables to learn how to prepare greens, enjoy them every morning – or at least a couple times a day. I know it may feel strange to have vegetables for breakfast, but try them.

My morning routine is often as follows: food-grade diatomaceous earth in pure water on an empty stomach, and/or a quart or large mug of warm water with either: lemon juice and a dash of cinnamon, Rye Tonic or tea (rosehip, raspberry leaf, or other) with or without chia seeds. In the next 10 minutes-hour: yoga, jogging on a mini-trampoline, or/and a walk, and then breakfast, choices depend on my day:

- I have this almost every day, it holds me for a long time and makes me feel the best: Miso Soup made with diced squash or carrot, peas or corn, Brussels sprouts, broccoli or cabbage, daikon or celery, and wakame, followed with steamed cabbage and greens and if hungry enough, a small bowl of hot cereal (oats, barley, etc.).
- soft-cooked grain with ground pumpkin seeds, dates, dried apricots or apple sauce, oat yogurt, etc.
- steamed rice or/and millet with Sesame Sprinkle, sauerkraut or Salt Brine Pickle, cooked greens such as collards, cabbage, kale
- a steamed bowl of cauliflower, carrots, broccoli and/or radish
- sometimes I skip breakfast and wait until 11 and have lunch: Layered Salad, grain/bean patties, just corn tortilla and lettuce with Bean-Naise or Sunflower Dream Cheese.
- I'll add to any of the above an hour or so later, My Favorite Smoothie, Green Drink, a Quinoa Muffin or Corn Bread if I made them.

When concentration and focus is needed so the day is set right, try Morning Tao or Grain Porridge with Sesame Sprinkle, fresh ground flax seed, a small side of sauerkraut or homemade pickle, and greens for an alkalinizing Zen breakfast . . . and chew, chew, chew!

Morning Tao

Even if this only holds you for an hour, start the day simply, allow the body to wake up in its own time. This food will de-tox and cleanse the body so a clarity and energy can slowly unfold. Give it time and permission, and it will give longevity and strength.

> a cup of Miso Soup (Soups)
> brown rice or millet, cooked and warm, 1 cup
> greens: dark leafy kale, collards, mustard, bok choy, cabbage

garnish soup with minced green onion or fresh parsley
sprinkle 2 teaspoons Sesame Sprinkle (Condiments) on grain
steam or blanch greens or cabbage (see Easy Steamed Vegetables)

Instead of rice or millet alone, try the Millet with Sweet Vegetables or Grain Porridge. And make a quick stir-fry of matchstick carrots and snap or frozen peas (see Matchstick-Cut Stir-Fry in Vegetables) and toss into the grain with Sesame Sprinkle or plain roasted or raw ground pumpkin seeds.

Morning Tao is a ritual of complete nourishment, grounded energy, and clear intention for the day.

Grains and sweet vegetables because of their natural, subtle sweetness, and if chewed well, nourish the organs, especially the stomach, spleen and pancreas by relaxing them. We crave sweets because they relax us and make us feel complete – good quality ones, that is. Providing this delicate sweetness through unrefined whole grains, root and round vegetables, we give the body a chance to heal itself. These foods are high in vitamins, minerals, and nutrients essential to health that give energy to the body and not take energy from it like refined foods do.

Grain Porridge

This is a staple breakfast, easy and quick. I have it almost every morning with Salt Brine Pickle and sometimes Sesame Sprinkle or apple sauce with fresh ground flax seeds. Add chopped dried or fresh fruit to the simmering grain, or diced/grated winter squash, carrots and onions. Place fresh or frozen berries in a bowl and top with hot cereal. Chop nuts/seeds and stir them in. If cereal is too loose, add ground flax, pumpkin seeds, or rolled oats.

> 1-2 cups cooked grain (millet, rice, oats, barley, etc.)
> ¼-½ cup water or water and juice for a sweeter cereal

place grain in a small pot, add water (and juice if using)
if adding vegetables, place in the pot first, then grain
add chopped fresh or dry fruit, soaked nuts, seeds, or leave as is
simmer, covered, 5-10 minutes, if using squash, simmer until soft
check liquid, more may be needed especially if squash was added
blend part or all if a smooth texture is desired, or mash with a masher

For variation, add after heated and in bowl:
- homemade pickle and Sesame Sprinkle, fresh ground flax seeds
- protein powder, vit. C powder (camu camu, acerola cherry, rosehip)
- ground flax, vitamin D oil, chia seeds, other seeds or nuts
- cinnamon, hemp seeds, apple or pear sauce

Soothing Barley
whole barley: earthy, light, full-bodied taste

> 1 cup whole hulless barley (not pearled), soaked (see Cook's Notes)

blend soaked barley in a blender with 2 cups fresh water for 10 seconds
place blended barley into a pot, add 2 more cups of water
bring to a boil while stirring, otherwise it will clump and stick
when boiling, cover and turn heat down, simmer 30-40 minutes, stir often
serve plain with steamed vegetables and Sesame Sprinkle
For variation: see Millet & Sweet Vegetables.

Millet & Sweet Vegetables

This dish has a deliciously simple and mild, sweet taste, a healing dish. It is based on a traditional macrobiotic recipe said to relax the digestive organs. See Morning Mashers for a different take on this combination.

> 1 large carrot, diced very small or grated
> 1 cup winter squash, diced very small or grated
> ½ onion, diced (½-¾ cup)
> ½ inch piece kombu or wakame or pinch of salt
> 1 cup millet, soaked if you have time or rinsed well (or 2-3 cups cooked)

If using uncooked millet soak first, see Soaking Grains in Cook's Notes.

place vegetables and kombu or salt in a medium pot
scatter the millet (soaked, rinsed or cooked) atop vegetables, do not stir in
gently add, down the inside of the pot, water (4 cups for raw millet, 2 cups if using already cooked millet)
bring to a boil, add salt if using, cover and simmer 30-40 minutes
mash or whip with a wooden spoon or blend half until creamy, then mix it back into the rest. Strain a bit of cooking liquid out if it is too loose or add a small handful of rolled oats and let it cook in 10-15 more minutes, stir often. The oats will thicken it up and smooth it out.

For variation combine the following ingredients in a pot:
- ¾ cup cooked millet, ½ cup cornmeal or polenta, ½ cup grated winter squash, ½ cup corn, 2½ cups water, stir well to remove any clumps. Bring to a boil, then gently simmer 30 minutes, stir often.
- instead of millet, use rolled or steel-cut oats and only 3 cups water (or 2 cups if using already cooked oats).
- coot the sweet vegetables with Soothing Barley (this section)

Chew very well, try each bite 50 times minimum before swallowing, the longer you chew, the "sweeter" it gets. Longer chewing transforms starchy grain into highly absorbable nutrition beyond the gluten and starch it contains. It unlocks the amino acids, fats, pure carbohydrates and beautiful energy our body utilizes almost immediately, the best "fuel."

Apple Sauce

Yield: approximately 2½ cups

3-6 apples, any will work especially bruised, broken, and lonely

wash apples, remove bruises, cut in quarters, remove seeds/core
cut in large dice, leave skin on, place in pot (about 5-6 cups)
add ½ cup of water (or a fruit juice), bring to a boil, add pinch of salt
simmer covered, 15-45 minutes, until very soft
blend until very creamy
If there is too much liquid after boiling the apples, strain and store for another use, add a bit of it to the blender if needed to get it going. Cool completely before storing in a glass container in the fridge. It freezes well.

For variation add:
-    plums, pears, apricots, peach, berries or dried fruit: prune, apricot, etc.

Pan-Seared Apple
Cut and core 1-2 firm apples (Granny Smith, Braeburn, Fuji) into cubes or thin slices, leave skin on. Gently knead a large pinch of salt into apples, then sauté until just brown, add a dash of cinnamon if desired. Nice with hot cereal, muesli, layered with Oat Yogurt and ground flax, even Creative Chef Salad or pilafs.

Cornmeal Porridge
blueberries, dates & apricots

½ cup yellow cornmeal (can use blue cornmeal if desired)
2-3 dates, chopped, may need more depending on size
2-3 dried apricots, chopped
¼ cup fresh or frozen blueberries
Sesame Sprinkle if desired

whisk together cornmeal and 2 cups water in a medium pot
bring to a boil while whisking so it does not form lumps
add dates and apricots, cover and simmer 10 minutes, stir often
stir in blueberries serve with a dash of Sesame Sprinkle . . . enjoy . . .

Hot Barley or Oats

Yield: 4 cups

> 1 cup rolled oats or barley flakes (or half and half)
> 3 cups water

bring cereal and water to a boil, watch that it doesn't bubble over
stir once, then turn heat down, cover and simmer 15 minutes for oats,
15-20 minutes for barley flakes or if using half and half
stir a couple of times during cooking
let set several moments off heat when done before digging in

Add anything and everything while simmering: grated carrot or squash, chopped dried apricots, prunes, dates, raisins, apples. Even simple and quick with applesauce and fresh ground flax and/or pumpkin seeds. Thick-cut oats need longer cooking, even regular-cut needs longer cooking, it just depends.

As it simmers, a creamy liquid gathers on top. If you scrape or gently pour this off, you can use it that evening in Creamy Mushroom soup.

Cinnamon Toast

> 2 slices of bread, Corn Bread, polenta, Magic Millet, or Rice Flat Bread
> 1-2 teaspoons nut/seed butter, see Almond Butter variation
> 2 teaspoons maple syrup, barley malt, date sugar, jam or apple butter*
> cinnamon to taste

toast or steam bread, spread with nut butter or Almond Butter variation
drizzle with syrup or sprinkle with date sugar, jam, etc.
sprinkle lightly with cinnamon
place in pan on burner or hot wood stove or under broiler
until warmed and toasted

* or try vegetable jam (see roannelewis.com for recipe) and spread on toast with cinnamon for an earthy natural sweet alternative.

Buckwheat-Rice Cereal
with amasake and flaxseeds

Buckwheat is a hardy, earthy tasting gluten-free fruit seed – not a grain. When roasted it is called kasha. It's good when there is physical work to do, or on cold days. It contains protein, magnesium and rutin, a bioflavonoid that helps with the absorption of vitamin C, as well as strengthens capillaries and has anti-inflammatory qualities.

> 1 cup kasha (roasted) buckwheat, rinsed
> 1 cup cooked brown rice
> almond amasake* see Glossary for more info.
> 1-3 tablespoons ground flaxseed and/or chia seed

simmer buckwheat in a pot with 2 cups water, 10 minutes
add rice and 1 more cup of water or "milk", simmer 10 more minutes
whip with a wooden spoon until roughly blended
serve drizzled with Amasake and sprinkle with ground flax or chia seed

To prepare kasha, rinse raw buckwheat, place in a dry skillet on medium heat. Stir often until just golden and a roasted aroma emanates.

In the northern colder climates (yin), more animal food, rich casserole dishes made with beans, miso and root vegetables are consumed to stay warm, buckwheat too; if eaten in abundance in a warm climate, one might find themselves out of balance, unable to cool down and relax.

Rye Tonic Porridge

This is a weird and wonderful favorite of mine. You need the soaked rye berries (and raisins) from making Rye Tonic (see Beverages & Smoothies). Blend the rye berries/raisins with enough water to get it smooth. Transfer to a pot and simmer 5 minutes, stir often. It cooks up loose, so my favorite is mixed with rolled oats, ground flax seeds and apple sauce (or apple-plum sauce). Let it sit so the oats can absorb the extra moisture.

Creamy & Sweet

¼ cup uncooked (raw) brown rice or millet, optional
½ cup rolled oats (if not using the rice, use 1-1½ cups rolled oats)
¼-½ cup date pieces or 6-8 pitted dates, chopped

grind rice/millet finely in a coffee grinder, so it resembles sand.
combine with the oats, dates and 2½ cups water, stir very well
simmer 15-20 minutes, <u>stir often</u> or it will clump up

For variation:
- use any other fruit, or a couple tablespoons maple syrup in the cooking. The dates make it taste like brown sugar
- instead of raw rice, use ¾ cup *cooked* rice or other cooked grain such as millet or barley and only 2 cups water, simmer 10 minutes
- instead of raw rice, use cornmeal/polenta, or use all oats (1 cup)
- add to the above recipe (Creamy & Sweet):
    1 cup butternut squash, diced small
    ¼ cup raw millet (grind in a coffee grinder like the rice above)*
    ¼ cup corn grits (polenta)
    1/8 teaspoon cinnamon
    2 cups water

* the millet can be blended until milky in a blender with the 2 cups water, then pour into pot and add rest of ingredients, simmer 30-40 minutes, stir often at first with a whisk until simmering, otherwise it will clump.

Creamy & Sweet . . . a different take

one onion, diced (about 2 cups)
½ cup cooked brown rice or millet
¼ teaspoon any kind of miso, optional

simmer onion, cooked grain, and add water to just cover for 40 minutes
add miso if using (richens the dish, but not necessary), simmer 3-4 minutes
If the cereal is too loose for your liking, add ¼-½ cup rolled oats near the end and let them simmer in and soak up the excess. Very soothing and delicious. I love this for breakfast. Adding grated carrot and/or winter squash is great too.

Muesli
cultured, creamy and sweet . . .

1 cup rolled oats
1½ cups liquid: water, vegetable steaming liquid, Rye Tonic, or "milk"
¼-½ cup Oat Yogurt (Miscellaneous), optional
1 tablespoon almonds, pumpkin or sunflower seeds, soaked*
1 tablespoon raisins, dried apricots, prunes or figs, chopped
¼-½ small apple, finely grated or chopped
pinch cinnamon
1-2 tablespoons fresh ground flax seeds

soak oats a minimum of 10 minutes (as long as overnight) in the liquid
stir all into the Oat Yogurt, allow to sit 5 minutes to let the dried fruit
soften, or if using dried fruit, chop and soak with the oats. Fresh berries,
peaches, or pears, etc. are great as well.

* see soaking seeds and nuts in Cook's Notes

Rice Yogurt Muesli
a simple breakfast . . .

Rice Yogurt (Miscellaneous)
prunes or other dried fruit, soaked overnight in warm water
1-2 tablespoons flax seed, ground fresh
¼-½ apple or pear, diced or grated
blackstrap molasses or apple sauce, optional

Place desired amount of yogurt in a serving bowl, a few prunes or other dried
fruit with a drizzle of its soaking juice, scatter ground flax, fruit, molasses or
other. Nice with a side of steamed greens.

For variation add:
-   chopped nuts or/and seeds, roasted or soaked

Oats & Quinoa with Squash
and Apple-Apricot Marmalade

1 cup rolled oats (or barley flakes)
½ cup quinoa (see Glossary for proper preparation)
1 cup winter squash, diced

place quinoa in a medium pot with oats and squash
add 2½ cups of water or "milk"
bring to a boil, cover and simmer 20 minutes
meanwhile, prepare the marmalade to grace this simple fare

Sometimes I trade out the oats for a cup of cooked millet, rice, barley flakes or use all quinoa and reduce water/ "milk" by ½ cup.

I do not advocate the use of quinoa flakes, they are not prepared properly before flaking, and become rancid very quickly on the shelf.

Apple-Apricot Marmalade

Use this tasty, tangy spread on hot cereal, toast, as a chutney with grain pilaf and curries. It will last two weeks in the fridge.

1 apple, diced (1½ cups)
4 dried apricots, chopped
dash umeboshi vinegar or pinch of salt
½ cup water or apple juice
½ cup orange or tangerine juice + ½ teaspoon grated rind, optional
1 tablespoon maple syrup, barley malt or rice syrup
fresh ginger, a few slivers, or 1 cracked cardamon pod, both optional

sauté on high the apple and dried apricots in vinegar or salt, 3 minutes
add rest of ingredients (if not using orange juice, use all apple juice or water)
simmer until apples are soft and most of the liquid is burned off

Use this as a topping along with chopped nuts, granola or ground flaxseed.

Continental Breakfast

Europe taught me how beauty fulfills the soul, from its cobblestone streets, eclectic and abundant art museums, little markets on every corner – that euphoric sense of independence travel gives you – and air of sophistication and peasantry.

1-2 cups cut vegetables: carrot, broccoli, cauliflower, cabbage, radish
1-2 slices Sourdough Sprouted Bread or other
almond butter, tahini, other nut butter, or coconut oil, optional
fruit-sweetened jam or Apple-Apricot Marmalade, Vegetable Jam*
¼ cup fruit of choice, dried or fresh, chopped
½ cup Oat Yogurt, or other
1-2 tablespoons roasted seeds, ground flax, or chopped nuts

steam vegetables 2-3 minutes, barely soft with a good crunch
place bread atop vegetables as they steam to soften and warm
spread warmed bread with nut butter or coconut oil and jam
layer yogurt, fruit, then seeds/nuts in a small bowl or cup
enjoy with a cup of Miso Soup or roasted barley or green tea
* see roannelewis.com under recipes

Tempeh Sausage

1 package tempeh, diced, simmered in water for 15-20 minutes
2 teaspoons *each*: crushed anise or fennel, thyme, chili powder, cilantro, mixed Italian herbs + pinch of cayenne
1 tablespoon garlic powder or 4-5 garlic cloves, minced
½ cup cooked grain
1-3 tablespoons shoyu
2 teaspoons fresh lemon or lime juice

drain tempeh, pulse with the rest of ingredients in a food processor
form into small patties, pan fry until golden on each side. They freeze well.

Leftover tempeh works great for this recipe. Add more cayenne or a minced jalapeño or habanera pepper for spiciness.

Pancakes

Yield: 13-15, three-inch pancakes

Delicious and rich, serve with steamed greens and Miso Soup – it'll help balance the sweetness. Use high oleic safflower, coconut, grape seed or sesame oil when frying. A well-seasoned, cast-iron skillet for pancakes/French toast works best (they require very little greasing, I only *very lightly* oil it once in the beginning, meaning just wiping the pan). Enjoy plain and simple or add to the batter: chopped fruit, nuts, or cooked vegetables (such as winter squash) for variation.

2 cups water or grain "milk"
½ banana, ½ cup cooked sweet potato, mashed or oat yogurt
1 tablespoon apple cider vinegar
3 tablespoons ground flax seed, *well ground* (grind with oats)
¾ cup rolled oats
1¼ cups rice flour or cornmeal (or half and half)
¼ teaspoon cinnamon
1 teaspoon baking soda
1 cup fresh or frozen raspberries, blackberries, blueberries, and/or cranberries, or anything of choice (grated squash, pear, apple . . .)

combine first three ingredients in a mixing bowl
grind flax seeds and rolled oats together in a coffee grinder
toss dry ingredients (ground flax/oats too) and berries in a separate bowl
add dry to wet, stir briefly, batter will be loose, let it sit 3-4 minutes, the flour and ground flax will absorb the liquid
spoon batter onto a greased skillet
flip when little bubbles form and the top starts to dry a bit

Before cooking, add chopped nuts or hemp seeds or try adding grated carrot or apple. Let batter sit a bit to firm up, or add water if too thick. They are delicate, and will work, just stay with them.

Delicious topped with applesauce and Oat Yogurt, then with or without maple syrup or Lemon-Walnut Sauce (see French Toast recipe).

French Toast

Read the information under Pancakes since it goes for French Toast as well concerning pans and what oil to use.

> 6 tablespoons flour (I use rice flour)
> 2 tablespoons *finely* ground flaxseed
> 1 tablespoon nutritional yeast
> 2 teaspoons cinnamon
> 1¼ cups "milk" (Miscellaneous), or warm water
> 1 teaspoon vanilla
> 4-6 slices whole grain bread

combine dry ingredients (first 4)
whisk in milk or water and vanilla and let sit 2 minutes, it will thicken
coat slices of bread covering both sides, if it gets too thick, add water
pan fry both sides until golden
serve with sauce below, or pure grade B maple syrup, or with Oat Yogurt and apple or plum sauce

I always just use water for this recipe, "milk" would be great but is not necessary. Careful about adding water when the batter gets thick, not too much, just a tablespoon at a time.

Lemon Walnut Sauce

> ½ cup brown rice syrup or ¼ cup maple syrup
> ½ lemon, juice only
> ¼ cup walnuts, roasted and chopped
> 2 teaspoons arrowroot powder dissolved in ½ cup cool water

place arrowroot mixture in a saucepan, add syrup
simmer while whisking until thickened and cloudiness clears
add lemon juice and rind if using and walnuts

Delicious atop pancakes, waffles, French Toast, a sauce into which Magic Millet or polenta cubes can be dipped.

Seed-Crisp Granola

Yield: approx. 7 cups

I rarely eat cold cereal for breakfast, and of course granola can be simmered in hot water or "milk" for a warm nutritious meal. Granola lasts several weeks stored in a glass jar. Sprinkle over puddings, pies, made into pie crusts, ground as flavored flour in baked goods, or just as is with "milk."

4 cups rolled oats
½ cup sesame seeds, soak all seeds (see Cook's Notes)
½ cup sunflower seeds, soaked
½ cup pumpkin seeds, soaked
½ cup chopped almonds, walnuts, or pecans, optional
½ cup shredded coconut, or oat bran or wheat germ
½ cup rice, barley, or millet flour
1/3 cup molasses or brown rice syrup
¾ cup apple juice (or other) or water
2 teaspoons vanilla
1 teaspoon cinnamon
¼ cup whole flax seed (mix into granola after it has been baked)

mix dry ingredients (first 7) in a large bowl even if the seeds are still wet
place wet ingredients in a saucepan and whisk together, heat slightly
pour heated mixture (wet) into dry and mix until well coated
spread evenly on two large cookie sheets, bake 20 minutes in 325° oven
flip granola and cook again until golden, 15-20 minutes
scrape onto flat surface and allow to cool completely
mix in flax, raisins, dried cranberries, chopped dried apricots, goji berries, etc.

Depending on your oven and the way it heats, it may need longer cooking time, and closer watching.

I usually double this recipe. I place the seeds and coconut if using (and nuts, but I rarely use nuts anymore) all together in a bowl, cover with water and salt and soak overnight. Even if it is longer than 8 hours, it doesn't matter. Then I pour them into a mesh strainer and set in a bowl (slant the strainer a bit to let as much water drain out as possible). I will often leave the seeds resting like this all day and overnight, and they will just begin to sprout.

Morning Mashers

Yield: 20 mashers

Morning patties, why not? They are like a very moist and soft cookie. Easy to take on the go, as a mid-morning snack, or along with a cup of Miso Soup and Skillet Greens or any steamed vegetable. Dip them in Sweet Mustard Sauce or spread with Sweet Bean Sauce, or just munch while looking at the mountains.

> 1 cup millet, soaked (see Cook's Notes for soaking grains)
> 6 dried apricots, soak overnight with raisins in 1 cup water
> ¼-½ cup raisins, soak overnight with apricots
> 1 cup butternut or kabocha squash or carrot, medium grated
> ½ cup *each:* onion and green or red cabbage, minced
> 1 apple or pear, roughly chopped or grated
> 2 tablespoons *each* or choice of: hemp seeds, chia seeds, flax seeds
> 3 tablespoons ground flax seed or ground sunflower/pumpkin seeds
> 1 teaspoon each: cinnamon and vanilla
> stevia or chopped dates if desired for sweetness

If you do not have time to soak the millet or the dried fruit, it doesn't mean the recipe cannot be made, it's just better to soak for digestion and assimilation. Just rinse the grain and chop the fruit.

drain millet, add apricots, raisins, squash, onion and cabbage
cover with 2 cups water + fruit soaking water, bring to a boil (3 cups total)
add a pinch of salt, stir once, cover and simmer 40 minutes
mash with a potato masher, stir in rest of ingredients
stir well and taste. Form into patties, pan-fry or bake on lightly greased skillet or baking sheets until just golden on each side.

For variation:
- use polenta instead of or along with the millet (half and half)
- mix in ½ cup minced roasted almonds, pecans or macadamia nuts
- mix in cocoa or carob chips, raw cacao nibs, shredded coconut, or any other dried or fresh fruit before forming into patties

Quinoa Muffins

These are not light fluffy muffins, but very moist, dense, tasty, and interesting. A great snack, addition to a meal, or hiking partner. See Cook's Notes on how to properly soak quinoa, Grains on how to cook it, and the Glossary for more information about it.

    1 cup sweet potato or carrot, grated
    1 apple or pear, minced
    ½ cup onion, minced
    ¾ cup apple sauce, this section to make your own
    1/3 cup molasses (black strap) or other liquid sweetener
    ¾ cup water + ¼ cup ground flax*
    4 dry apricots, chop very small
    2 tablespoons raisins (chopped) or currants (no need to chop)
    1 cup cornmeal or millet/rice/oat flour
    ¼ cup arrowroot starch
    1 teaspoon baking soda
    2 cups cooked quinoa**
    2 teaspoons cinnamon, optional

mince or grate vegetables and apple/pear very small, or pulse in a food processor – it's what I do - potato/carrot first, then fruit and onion
mix pulsed/minced vegetables/fruit together with rest of wet ingredients
place dry ingredients and cooked quinoa in a food processor
pulse until blended, transfer and mix into wet ingredients
(if not processing, mix dry with quinoa, then into wet ingredients)
scoop into greased muffin tins (12), bake 350° oven for 45-60 minutes
allow to cool 10 minutes in tin, then loosen around edges with a knife
gently remove and set on cooling racks upside down to allow to cool

Keep in the fridge up to a week, they freeze well. I have also made them by blending a fresh pear and a handful of small Italian plums (very sweet!), with the water and flax seeds instead of using the applesauce, and add a few more tablespoons of cornmeal/flour. Add nuts or seeds if desired as well.

* whisk the ground flax and water together with a fork until thick before adding to wet ingredients (or blend whole flax seeds and water until frothy)

** ¾ cup quinoa cooked in scant 1 cup water = approximately 2 cups.

Scrambled Tofu (or polenta)   Yield: 2-3 servings
savory & turnip, wild & turmeric

Tofu (polenta too) easily lends itself to manipulation through taste and texture. This recipe can be combined and changed many times, so experiment. Try it with polenta instead of tofu, see first variation below. Add traditional ingredients such as peppers, tomatoes and black pepper if desired, use different seasonings, and check out the suggestions below for more ideas. See tofu in Glossary.

> 1 cup onion, diced (see Glossary on how-to-cut)
> 2-3 cloves garlic, chopped, optional
> ½# firm tofu, squeeze as much water out, then crumble (or polenta)*
> ¼ cup carrot or peeled winter squash, finely grated
> ½ red pepper, zucchini or leek (white and green parts), diced
> ¼ teaspoon salt or 1 teaspoon shoyu, or to taste
> 1 tablespoon *each* parsley and green onion, minced
> ¼ teaspoon turmeric powder

sauté onion and garlic if using, 5 minutes in covered skillet, stir often
add rest of ingredients and sauté 4-5 more minutes
pour in ¼ cup water if it seems dry, if not cover anyway and cook on high until steamed through, a moment or two

* use polenta (pg.98) instead of tofu (cut it in small dice instead of crumbling)

For variation:
- toss in roasted pumpkin seeds near the end
- season with lime or lemon juice and a dash of cayenne pepper

Enjoy as is, or:
- with a side of cooked grain and a cup of Miso Soup
- rolled in a tortilla with beans, steamed greens, and salsa
- with Roasted Roots and Green Chile Sauce
- simply with steamed or blanched Greens
- mix in Sun-Dried Tomato Mayonnaise or Bean-Naise

Beverages & Smoothies

A smoothie can be a meal in itself, a snack, or maybe it just answers the need for something creamy and sweet. I believe chewing is so important, that blended drinks are best for occasional treats. When food is not chewed, thus mixing with salivary enzymes, then it is not digested well and too much "sugar" is released in the body.

The Ginger Mint Lassi, an Asian probiotic drink, is a tasty, creamy, cultured creation. Its base is oat yogurt, that you make yourself (Miscellaneous), then blended with classic digestive herbs (although any fruits, herbs, or vegetables can be substituted), and like kombucha, it is thought of as a cleansing and healing drink. *For the Love of Eating's* My Favorite Smoothie, Ginger Mint Lassi, and Rye Tonic are necessary health drinks as well as homemade pickle and cultured salads mandatory on a daily, or at least, weekly basis to keep up friendly bacteria crucial to health.

Also see Remedies Internal & External for other drinks, namely teas for daily enjoyment, not just healing.

It is our job to understand which foods have an acidic or an alkalinizing effect, and to balance them. Too much salt or salty foods makes us thirsty and leads to cravings of liquids and sweets. Then the pendulum swings back, and after full-filling that craving with liquids and sweets (and/or alcohol, over-eating, drugs, etc.) we need contracting salty and heavy food again. Following *For the Love of Eating's* guidelines takes patience to practice, as does changing anything that is so important as your health.

Include an abundance of vegetables, both raw and cooked, in every meal; deep breathing and exercise; avoid dairy and meat and limit salt, sweets, and flour products; avoid processed foods. What you need is not always what you want.

Keep an open mind, this is imperative to enjoying an incredibly rich and vital life. Be brave, know you can nourish yourself with organic, non-gmo, fair-trade more than you can through supplements, super-foods, and packaged, frozen, processed foodstuffs – even if they are organic. And even if you are plagued with disease, allergies, or a bad case of incredibly convincing media. You can do it.

Breakfast Smoothie

    1½ cups water, "milk", or juice, or tea*
    2-3 dried fruit: prunes, apricot, fig, etc., soaked overnight in water
    ½ pear or apple, optional
    ½ cup frozen or fresh berries of choice
    1 teaspoon spirulina, chlorella, or other greens powder OR
    handful greens: spinach, kale, collards, etc.
    1 scoop hemp protein powder, whey, or one of choice
    2 tablespoons flax seed, whole or ground
    ¼ inch slice (or more) fresh lemon, cut yellow part of rind off
    ¼ teaspoon cayenne powder, or to taste

soak extra fruit and keep in fridge for later use or to sweeten hot cereal
lemon, leave as much of the white as possible, pit and cut in small chunks
combine all ingredients in a blender, blend until very smooth

* I use water only and sometimes a splash of apple/prune juice or Rye Tonic.

Drink up, it will thicken as it sits. Fresh lemon (especially with its rind) with water and cayenne is a food source of natural vitamin C.

For variation add:
-   vitamin C powder such as acerola cherry, amla or camu-camu
-   soaked sunflower or pumpkin, chia or hemp seeds
-   banana, peach, apricot, cooked winter squash
-   Oat or Rice Yogurt (see Miscellaneous), aloe vera, herbal tinctures

MY FAVORITE SMOOTHIE
It's simple I know, but I love the lemony-vanilla, non-sweet simplicity.
    1 (or so) cup water, or tea such as chamomile, nettle, rose hip, etc.
    1 scoop vanilla protein powder
    2-3 tablespoons flax seeds, dash cayenne
    ½ lemon, diced, remove only outer yellow part of skin
    ¼-½ cup Rice or Oat yogurt
Blend until creamy, add soaked prunes, prune juice or frozen berries. Use more or less water/tea for desired consistency, it will thicken as it sits.

Creamy Nut-Milkshake

1 cup nut milk (see Miscellaneous)
1 frozen banana

blend ingredients, add ice (and water) as needed to get the blender going
keep it thick and creamy

Or, if you have a great blender, just add ¼ cup soaked (see soaking nuts in Cook's Notes) almonds or cashews, 1-2 fresh or frozen bananas, ice if using fresh banana, and 1 cup water. Blend until very smooth. Instead of banana, try dates, stevia, or apple sauce to sweeten.

For variation add:
- raw cacao, cinnamon, fresh ginger or turmeric, dates
- instead of banana use cooked winter squash and sweeten with a few drops of stevia, dates, or other dried/fresh fruit, or barley malt

High Mountain Berry Smoothie

1 cup berries: blueberries, raspberries, cranberries, etc.
1 cup apple or pure concord grape juice, or a mix
handful of ice if berries are not frozen
5-6 pine needles or/and juniper berries
½ cup rosehip tea (see Remedies) and lemon juice to taste

Combine all ingredients in a blender and blend until very smooth.

Use a combination of berries. If you can, pick fresh pine needles, they contain vitamin C, A, may aid in breaking up mucous in the lungs and is said to help heal infections in the respiratory and urinary systems. Rosehips are a natural source of vitamin C, antioxidants and bioflavonoids – simmer a handful in a quart of water 20 minutes. Drink the liquid, and then refill with water and simmer again, and even a third time. The water will get pinker each time. If you cannot pick your own rosehips (available in the fall in many mountainous places), and you cannot purchase them, use hibiscus tea.

Mellow Smoothie

Many smoothies use bananas for sweetness and creaminess and though touted as a health food, I disagree. Bananas are very different then how they appear in nature (hybridized, picked early, etc.). And many foods contain high amounts of potassium as well as adding that creaminess, but without the tropical sugar bananas contain. So here is a smoothie with squash (high in potassium) for a mellow sweetness and soothing texture.

> ¼ cup sunflower seeds or almonds (or a bit of both), soaked
> ½ cup cooked winter squash (butternut, kabocha) or sweet potato
> 2 tablespoons aloe vera juice or gel
> 1 teaspoon greens powder, optional
> 4 dates, pitted, optional
> ½ cup apple or pear juice or sauce
> dash of cinnamon, fresh ginger and ice if desired

soak seeds/nuts (see soaking seeds and nuts in Cook's Notes)
drain in the morning, place in a blender, add 1 cup water
add cooked squash or sweet potato and blend until creamy
add rest of ingredients and blend until very smooth
taste, you may want a few ice cubes blended in to chill it

For variation:
- use pumpkin seeds or hemp seeds instead of sunflower seeds
- use ½ a ripe pear or apple instead of juice
- use soaked dried apricots or prunes instead of dates

Orange Cream Smoothie

> 1½ cups nut, coconut milk or rice/grain "milk"
> 1 orange, scrubbed and cut in large chunks, leave skin on
> 1 frozen banana
> 1 scoop vanilla flavored protein powder or just vanilla extract

Blend all until very creamy, add ice to get it chilled and frothy.

Grain "Cappuccino" or Hot Cocoa
. . . this creamy cup of goodness settles the soul . . .

1 cup Amasake (plain or other), see Glossary for amasake
2-3 tablespoons grain coffee powder, also see in Glossary

stir ingredients + ¼-½ cup water in a small saucepan
simmer a few moments, enjoy as is or blend to get it frothy
The amount of water and grain coffee is up to you. Taste and adjust.

Golden Elixir

1 cup dried apricots, prunes, golden raisins or a combination
¼ teaspoon umeboshi vinegar (or umeboshi paste)
1 tablespoon fresh turmeric root or 1 teaspoon dried
1 green tea bag
½ cup fresh cilantro
1 tablespoon fresh grated ginger
2 tablespoons raw honey, barley malt or maple syrup, or 20 drops stevia
1 lemon or lime, juice only

soak dry fruit in water to cover overnight
boil 1 quart water, simmer fruit, vinegar and turmeric, 10 minutes
remove fruit and use in morning cereal, a smoothie, etc.
add tea bag and cilantro to hot fruity liquid, cover and steep 4 minutes
discard tea bag, add rest of ingredients, cover and let sit 5 minutes
strain and sip straight or mix into water, Rye Tonic, over crushed ice,
or in hot tea. Keeps 10 days in the fridge.

For variation:
- after removing fruit and tea bag, blend in cilantro and ginger
- use fresh fruit instead of dried fruit

If you do not soak the fruit overnight, simmer it in the water with the vinegar
and turmeric. If you did soak it, use its soaking water as part of the quart of
water.

Green Drink

> 1 cup dark leafy greens: kale, collards, bok choy or spinach
> ½ cup cucumber or bok choy (the white part, use the green part
> for the dark leafy greens part of this drink)
> ½ stalk celery, optional
> ½ inch fresh ginger root and/or fresh turmeric root
> handful parsley or cilantro
> 1 small green apple or pear, core removed, cut in chunks
> ½ lemon, remove yellow part of rind, keep white inner rind
> Rye Tonic, water, tea or juice

place all ingredients in a blender that can handle pureeing really well
blend, add Rye Tonic etc. preferably warmed, until desired consistency
OR, if you have a juicer, juice all ingredients and add Rye Tonic after
drink immediately on an empty stomach

Ginger-Mint Lassi

A Lassi is a fermented yogurt-type drink traditional in India and Pakistan
where it is often served as a before dinner, beneficial digestive tonic. Prepare
Oat Yogurt (or Rice Yogurt) in advance (see Miscellaneous for recipes).

> ½ teaspoon fennel seeds, soaked, if no time use anyway
> 1-1½ cups Oat Yogurt
> 1 teaspoon lemon or lime juice
> ½ inch fresh ginger, peeled, minced
> 4 fresh mint leaves

soak fennel seeds, 8 hours or overnight in water and dash of salt
blend all ingredients very well in a blender until smooth
enjoy before dinner or meals . . . or anytime

For variation add:
- some banana, a soft pear, some berries
- soaked prunes or prune or apple juice

Rye Tonic (a.k.a Rejuvelac)

I learned about Rejuvelac from Ann Wigmore, an incredible health pioneer and advocate of raw and cultured foods. When I contacted her foundation for permission to use it here, they were very strict in not wanting any confusion as to her method, the correct method, of preparation. Since I have changed it, know that it is not the "real thing." It is a slightly fuzzy fermented, natural probiotic, enzyme-rich healing beverage better than kombucha I think in that it uses no processed sugar for the culturing process (I add raisins in the second soak).

>   1½ cups rye berries*, soft wheat, or whole (not pearled) barley
>   ¾ cup raisins, optional

place grain of choice in a clean glass gallon jar and cover with water
fasten with cheesecloth and rubber band, let soak overnight
morning, drain, slant on its side in dish drainer, cover with a tea towel
rinse grain 2x/day for the next 2-3 days, until 1/8" sprout appears
fill jar with fresh water, let sprouted berries soak 24 hours or longer **
strain tonic and fill again with water, add raisins, let soak 24 hours

* my favorite, other grain can be used as well: rice, millet, buckwheat, oats.
** keep in mind that during colder weather, fermentation takes longer. If having trouble, see Troubleshooting in Glossary.

Drink this tonic daily (it lasts weeks refrigerated), use in making seed/nut cheese, sourdough and in any baked recipes, smoothies, as your morning drink cut with tea or fresh vegetable/fruit juices instead of diluted with water. What to do with the soaked grain afterwards? See Breakfast for Rye Tonic Porridge.

Include cultured foods and drinks 3 times a day: Rye Tonic in the morning, Oat Yogurt Muesli or smoothie, homemade pickle or sauerkraut, cultured salads as part of lunch and dinner.

Cultured foods help stimulate the colon, boosts immune function, aids the liver in releasing radiation from the body, restores alkaline/acid balance, helps with food cravings, and more. The transition to a healthy eating regime and lifestyle begins in the kitchen. Cultured foods made at home provide optimum quality. They are essential live "friendly" bacteria needed for health.

The rye/wheat has been sprouted and fermented, so its gluten content changed, and is possibly tolerated by those sensitive, I repeat, possibly.

Miscellaneous

From nut and seed "milk" to spice mixes, soup stock, roasted salt, Oat and Rice Yogurt, Miscellaneous is made up of important recipes for the eclectic, home-remedy and healing chefs we innately are.

It is a talent that grows as the method of whole food cooking, eating, and healthier lifestyle is established within ourselves and our family. Over time and with experience, genius from your hands will emerge concocting ingredients, leftovers, palettes, and seasons that will blossom into easy and integral meals. I only eat organically, it's superior in taste and nutrients than commercial, and stay away from processed, boxed, and canned foods, yet still enjoy samples at health food stores or farmer's markets, going out on occasion, etc. – canned beans are fine when time is short.

As we learn to use leftovers, odd chunks of vegetables, excess sauces in meals, etc., we truly take on whole food cooking and taking care of ourselves and our family through this age-old wisdom and custom of cooking. We can be proud that we are handling our health, lives, and healing through what we eat, getting what we need through food alone. If we shop local as often as possible at farmer's markets, and possibly grow a little on our own, the nutrients are rich and viable. Relying on the whole plant more often than supplements made from that plant, is what our body recognizes and craves. The body can break down, absorb and assimilate bio-available food (fresh vegetables, whole grains, beans, etc.) and prefers them.

A plant-based diet has fed me and my family for decades. It takes time to learn different cooking methods, and figure out what fulfills your palette and lifestyle to make it work. Learn the language, your health and vitality will show it as time moves on. Age will not be a burden, the body can weather the storms of life if given the food it needs and thrives on.

If I crave salt, crackers or fried foods, I'll have them, but balance with Easy Steamed Vegetables, Sweet Winter Squash, Vegetable Soup, Sweet Rice Balls, Carrot-Daikon Drink, Rye Tonic and Rosehip Tea – an example of how to take necessary steps to stay on the path. Learn healthy alternatives that *For the Love of Eating* offers, they will save your life. I am not talking about a vegan agave-sweetened raw cacao truffle dense cake sensation in place of the regular fudgy ice cream marshmallow goo you want. I mean, eat clean for several weeks (at least 12 initially) and your body will crave the clear, light, hopeful feeling healthy food gives you, and the body will be able to do without the amount of sweets, salt, fat, fried food, meat, processed food stuffs it has been used to. And so, the healing journey begins . . .

Making Sprouts

1. 2-3 tablespoons sprouting seeds: red clover, radish, alfalfa, etc.
2. ½ cup peas (sprouting peas), mung beans, lentils, adzuki beans
3. 1-3 cups garbanzo beans, or other bean or whole grain (rye berries, soft or hard wheat berries, whole barley, etc.)

Choose one from either line 1, 2, or 3. A sprouting jar (quart-sized glass) works great with a screen top or rubber band with a piece of cheesecloth. For beans use a gallon jar, unless only sprouting a small amount.

place seeds, beans, or whole grain in jar, one kind or different ones as long as they are the same size
cover with water, let seeds soak 2-4 hours, overnight for grains/beans
drain, rest mesh end down on an angle in a bowl or dish drain
rinse 2-3 times a day, after each time, set on a slant to drain, out of sun
keep the jar out of sunlight, gently shake once a day to loosen
sprouts will form in 1-3 days
sunlight is great for them now and will turn them green
store in a glass container in the fridge

See Sprouted Sourdough Bread for using grain sprouts (for grain sprouting, only allow an 1/8-inch sprout, otherwise they will get too chewy/stringy). I love lentil sprouts simmered a few minutes in Miso Soup, or added to salad with cooked rice or millet, tossed with Sliced beets, lettuce, salad dressing.

When sprouting beans, do the initial soak (see soaking beans in Cook's Notes), then drain and place them in a mesh strainer (or a gallon jar as above, but a strainer works just as well for beans), rinse a few times during the day until a sprout emerges. Store in the fridge until ready to use. They can be simmered with kombu until soft (see Beans for cooking instructions), and need less water and half the time to cook; or steamed briefly or tossed into stir-fries for quick cooking. They can be eaten raw in their sprouted form, blended into dips, even roasted. But I think digestion is enhanced by at least some cooking. It softens the fibers and texture and taste is better overall.

When sprouting seeds such as clover or alfalfa: once the sprout emerges, rinse the seeds several more days to get them ½-1 inch or more, then place in the sun (while still sprouting in the jar) and they will turn green.

Quick Grain Milk

This is a basic milk. If desired, add a few drops of stevia or 1-2 tablespoons rice or maple syrup, even a half teaspoon pure vanilla extract. If you have just made fresh grain, there is no need to simmer it again since it is hot and wet, just blend with the water.

>   1 cup *cooked* rice, millet, barley, oats, or a mixture
>   2 cups water

simmer grain (if cold and/or dry) and water for 5 minutes
purée in a blender for 1 minute
add more water if it seems too thick
pour through a strainer into a bowl, then strain again if you want it light
discard pulp, or use in soups, bread, breakfast cereal, or molded with beans into patties, etc.

Allow to cool, stores several days in fridge, freezes well.

Sesame Rice Milk

This milk is a superb alternative to regular milk. It has natural fat and higher protein content (than regular brown rice) from the sweet rice, minerals and oil from the sesame seeds, and a mild sweetness from the two kinds of rice. It can make one gallon, unless you want it thicker. See Cook's Notes for soaking rice and seeds.

>   ½ cup sweet brown rice, soaked
>   ½ cup long grain brown rice, soaked
>   2 tablespoons brown or white sesame seeds, soaked

roast grains and seeds separately in a dry skillet
soak all ingredients together in water to cover overnight
drain in the morning, and add 4 cups fresh water
boil rapidly 5 minutes, then simmer covered 2 hours
blend well adding water to equal one gallon, pour through a mesh strainer, then again through a finer one
save bran left each time in the strainer for another use. Let it dry and store in a jar.

Almond or Cashew Milk

A good blender is necessary to make creamy milk.

> 1/3 cup raw almonds or cashews, soaked
> 2 cups warm water

soak nuts (see soaking seeds and nuts in Cook's Notes)
drain water and blend with fresh warm water until smooth
add small amounts of water if too thick
pour milk through a mesh strainer

If you have no time to soak nuts, simmer them in 1 cup water for 10 minutes (after the first minute you can pinch the skins off the almonds, after placing them in cold water so you can handle them and discard), strain and blend with the fresh warm water.

For variation add:
- vanilla or almond extract and rice or maple syrup or stevia
- dates or dried and re-constituted apricots while blending

Use as you would milk. If you strain out the pulp, use it in soups, stir-fries (unless sweetened), fermented in sourdough bread, blended into smoothies, in breakfast cereal, or molded with beans/grain into patties.

Seed Milk

> ¼ cup soaked seeds: sunflower, sesame, pumpkin

Follow directions for almond milk.

Potato Water

Use half to one cup in cakes or bread recipes to add moistness.

 1 small potato (red preferred), diced, about ¾ cup

simmer potato in 1 cup water, 10 minutes, until very soft
blend until creamy while adding an additional cup of cold water
strain and allow to cool. Freeze in an ice cube tray for future use.

Sweet Potato Puree

Use in recipes to replace oil, add moistness and sweetness. I use the Japanese sweet potato. They have a dark skin and cream-colored flesh.

 1 cup sweet potato, diced (leave skin on)

simmer potato in water to just cover, 10-15 minutes, until soft
purée in a blender, add small amounts of the cooking liquid until very smooth, cool and store in fridge or freezer

Plum Sauce

Tangy and sweet, adds flavor and body to oil-free dressings, over pancakes, Corn Bread, hot cereal, or plain out-of-the-jar. Freezes well.

 1½-as many as you want cups of fresh plums, any that are sweet*

clean and pit plums, roughly chop or not, just pile whole into a pot and,
simmer plums with an added tiny pinch of salt, 5-20 minutes
stir often, the plums will soon cook in their own juice
transfer to a strainer over a bowl, when cool, search for all pits and remove
puree in a blender until smooth

* add (black)berries, diced apples/pears to the cooking plums, a real treat.

The simmering time varies depending on the plum: juicy plums need less time; if firm and/or tart may need longer + a bit of juice to the simmering.

Soup Stock

Use as a base for any soup, sauce, salad dressing, for cooking grain, braising vegetables; rich in minerals and nutrients and adds flavor to any dish.

> 2 inch piece kombu
> ¼ inch slice of fresh ginger, sliced
> 2-3 dried shiitake (or other) mushrooms, broken into pieces
> 1 each of carrot and stalk celery, diced
> ¼ onion, diced or/and ¼ cup dried daikon (see Glossary)
> handful parsley, optional

combine ingredients in a pot with 5-6 cups water, simmer 20 minutes
strain, use carrot, celery, shiitake and kombu in another dish or discard

For variation:
- save vegetable ends of everything: scallion/leek roots, clean onion skins, peelings of squash/apple/cucumber, strawberry leafy ends, cobs of corn, etc. Store in a bag in freezer until you have enough (6-8 cups or so), simmer in water to cover 20-30 minutes
- for a salad dressing base, do above or simply simmer the kombu or wakame alone or with other vegetables in water 10 minutes, strain

Squash Stock

Cut any winter squash in half, trim ends, remove seeds/guts and place in a pot with anything else if desired: onion parts (if adding skins, remove from stock 1 minute after putting them in otherwise broth may become bitter), celery ends, cauliflower leaves and core, scallion root ends, etc., cover with water, simmer 20 minutes. Strain, use this stock/broth in recipes.

I rarely add the actual squash saving it for another use. But you can add some to make the broth richer and sweeter. This recipe uses squash parts generally discarded.

Corn Stock

In summer we eat a lot of corn-on-the-cob. I boil the corn in an inch or so of water for 8 minutes, and use that stock to cook grain, in stir-fries, morning oats, etc. And then, after eating the corn, I boil the cobs in plenty of water for 20 or so minutes. Great stock. Add other vegetable ends if desired. Freeze the cobs if you cannot get to making stock out of them just yet.

Seasoning Alternatives

When cooking beans, pour off their thick stock and simmer with salt or miso, balsamic or umeboshi vinegar, garlic, pinch basil, celery seed, sage. Make it strong, strain it and freeze in ice cube trays to have on hand, use instead of shoyu, tamari, or Bragg Liquid Aminos.

Miso/shoyu substitute: if you do not want to use miso, substitute shoyu, Bragg-Aminos, good quality vegetable broth powder or homemade broth. If avoiding soy/gluten, cook in a bit of salt with bean liquid (as above), vinegars, lemon, spices, herbs, bouillon, or vegetable broth powder – but watch broth powders and bouillon, they often contain MSG disguised under many different names (see Glossary) as well as too much salt and a lot of poor quality oil.

Cajun Spice

    1 teaspoon fennel seeds, ground
    ½ teaspoon cumin seeds (or powder)
    2 tablespoons paprika
    1 tablespoon onion powder or granules
    ½ teaspoon cayenne pepper and black pepper (or more)
    1 tablespoon oregano
    1 tablespoon thyme
combine first 2 ingredients in a coffee grinder, blend well
add rest of ingredients and blend briefly. Store in a glass jar.
Alternate: 1 teaspoon cumin and paprika or chili powder, cayenne to taste

Roasted Salt

I rarely salt food without cooking it in, but, on popcorn, in Walnut Cheesy Sprinkle or when making hummus, etc. I'll roast ¼-½ cup in a dry skillet for 10 minutes or longer (it smokes a little). Then grind it in a suribachi or mortar and pestle until very fine and store in a jar. Roasting salt breaks it down, so it is not so extreme in its acidic nature of reacting in the system. It is a highly concentrated seasoning, best if used sparingly. If no time, of course use un-roasted salt, either way choose wisely: Himalayan, Real Salt, Celtic, Si, unrefined sea salt. See section on How To Cook for more information on salt.

Oat Yogurt

Yield: 2-2½ cups

Many recipes use this as an ingredient: Ginger-Mint Lassi, Indian Lentils & Greens, Muesli, My Favorite Smoothie, or just as a topping for curry, grains and beans, rolled in tortillas with cultured salads and stir-fries, stirred into cut fruit and nuts, on pancakes with apple sauce – anything yogurt is used for.

    1 cup rolled oats, or ½ cup whole oat groats
    ½ teaspoon (scant!) light or red miso

simmer oats in 2 cups water for 5 minutes (makes 2 cups cooked)
or simmer the oat groats in 1½-2 cups water until soft, almost an hour
cool the oats to slightly warmer than room temperature
mix the oats and miso together
cover with a bamboo mat or light cloth
set aside in a warm place such as on a kitchen counter for 3-4 days
when done, it should smell sour but not overly fermented
blend until smooth in a blender, if too loose, strain before blending

The time depends on how warm or cool the room is as it ferments. It will have a mild sour smell and a subtle sweet taste when done.

Alternate: mix 2 cups water, 1 cup rolled oats and ½ teaspoon miso, all raw, let it ferment as above until you can smell a sourness.

This yogurt can be used in batters (pancakes, quick breads, muffins), then set out to ferment where it *may* puff or rise *very* slightly, then steam to cook (see Steaming "baked" goods in Cook's Notes) for steaming instructions.

Sometimes it turns out quite loose and I'll strain it before blending, and keep that liquid to use in batters for Corn Bread, Quinoa Muffins, as the milky liquid over hot cereal . . . store in fridge up to two weeks.

Rice Yogurt

If sensitive to the gluten in oats (gluten-free oats are available in some health food stores or you can order online), use 2-3 cups cooked short-grain brown rice in place of oats. Let ferment 24 hours only. It will have a slightly sour smell. Blend to desired consistency, store in fridge. See Rice Yogurt Muesli in Breakfast section for ideas.

get healthy to the core and live simply

Remedies Internal & External

Cleansing or detoxing reactions are often experienced when eating the *For the Love of Eating* way, such as increased symptoms of what you are trying to clear: headaches, skin conditions, bloating, constipation, diarrhea, mental fogginess, weight issues, etc. The body is opening, letting go of toxins it has been holding onto for so long in the muscles, tissues, organs. On occasion, it's great to help the body out with a little more kick than just including greens every day. This section has ideas on cleansing, as well as drinks (Carrot-Daikon, Ume-Kuzu, Ginger Tea) and foods (Raw Daikon) to clear out debris. These are inexpensive, easily found ingredients in health food stores, to bring on increased healing and a sense of balance.

Remedy Drinks help in many ways:
- when starting a whole food regime, elimination is more active, remedy drinks aid in the quick and gentle removal of toxins.
- they can temporarily alleviate conditions although unless there is a change in lifestyle, symptoms may come back.
- safe and mild, most are made from easily found foods.
- recommended for a short time, 1-3 days-week, then a few days off to let the stimulated organs adjust to the change, then on again.
- best taken on an empty stomach but some aid in digestion after eating heavy foods such as Ginger Tea, Ume Kuzu)
- many are based in macrobiotics, a radical healing diet through food alone. I have made some changes to make them work for me.

Easy Cleansing and detox tips:
- upon rising, drink (one glass – 1 quart) warm water or bland tea: rosehip, marshmallow root, nettle, kukicha or other with or without lemon or Rye Tonic (see Miscellaneous). Wait 30-60 minutes before eating. In that time, exercise: yoga, mini-trampoline, Qi-Gong, go for a walk, etc.
- take food-grade diatomaceous earth (Glossary) in water (distilled is best – anything but tap) on an empty stomach only, upon rising or before bed, wait 30-45 minutes before eating.
- prepare vegetables for breakfast: Miso Soup, steamed greens, Easy Steamed Vegetables, Quick Blanched Vegetables, along with other foods of choice. Try not to season breakfast too strongly.
- weekly: include a Green Drink, fresh juiced vegetables, Rye Tonic, Golden Elixir, My Favorite Smoothie, or Ginger-Mint Lassi often.
- if experiencing sweet cravings, or any cravings, try including more steamed/braised winter squash, onions, green cabbage,

carrots, and steamed greens. When the craving hits, chew on a piece of nori, take a few bites of rinsed sauerkraut or homemade pickle, go for a quick walk (get your mind off the craving), have tea with ginger.

- skip dinner a few nights a week, and if hungry, prepare steamed or braised vegetables, greens or cabbage. And have a mug of tea.
- daily oil-pulling, an Ayurvedic method that helps remove toxins, aids in circulation, and so much more, look it up on the net. I do it every morning after brushing my teeth and on an empty stomach.

For one month:
- avoid meat and dairy foods (and then for the rest of your life)
- use nuts and seeds sparingly, avoid oils and nut butters
- eat no flour products at all, yet corn or sprouted grain tortillas or homemade bread (such as Sour Millet Bread, Sprouted Sour-dough Bread, Corn Bread) when desired
- never salt food, always cook the salt in, be *very* light with it
- consume no *processed* food, desserts/sweets, fruit in moderation

Lifestyle:
- do not eat 3 hours before going to bed
- dry or wet scrub skin daily (see Glossary under Wet Scrub)
- exercise 3-4 times/week: mini-trampoline, early morning walks (45 minutes), hike, bicycle, etc. – and outside as often as possible.
- keep the mind active in some way, even through reading, learning a language, journal writing, memorizing poems (or anything), meditation – do what you love; find ways to naturally relax.
- find recipes to help minimize cravings.
- plant vegetables, start a garden, garden pots.
- walk barefoot on early morning grass or sand, as often as possible
- eat less whenever possible. It is the key to health and longevity.
- instead of shampoo/conditioner, wash hair with baking soda (¼-1 teaspoon dissolved in water, then rinse); follow with an apple cider rinse (2 teaspoons mixed into water); rinse with cool water.

Cleanses/fasts: eat clean for 3-21 days, then a 3-10 day juice fast such as:
- Master Cleanse or Lemonade Diet
- Check out Paavo Airola, a health pioneer on fasting and cleansing
- *For the Love of Eating's* Miso Soup, cultured foods, whole grains, beans, vegetables and chew each bite 100 times.

Carrot-Daikon Drink

This is a popular macrobiotic remedy drink used in many situations. It helps to dissolve fat deposits deep in the body as well as removing excess water and weight. I use this after over-eating or feeling a bit too indulgent. It helps to slim down and move excess out of the digestive tract and colon. It's a good cleanout, especially if done on an empty stomach in the morning at least 20-30 minutes before breakfast for 3-10 days.

> 1/3 cup *each* daikon radish and carrot, both *finely* grated
> 1 cup water
> ½ sheet nori, torn in small pieces, optional
> 1 minced scallion, optional

simmer daikon, carrot in water, 2 minutes
place nori and/or onion if using, into a mug
pour hot beverage over. Drink and eat as hot as possible

This can also be taken raw before a meal, just carrot and daikon, with a squirt of fresh lemon juice. Watch it, radish burps follow when eaten raw.

Raw Daikon

Or *mula* in Nepal where I sat waiting for a bus one hot and blue morning. Beautiful Nepalese women engaged in conversation hanging out the windows exchanging rupees for large chunks of white daikon. They would peel the thick skin and eat it in large round slabs, laughing large and bright. What a great snack I thought, especially the larger ones which tend to be less pungent. I eat if often (cooked too). And if you can find it attached to its leaves, steam those up as part of your dark leafy green repertoire.

Raw daikon (Japanese white radish) is especially helpful after a fatty/oily meal, or if nauseous from heavy foods such as nut butters, bread, sweets, meat, etc. The pungency of this deep root radish helps break up hard-to-digest food or knotted feelings in the gut. Keep in mind, it will give you unpleasant (smelling) burps for about an hour after ingesting. Chew on some fresh parsley along with it . . . or just stay away from people for a bit!

Ginger Tea

Ginger, a pungent root spice, with many healing qualities; helps with nausea in general and during pregnancy (it is said to be safe), over-eating, car sickness, or after a fatty/oily/heavy meal. Ginger helps digest proteins and fats, cuts through and helps break down stagnant, undigested energy, stimulates circulation and so many more conditions such as but not limited to:

- cold/flu feelings
- anti-inflammatory
- bloating, indigestion
- an overall uncomfortable feeling from food or life in general

Ginger is available in tea bags, but is best to use fresh. Grate it finely, hold the juicy pulp in your hand and squeeze into a mug, then pour hot water over (and wash your hand very well). Or finely slice it and add to tea or hot water. The grating/squeezing method is more potent and works better as a digestive aid. Daily, I grate it on a macrophage zest grater and add it to hot water or tea and Rye Tonic.

Umeboshi-Kuzu Drink (Ume-kuzu)

Another classic macrobiotic elixir, yet I have changed it to how I prepare it – without shoyu. It strengthens and promotes good digestion, helps to restore energy after over-eating, nauseous or bloating. It is also a deep immune booster, alkalinizing, restores balance and settles the stomach. See Kukicha Twig Tea for an easy version. Yield: enough for one person.

> ½ umeboshi plum or ¼ teaspoon umeboshi paste
> 1 heaping teaspoon kuzu (do not substitute with arrowroot)
> 3/4 cup water
> 1 teaspoon finely grated ginger, (and minced green onion) optional

cut flesh from pit of the plum, chop and add + pit (or leave the pit for the next one you make) to a small saucepan
mix together kuzu with water (best with fingers) and pour over plum
gently simmer 5 minutes until cloudiness disappears, stir often
place ginger in a mug, pour hot drink over, and green onion for a real digestive soup-like soothing drink

Flu/Cold Elixir

This is simple magic, and can drive out any cold, flu, or feelings of "coming down with something." It'll help nip it in the bud. I worked with Madeline Goulard, an incredibly spirited, intuitive and wise healer at her Simple Life Health Center in New Mexico. This is a rendition of her recipe.

In a large mug, combine:

> ½ lemon, juice only
> ½ teaspoon ginger powder or 1-2 teaspoons fresh grated
> ¼ teaspoon cayenne powder, more if you can take it
> 1 teaspoon-1 tablespoon raw honey
> 1 clove garlic, minced, optional

pour hot water over, as hot as you can take it, and drink it all down
repeat as many times in a day as you like

For variation add:
- vitamin C powder (camu-camu, rosehips), aloe vera juice, etc.

Worm/Parasite Purge

For three days, 1 hour before breakfast, on an *empty* stomach, chew very very well until milky in your mouth:

> 3-4 tablespoons short-grain organic brown rice
> 1 teaspoon minced green onion
> 1 tablespoon raw pumpkin seeds
> 1 small clove garlic, optional

If you find the rice too hard on your teeth to break it down, soak it overnight in a small amount of water, the next day chew it with the other ingredients and drink the soaking water too. Remember, empty stomach only. It works better raw, I have a hard time with it, but holding it in my mouth and moving it around, masticating slowly and steady, it softens enough to chew it up.

Repeat procedure the next week for three days. Check out Hulda Clark's parasite purge as well using herbs. See Diatomaceous Earth in Glossary.

Kukicha Twig Tea

Also known as Bancha Tea. It is made from roasted twigs, stems & leaves of the mature green tea bush; aids digestion, contains calcium and only trace amounts of caffeine, a calming, slightly alkaline tea with an earthy taste. Purchase in bags (Eden or Choice) and brew according to directions. Or in bulk, see Resources, and simmer 5 minutes or longer. These twigs can be used many more times, the tea will weaken each time. Once brewed, enjoy as is or add lemon, ginger slices or juice (see Glossary), chopped umeboshi plum or paste which makes it a quick alkalinizing drink (see also Ume-Kuzu).

Rosehip Tea
the fruit of the wild rose

Simmer rosehips (½ cup or more) in a large pot of water (3-4 quarts), 20 minutes or longer. I often just leave it on my woodstove in the winter, and drink it throughout the cold days. Rosehips contain a good amount of vitamin C, pectin and other nutrients, aids in flushing out the kidneys/urinary tract, strengthens resistance to infection. Nice with other teas, smoothies, etc. Use the rosehips again – they will simmer up pink several more times.

Tea Tree Steam

A good friend, mentor and very intuitive Naturopath suggested this to me when I was intensely congested. Tea Tree Oil is an incredible, very strong healing remedy used in many external-only applications. In this instance, it clears sinuses when congested, infected, or blocked. Start with one drop, it is very strong.

boil water and pour into a mug that is kept for this purpose only
add 1-3 drops tea tree oil then place your nose and mouth over opening
cup your hands around to form a loose seal, and breathe deep, repeat
re-heat if it loses its steam

Ginger Compress (external remedy)

The ginger compress is a deeply effective and inexpensive herbal remedy easily done at home. I learned about it at the Kushi Institute and again from Kaare Bursell, a macrobiotic counselor. Ginger is a miraculous healing root, used both internally and externally, beneficial for many situations:

- on the kidneys or liver/gall bladder area to relieve pressure and pain from kidney or gall stones respectively.
- on the lower intestines for breaking up old impacted material in the colon, helping peristalsis, dissolving sticky fats and old proteins, and bringing in needed circulation to this area.
- in general, used for circulation which makes the skin red, this rushed blood into the area helps to cleanse and carry out toxins.

Read about the original method at Kaare's website (see Resources). I do the following method only, it is easier, which for me, makes me do it. It feels good to relax for half hour and experience the deep, penetrating heat.

boil enough water to fill a hot water bottle
grate 1/3-½ cup fresh ginger, loosely packed, need not be organic
lay a wet washcloth on a small plate, spread the ginger on half the cloth
fold the cloth over, pour a small amount of boiling water over so it is nicely dampened and the ginger juices release, but not too wet
pour the rest of the water into the hot water bottle, press the bottle against you to press the air out and the water comes to the top, then screw the lid on. You don't want air in there with the boiling water
place hot water bottle on top of the folded ginger cloth to get it warm
get comfortable for 30-40 minutes so you don't have to move
place the folded washcloth containing ginger in it on the ascending colon
then the water bottle on top, and lastly a small towel to cover it all
tuck in parts of the towel if the hot water bottle touches your skin

If doing the intestines, every 5 or so minutes move the whole thing to your transverse colon and then descending colon, then across lower belly, repeat until time is up. You can do the kidneys with this method if desired, but it is more difficult because of having to reach around, unless you can get help.

The area being administered will become very red and even blotched with white spots – indications of blockages, mainly from old fats and dairy, stagnant in this area. Even the next day faint blotches may still be there and will go away until the next ginger compress. Apply 2-4 times/week.

Glossary

ADZUKI: (aduki, azuki) means small bean; they are high in protein and easy to digest because of their low-fat quality; helps strengthen the kidneys and can even aid in regulating menstruation in women, if eaten often as well as following a "clean" diet such as *For the Love of Eating*.

AGAR AGAR: see Sea Vegetables

AGAVE SYRUP: I do not advocate agave syrup, it can be substituted (and is a cheaper alternative) to maple syrup or honey if desired; high in fructose which is detrimental to the system for many reasons; made by expressing juice from its core, then filtered and heated to hydrolyze carbohydrates into sugars; fructose is often under several names: chicory, inulin, iso glucose, glucose-fructose syrup, crystalline fructose, dahlia syrup, tapioca syrup, glucose syrup, corn syrup, fruit fructose, agave. I don't think it is as good as it is said to be – and it is not raw.

AMASAKE: a delicious creamy drink made from sweet brown rice that has been naturally cultured to convert the starches into maltose & other natural sugars; available in health food stores in the refrigerated section.

ARROWROOT STARCH: a starchy flour from a tropical tuber; gluten-free; used as a thickener; can be added to baked goods or gluten-free flours to add a smooth consistency or binding quality; first mix into a small amount of cool water (or if baking add to dry mix) then add to gravy, pie filling, etc., whisk over heat until thickened, let bubble 10 seconds and remove from heat. Cornstarch is similar yet highly processed and treated with chemical bleaches and toxic extracting agents as is potato starch.

BAKING POWDER/SODA: baking soda (BS) is pure sodium bicarbonate; an acidic ingredient (vinegar, lemon juice, cocoa, molasses) is needed with baking soda to create a rise in a baked good; bubbling action begins immediately upon mixing so the item must be cooked/baked right away; yields a bitter end-product unless an acidic ingredient is used along with it; baking powder already contains this acidic ingredient and is often used in more subtle and delicate baked goods. Regardless, I use only baking soda.

    Baking powder (BP) contains sodium bicarbonate combined with cream of tartar (the acidic agent) and generally cornstarch; single-acting bubbles right away and must be baked immediately upon mixing, double-acting can wait before baking. If you substitute BP for BS, more is needed. If you substitute BS for BP, add a teaspoon of apple cider vinegar or lemon juice to batter, ½ teaspoon BS = 2 teaspoons BP.

Recipe for your own BP:
2 parts cream of tartar, 1 part baking soda, 1 part arrowroot starch
Mix together and store in a glass jar.

BARLEY: whole hulled barley has had the inedible hull and one hard outer layer removed leaving most of the nutritional value intact; pearl barley has had the hull and two hard outer layers removed putting it nutritionally in the class with white flour and white rice; choose hulled over pearl more often, it takes longer to cook, prepare in advance and freeze in batches for quick use.

BARLEY FLOUR: a workable substitute for white flour for muffins, pie crust, cakes, etc.; not gluten-free, can be used for those allergic to wheat.

BLACK SOYBEANS: different from the white or beige colored soybeans; they nourish the reproductive organs and have a lubricating quality to the bronchi and throat, the large intestine loves them; high in iron and calcium; can be replaced with regular black bean, which are great but medicinally not the same.

BRAGG-Liquid AMINOS: I avoid it. It is a refined product of un-fermented soy origin; not easy to digest; though high in amino acids, there are many other foods not as concentrated or refined.

BURDOCK: hardy wild plant which grows throughout the United States; strengthening qualities; astringent and diuretic qualities when dried and chopped; also called Gobo.

> **shaved burdock method**: gently scrub the root leaving its bark-like roughness, then, hold it in one hand at the end, at a slight angle over a bowl. With a knife in the other hand, shave pieces off so they look sort of like pieces of bark – small, angular and thin.

CHESTNUT: considered "the grain that grows on a tree" because of its low fat and high trace mineral content; 2½ nuts = 1 gram protein; available frozen, dried, or jarred; sweet, smoky flavor, delicious in many recipes, easy to digest; if dried, soak overnight (½ cup in 1½ cups water), drain but keep the soaking liquid and remove hard, dark veins. Simmer 1 hour or more until soft in plenty of water; or add them plus soaking liquid to beans or grain (pressure cook with grain) to cook along with them, though I often find they need longer cooking; if frozen, simmer until tender. Jarred should be ready to use. Sweet and rich in dessert recipes; check out Sweet Rice Balls where blended chestnuts blended into a creamy topping is used; outrageous in brownies.

COOKING POTS: I use stainless steel, tinted glass (pyrex) and ceramic. I strongly advise against Teflon (or anything like it, even the newer varieties coming out) and aluminum. They leach into the food no matter what the manufacturing company or media says. They are dangerous in the most serious way. Well-seasoned cast-iron is exceptional as a "non-stick" alternative.

COUSCOUS: a type of pasta made from semolina (wheat); makes excellent cake-like recipes when one wants to avoid flour products to keep the diet more healing; millet can be substituted for couscous although it does not have the same lightness or texture.

DAIKON: (white radish) long white roots, pungent and spicy; their greens are edible and delicious when cooked; aids in digestion especially of fats and oils; helps dissolve mucus; helps eliminate excess water and reduces weight. Drying lets it reach deeper in the body and gives it an odd, butterscotch smell and interesting texture to cooked dishes; best to reconstitute in water before cooking.

> **Dried daikon** method to make your own: wash and scrub a few daikon roots, slice on the diagonal in thin long oval pieces, lay atop each other folded down like dominoes, hold with one hand and then slice into thin matchsticks. Spread evenly on a flat pan, allow to dry several days in an un-heated oven (one with a pilot light), in the sun, or in a dry place out of the way. Drape a light cloth over to keep dust off. They are done when beige-colored and have wrinkled and shrunk to half their size. Store in a glass jar in a cool dark place. Lasts for years. Or, dried daikon can be purchased at Oriental markets or online at Goldmine or The Natural Import Co. (Resources), etc. If unavailable, use freshly grated, diced, or daikon matchsticks raw and cooked in recipes.

DIATOMACEOUS EARTH (food-grade): a silica-rich powder looks and tastes much like clay; has a honeycomb-shaped skeletal form called diatoms; age-old fossils that dismantle bacteria, parasites, heavy metals, environmental pollutants, yeast, parasites, bacteria, viruses, and aids the body in de-toxing. It dismantles these toxins at a microscopic level – functionally, not chemically; safe and non-toxic for all ages, even during pregnancy, pets too; may help regulate blood pressure and aid in preventing kidney stones, helps repair and maintain lung tissues (protecting them from pollution); raises *good* cholesterol; the body cannot assimilate calcium without silica; best if taken on an empty stomach, preferably in distilled water, but not critical. I take it every other day upon rising.

FERMENTED FLOUR: use in cookies, cakes, non-sourdough breads, Corn Bread, etc.; place 3 cups flour or cornmeal in a food processor, add ½ cup oat/rice yogurt and 3 tablespoons apple cider vinegar, pulse until combined. Transfer to a glass or ceramic mixing bowl, cover loosely with plastic and let sit 24 hours. A little more may be needed when replacing for flour in recipes. Store in the fridge, keeps a couple of months.

FLAME TAMER (heat diffuser): a flat metal disk with perforated holes in it, placed between cooking pot and burner; it diffuses heat. Used in situations when the stove does not simmer low enough to slowly cook grain, beans, etc. Great used on woodstoves, and especially electric burners for controlling the heat.

FLAXSEED: small brown/blond seeds containing soluble fiber which assists in regulating cholesterol levels; contains lignan, an anti-cancer agent; highest known source of linolenic acid, the omega-3 essential fatty acid commonly lacking in the diet; helpful in relieving arthritis, asthma, promoting colon and breast health, improving moods, producing healthier skin, reducing allergic responses, and increasing vitality and energy. Whole flaxseeds can be stored at room temperature 2-3 months or up to 1 year in the refrigerator or freezer. To use, grind seeds and add to baked goods, smoothies, sprinkle on foods; no need to soak flaxseeds for general use.

I do not use flax oil, it is too delicate, and must be kept refrigerated. Once opened, use within 3-6 weeks, or store in the freezer for longer. When finished there may be debris (lignans) at the bottom, cut the bottle in half, use these lignans in sauces, dressings and pesto. I use only the whole flax seed, freshly ground, 1-2 tablespoons per serving; add whole or ground seeds to smoothies, pasta, grain, dressings, pesto, morning cereal, Corn Bread, pancakes, etc.

GINGER: an ancient super food prized for its healing properties; a natural anti-inflammatory, stimulates circulation, antioxidant qualities, digestive aid for gas, bloating, nausea, safe in pregnancy and for all ages. For its juice, use fresh organic root, no need to peel, finely grate, place all in your fist or in a piece of cheesecloth and squeeze on vegetables, into dressings, sauces, dips, for marinades, or into a mug of tea.

GLUTEN-FREE: see sections, How To Cook and Cook's Notes.

GRAIN COFFEE: roasted carob, fig, chicory, barley, dandelion root, by themselves or in combination; lends a strong coffee-like flavor to the Grain "Cappuchino" and/or hot cocoa recipe in the Beverages & Smoothies section; mix with hot water and hot grain/nut/almond milk for a delicious coffee-like beverage, sweeten with stevia, amasake, or other sweetener; use with cocoa or carob for a mocha flavor in drinks and desserts. Roasted dandelion tea is rich, and coffee-like too, available in tea bags, bulk or ground as a dark powder.

HEAT DIFFUSER: see flame tamer

How-to-cut: see Onions

KAMUT: rediscovered 6,000 year old ancient wheat; 20-40% higher protein content than whole wheat, with a lighter texture; those sensitive to wheat can often tolerate kamut, but it does contain gluten. No adjustments are needed in recipes substituting kamut for wheat.

KINPIRA: this macrobiotic style of cooking combines sautéeing and simmering of vegetable matchsticks (cut in matchsticks size or julienne, see onion in glossary for cutting technique).

KUZU (kudzu): a wild starchy root that grows in the south; used as a thickener with medicinal value; helps relieve discomfort in the intestines caused by over-acidity, bacterial infection, and in the case of diarrhea, excess water; high in naturally occurring flavonoids (antioxidants). In many cases of stomach aches and intestinal irritation, a mug of Ume Kuzu (see Remedies) brings quick relief. Kuzu may curb the desire for alcohol as well as its effects on the body. Use approximately 1½ tablespoons kuzu/cup of liquid to thicken sauces, and double that for jelling liquids. For most preparations, completely dissolve the measured amount of kuzu in a little cold water (using your fingers), then add to the other ingredients near the end of cooking time. Bring the mixture to a simmer, stirring constantly while it thickens and becomes translucent.

KUKICHA: tea, see Kukicha Tea in Remedy section.

LOTUS ROOT: root of the water lily, a beige colored multi-holed root that when cut, looks like a side-angle of the lung: aids in discharging mucous and congestion; also sold as a powder (a delicious tea). You can also make tea from the fresh or dried root; delicious sliced thin and cooked into stir-fries.

MIRIN: sweet liquid seasoning used to balance the salty flavors of soy sauce or miso in Asian cuisine. Look for those naturally and traditionally fermented made only with rice, koji (Aspergillus oryzae), water, sea salt.

MISO: a fermented, soy-based paste that comes in many different ferments and colors. Soy tends to block enzymes needed to digest protein. It also has high levels of phytic acid which can block the absorption of iron, calcium, magnesium, and zinc – all crucial minerals. But miso is *fermented* which breaks down the phytic acid rendering a product high in enzymes and friendly microorganisms that help restore healthy bacteria and can possibly aid in the removal of radioactive elements from the body.

It is made from cooked yellow soybeans, salt, grain and koji, aged several months to years. By varying ingredients (grains, etc.) and length of ferment, a wide range of flavors is produced. I use a ½ or heaping ½ teaspoon of dark barley miso (which contains gluten, use chickpea miso if sensitive) per serving in my miso soup recipe.

> **white miso**: soybeans fermented with a large portion of rice. It has a sweet taste; use in dips, sauces, dressings, summer or light soups.
> **yellow miso**: made from soybeans fermented with barley and sometimes a small amount of rice. It is stronger in flavor, yet still mild. I use yellow and white interchangeably, and refer to it in *For the Love of Eating* as light miso.

red miso: made from soybeans and barley or other grains and fermented longer; use in stronger tasting dishes such as bean soups, gravies, braises.
dark barley miso: fermented a long time, strong taste, very healing; use mainly in soups (Miso Soup) and where red miso is used.

Use miso like vegetable or beef bouillon:
white, yellow/mellow miso = chicken or vegetable type seasoning
red, barley miso = beef type seasoning
mix red and white for a richer "chicken" type seasoning

MOCHI: sweet rice cooked and pounded into flat square bars; said to be good for lactating mothers as it promotes production of breast milk; also good for gaining weight (if one eats a lot). When finely grated it melts like cheese, though it must be in-between something to melt, such as vegetables and sauce on a pizza, or in-between rice and beans in a tortilla, otherwise it remains dry. If grating to melt, use a macrophage grater (the one for zesting). They are worth the investment (for grating garlic, ginger, citrus rinds, as well). You can cut it into thin strips and place on a hot well-greased waffle iron and get incredible puffy crisp waffles! Mochi is available in the refrigerator section in most health food stores. I often grate extra and freeze it, or cut block of mochi in 4 squares and freeze for later use, holding one out in the fridge for daily use. It will mold within 10 days-2 weeks or so.

I use a macrophage grater for grating mochi, it takes a long time, but grates it very fine so it melts fast and even. For pizza, sometimes I'll grate mochi on a regular small grater. For chopped or small diced mochi, slice it very thin, then in thin strips, then chop in tiny pieces, just keep in mind, small is best unless simmering it in a recipe (such as Mac 'n' Cheez, then larger cubes are fine.

¼ block Grainessence plain mochi (3+ ounces)= 1 cup loosely packed grated.

MSG: Monosodium Glutamate; a dangerous flavor enhancer "added to" or "found in" many foods; an excitotoxin and should be avoided; under different names such as but not limited to: natural flavors/ing, hydrolyzed (vegetable) protein (HVP), yeast extract, glutamic acid, calcium or sodium caseinate, yeast nutrient, gelatin, hydrolyzed milk protein, natural beef flavoring, autolyzed yeast, kombu extract, bouillon, natural pork flavoring, RL-50, broth, natural seasonings, textured protein, calcium caseinate, gourmet powder, seasonings, sodium caseinate, glutavene, subu, flavorings, glutacyl, spices, malt extract, hydrolyzed oat flour, tamari, malt flavoring, hydrolyzed plant protein and the list goes on. See truthinlabeling.org for more information on this dangerous neurotoxin.

NATTO: a traditional Japanese fermented food made from soybeans and a bacteria (bacillus natto) that produces enzymes, vitamins, amino acids and other nutrients. It is these elements that give natto truly unique and health-giving benefits; has a specific taste and texture, one that takes getting used to, similar to a strong cheese; superior protein value and cultured food benefits; careful in Oriental markets, often sugar or other unwanted ingredients are added; can make your own.

NISHIME: a macrobiotic style of long simmering of vegetables over low heat with very little water allowing vegetables to cook in their own juices; a warming dish, providing calm, deep energy, see Nourishing Root Braise.

NOODLES/Pasta: choose whole grain varieties. Depending on the noodle, I usually boil them for 5 minutes, then cover and turn off heat, let them sit in this hot liquid 5-20 minutes. Japanese varieties such as udon and soba (buckwheat) are my favorite, though made with wheat. They already contain salt so adding salt to the boiling water is unnecessary. Noodles in my recipes can be substituted with your choice. See also the chapter, Noodles.

OILS: I rarely use oil in any of my cooking and baking/steaming, and when needed, I use only organic, cold pressed: sesame (plain, toasted), extra virgin olive and coconut, grape seed. I never use canola oil – no matter what studies have been done, my research is completely unfavorable to it – nor do I use peanut, corn or soy oils. Keep use of oil minimal, and never highly heat it, Three things damage oil: heat, light, oxygen, so best to buy in preferably glass and dark containers.

> **Canola oil:** genetically-engineered rape seed; a lubricating oil used in small industry; not meant for human consumption; derived from the mustard family, considered a toxic and poisonous weed; a trans-fatty acid; supposedly has a cumulative effect taking almost 10 years before symptoms manifest; may inhibit proper metabolism of foods and normal enzyme function that can manifest as loss of vision, emphysema,

anemia, constipation, irritability, even eye problems in animals and humans; antagonizes the central and peripheral nervous systems and depresses the immune system. It's cheap and tasteless. Be careful about its unsaturated qualities (omega 3,6 and 12) and its ability to be easily digested. Don't buy into it, but do your own research.

Butter/ghee: ghee is clarified butter, its milk fat boiled away. I lived in Nepal and reveled in ghee's use in cooking to hair grease and skin oil. I don't use it or butter.

ONIONS: how-to-cut . . .

Yellow/red: prepare onion by cutting ends off, slice in half from root end to top end. Peel halves leaving as much onion as possible. Lay each half cut side down on cutting board. Keep fingers curved away from knife while cutting. When nearing the end and it's hard to hold, turn face down and continue until the very end, include core ends on cuts.

thin slices: cut onion end to end or with the grain in thin or thick slices.

half moon: same as thin slices.

quarter moon: cut onion in thin slices or half moon, then in half again.

finely diced or chopped: cut onion in thin slices, turn and cut in thin slices cross-ways, resulting in small pieces.

minced: cut onion in thin slices, turn, hold it firmly and cut in thin slices again to get small pieces, then mince keeping tip end of knife on cutting board and raising handle end up and down.

green onions minced: trim very ends of white roots, but keep most of the roots, clean very well. Cut down the onion from inside green shoots to root ends. Clean very well, separating root ends to get grit out. If dirt is locked in too tight, cut the whole root end off. Cut each half lengthwise again and again so you have several long spears, then mince from roots up to tips.

Matchsticks: means to cut the vegetable into fine matchstick cuts. Cut the say carrot, into long oblong thin ovals. Then push them over like a line of dominoes so they overlap each other. Hold firmly to the pile, curl fingers in, and slice thinly into thin pointy matchsticks.

PASTA: see Noodles

POTATO: the carbohydrates in white potatoes (and *refined* grains) elevate sugar levels; they are absorbed quickly and easily, thus requiring large surges of insulin. Sweet potatoes and yams are tubers, not potatoes, nor are they related to each other. Sweet potatoes are what we find in the United States, yams are mainly found in other countries. Recipes in *For the Love of Eating* uses mostly Japanese sweet potato which has burgundy skin and light colored flesh, and then the other sweet potato or garnet yam with dark skin and orange flesh.

PRESSURE COOKER: a special pot that uses great pressure to cook foods not allowing air or water to escape. It is an intense way to cook food, a method I do not suggest very often. It cooks beans very nicely and quickly, but I prefer to boil them as with grains. It is convenient when time is short though. See chapter on Beans.

PROTEIN: a plant-based, whole food diet provides enough protein to nourish everyone if done correctly. Include daily: whole grains, a variety of vegetables, beans, and augment with nuts, seeds, cultured foods, seaweeds, etc. Try to plan ahead and prepare foods properly as suggested in *For the Love of Eating*.

QUINOA (KEEN-wah): originated in South America and sacred to the Incas; member of the goosefoot family (Chenopodicum quinoa), a high altitude, hardy pseudocereal, not a true grain; cooks quickly, 15-20 minutes, into a light fluffy grain with little sprout-like curls; has an unusually high protein content, is gluten-free, rich in lysine and other nutrients; a substance on its surface called saponins, a natural insecticide, requires soaking preferably for several hours or overnight in warm water (or at least thorough rinsing in warm water) before cooking or it will be bitter. This step of cleaning and rinsing is done in most packaged quinoa, but not all, so take the time to do this step. See Soaking Grains in Cook's Notes.

RICE PAPER: found in health food stores or oriental markets; made with white rice flour and often tapioca; they need to be re-constituted under water, laid flat on a surface to soften, then filled and rolled. See Salad Wrap.

ROASTING Nuts and Seeds: see Soaking Nuts and Seeds in Cook's Notes as the step to do before roasting. After soaking, set nuts or seeds onto a baking sheet to dry on top of a warm wood stove, in a low oven (150°), or in the sun. Or slowly roast in a skillet set over a very low temperature. The burners on my range do not go low enough and often use a flame tamer between the skillet and burner. Stir often until golden. For salt, see Roasted Salt in Miscellaneous.

SALT: sea salt, shoyu, tamari, umeboshi vinegar, etc.; best cooked into food, not sprinkled or shaken on top. Cooking salt into food enhances flavor and calms its highly concentrated state making it easier for the body to assimilate, creating less cravings. Look for Si salt, Celtic sea salt, unrefined sea salt, Real salt, Himalayan salt. When I use it raw, meaning just sprinkling it on top of food, I try to dry roast it first and store in a separate container to have on hand, see Miscellaneous for Roasted Salt.

SEA VEGETABLES (seaweed)**:** are detoxifying, alkalinizing due to their high mineral content, and because of their assimilable food-form, the minerals and elements are integrated into living plant tissue not isolated as in supplements or bound to tough proteins such as in dairy products.

> **agar-agar:** I refer to it as agar in this cookbook; processed from several different seaweeds into an odorless white or translucent bar, flakes, or powder; heated with liquid and cooled, gels similar to gelatin; contains calcium, iodine, and other trace minerals and is good for the intestines; known as kanten in Japan, it is used to make Jell-O type desserts, aspics, jam and jelly. I use it for puddings, pie fillings, frostings and cake fillings. Get familiar with it, it is worth the effort. If you purchase agar from an Oriental Market (in sticks, make sure it is natural, no added dyes), break them up, whiz in a food processor and then in a coffee grinder, store in a jar. It is easiest to use agar powder, order it through Goldmine Natural Foods or Now, two I know of. The powder dissolves quicker and leaves no clumps like the flakes often do.

> 1 tablespoon flakes = ½ teaspoon powder

> **kombu:** grows in deep ocean waters creating vast fields of long upward-growing fronds attached to the ocean floor; used to make soup stocks, cooked with vegetables, beans or grains, balances acidic and/or protein content of beans; used as a commercial thickener but called carrageenan. One piece can be used several times for soups, then sliced thin and eaten along with the dish it was cooked in; after soaking in cold water for a few minutes it doubles in size; contains vitamins A, B2, C, calcium, and iodine.

wakame: a leafy sea vegetable, delicate flavor, quickly reconstitutes in water (expands to 4-5 times in volume); add soaked and sliced wakame to salads or dry (break it up) to soups, any vegetable, bean or grain dish, or ground into Sesame Sprinkle; requires little or no cooking; high in iron, calcium, vitamins A, C, niacin and even protein.

hijiki: a dark-brown, branched sea vegetable that has a firm texture and strong ocean taste; reconstitute in a lot of water 30 minutes before using, triples in size; best to simmer in water (20 minutes) or cook before eating; great in coleslaw-type salads, stir-fries or a simple side dish such as Hijiki & Shiitake (see Sea Vegetables); rich source of calcium (higher than dairy products), protein, iron and a wealth of trace minerals.

dulse: red/purple in color, high in iron; great in fleck or powdered form and ground into Sesame Sprinkle or reconstituted and mixed into cultured salads. It does not need to be soaked before using, it is quite salty if not soaked, and check for little shells or other ocean debris.

arame: a thin dark brown sea vegetable which is parboiled, shredded, and diced by the time it reaches the shelves; has a delicate texture and flavor; often cooked with other vegetables, in salads, or in medicinal preparations and baths; reconstitutes quickly; use it raw (reconstitute first), marinated in salads or quickly cooked in sautés and soups; high in fiber like most seaweeds, niacin, calcium, iron, iodine.

nori: large square sheets rolled around rice and vegetables, then sliced, called norimaki (maki means roll) or Nori Rolls (vegetable sushi) in *For the Love of Eating*. This versatile vegetable has endless uses: quickly toasted over a burner its dark color turns green (unless it is already toasted), then broken or cut in strips and garnished in soup, ground finely and sprinkled over popcorn or noodles, ground up in Sesame Sprinkle, eaten like a large thin potato chip (helps to quench any sweet or chocolate craving); contains carotene, B vitamins including B12, vitamin C, calcium, and iron.

SEEDS: see Cook's Notes for soaking, and Glossary under Roasting

SHIITAKE: a brown mushroom that grows on decaying oak logs; powerful anti-microbial, anti-tumor components, anti-viral and deep immune boosting properties; used mainly in its dried form in macrobiotic cooking and medicinal drinks; the dried fruit is concentrated and has a higher amount of natural sugar than fresh. However, mushrooms are high in polysaccharides (complex sugars) essential for health and eating them dry will deliver more medicinal value. Dried shiitake helps the body rid itself of excess old fats and salt as well as providing.

> When preparing dried shiitake (or any dried mushroom), soak in water placing a plate on top to keep them under, 10-15 minutes to soften. Slice thin and use in any recipe. I leave the stem on, many take it off saying it is tough. I like the chewiness. Decide for yourself.

SHOYU (soy sauce): produced through fermentation of soybeans, water, salt, koji, and wheat. Shoyu is the Japanese version of soy sauce, and is generally less salty. See also Tamari (which is usually wheat-free and saltier) in Glossary. Look for natural brands such as Oshawa, Mitoku, San-J, etc.

SOY FOOD: there is a proliferation of GMO's (genetically-modified organisms) and soy is one of the largest crops therefore hard to trust. I have recipes calling for tofu and the more recommended fermented soy products (tempeh, shoyu, miso, natto) that I believe, are the only ones to consume; they are easier to digest since the protein is broken down. All others: soymilk, soy "meats", soy "cheese," TVP, soy protein powder, even Bragg-aminos and edamame, I strongly advise against. Tofu is not fermented so I do not include it in my diet very often, but it is quick and easy, and provides diversity, and I must say, I love it. So, I was happy when the company, Wildwood Organics, put out *sprouted* tofu and is the only one I buy – yet sprouted or not, the American-grown soybean is controversial in its gmo origin, and I still do not eat it often. Sprouted or not, tofu can be fermented into a "cheese" (see Tofu "Cheese") thus making it much more digestible, and quite delicious.

Tofu comes in different forms: soft, firm, extra firm, silken. I buy firm or extra firm since it holds up better for stir-fries, crumbling, etc. Soft is generally for blending or mashing into creamy dips, etc. but not necessary, the firm blends beautifully into "sour cream." Silken comes in aseptic containers, does not need to be refrigerated until opened and is extremely delicate, even the firm variety.

I am not an advocate of blending tofu with sweets for desserts, the combination is hard to digest. See roannelewis.com for a whole grain pudding recipe.

There are many ways to get protein: whole grains, beans, nuts, seeds, land and sea vegetables. The necessity of providing a full spectrum diet – eating a wide variety of plant-based foods to provide what we need – is imperative for health, energy, and happiness.

SPELT: an ancient grain, closer to bread wheat than Kamut although similar in nutritional content. Those allergic to wheat can often tolerate spelt, but like wheat, it contains gluten; requires less liquid (or more flour) than whole wheat in recipes; approximately 1¼ cups spelt flour in place of 1 cup whole wheat flour or decrease the liquid from 1 cup to 2/3-¾ cup.

STEVIA: an herb native to Paraguay; a sweetener, but can only be referred to as a "dietary supplement" according to the Dietary Supplement Health and Education Act; has a licorice-like flavor; cannot replace cup-for-cup for other sweeteners, 1 teaspoon stevia powder = 1 cup of sugar in sweetness; best to use the whole plant extract in powder or liquid form (green color and much stronger tasting) instead of the refined white powder made from it. Mix it into apple sauce or sweet potato purée (see Miscellaneous) to use in baked/steamed recipes which will serve as the sweetener and fat replacer.

SURIBACHI: a serrated, glazed, clay bowl used with a pestle (surikogi); used for grinding and puréeing foods such as Sesame Salt, salad dressings, sauces, even baby foods.

TAMARI: produced through the fermentation of soybeans, water, salt and koji (Aspergillus) spores made from the liquid that collects with the making of miso. It generally does not contain wheat (check the label), and has a stronger taste compared to shoyu, and is thicker. It is used more frequently in food processing and tends to be used in longer cooking dishes where its flavor softens, and adds a darker color to it.

TEMPEH (also see SOY FOODS in Glossary): an Indonesian soy food made by inoculating cooked soybeans with an edible mold spore. The mycellium bind the beans together into a cake-like mass which is then cooked for making other dishes; high protein food, it is also a supposedly very minimal source of B-12 but not to be relied on.

TOFU: see SOY FOODS

TROUBLE-SHOOTING:

Cultured Salads: sometimes more salt (or umeboshi vinegar) is needed to get the juices going, especially if the cabbage/vegetables is tough or cut large. As you knead the vegetables, add salt until it really sweats and is getting wet. Consequently, after the salad has cultured it may be too salty. Just rinse it under water and squeeze out or let drain in a mesh strainer. Do not worry about letting the salad press/culture for a longer time than recipe calls for. Several hours to overnight, even a day or two is fine, it's what I usually do. I like more of a fermentation, especially with cabbage, but not with say, cucumbers.

Rye Tonic: it is possible for Rye Tonic to go bad (as any fermented food or beverage can). You can tell by the smell and taste – it should be slightly sour, which is good. It will keep in the fridge for many weeks. Hot weather may encourage the growth of pathogenic organisms before the beneficial ones get started and the culture will smell putrid. In this case, I use it as the liquid in recipes (Corn Bread, Sourdough Sprouted Bread, Pancakes, etc.) where its fermentation can be applied and taste diminished.

Patties: I use an ice cream scoop to form patties (4-tablespoon size, spring action release); wet hands each time you mold or drop it from scoop into your hand, and press into patty. After cooking, let cool on wire racks. If they fall apart, the batter may be too dry or not blended enough (mash it with a potato masher, with your hands or blend part in a food processor and add a tablespoon at a time of water or broth). If too wet, add 1 tablespoon at a time of flour or arrowroot starch.

Quesadillas: I use very little oil in all my cooking, and use a well-seasoned cast iron skillet: warm over burner, wipe *very lightly* with oil, add a dash of water, place filled quesadilla. As it warms, add dashes of water, it will sputter and steam, gently move quesadilla with a metal spatula to let steaming water get under. Flip and repeat.

UMEBOSHI PLUM: salt-pickled fruit, member of the apricot family; salty-tart flavor and medicinal qualities; powerfully *alkalinizing*, anti-bacterial, strengthens and balances; stimulates appetite; aids digestion; shiso leaves lend the reddish color and natural flavoring during pickling; sold whole, in the form of paste, as concentrate, or in balls easy for traveling.

UMEBOSHI VINEGAR: not a real vinegar, ume su (vinegar) is the liquid which is expressed during the processing of umeboshi plums; sour and salty; unlike most vinegars, it is *alkaline* rather than acidic.

UME-SHISO POWDER: dried and ground shiso leaves usually tangled in umeboshi plums; delicious, healing condiment adding intense flavor; replaces salt in Sesame Sprinkle and any other cooking. I buy several packets and store in the freezer. Available through the Natural Import Company and others (see Resources) or possibly a health food store.

VEGETABLE STEAMING LIQUID: when steaming vegetables, the water or liquid in the steaming pot is great to use in salad dressings, sauces, soups, to cook noodles, grain or vegetables. Taste it first to check for bitterness.

WASABI POWDER: a dried and powdered root used mainly with sushi; hot and pungent, clears the sinuses; watch for additives and colorings; purchase only pure; dry mustard may be added and chlorophyll or spinach powder for coloring; mix with water into a paste, then shoyu as a dip for Nori Rolls.

WATER-SAUTÉ: *For the Love of Eating's* preferred method of sautéing; see Easy Vegetable Sauté, pg. 46; I only sauté in water, and depending on what is cooking, only dashes is needed, if any at all; mushrooms and onions need none at first, cover while cooking to retain moisture, if they brown or dry too much, again, just dashes of water, vegetable steaming liquid, or broth. I often sauté vegetables with no liquid, and a dash of shoyu or umeboshi vinegar which pulls the juice out of the vegetable, and cooks in its own liquid. Keep it quick, covered, and toss often.

WET SCRUB: aids in releasing toxins, "stuck" energy, and thoroughly cleans the skin, the largest eliminative organ in the body. It is different than taking a shower with a loofa or something similar. The action of scrubbing incorporates and utilizes internal energy otherwise latent, into the method.

This wet scrub, similar to dry brushing (but better I think), activates blood circulation that helps with relaxation and detoxification. I believe it (as well as diet change) is one of the most important things to do as part of a whole lifestyle change. Perform daily as your method of washing, or before showering in the morning or evening.

Use a regular sized washcloth, wet with hot water, wring out. Scrub gently, yet enough so the skin turns pink.

Start with:
1) face, neck, back of neck an d then,
2) right foot toes, rub each one, then foot, work up leg, repeat left side
3) then fingers on right hand, work up arm, shoulder, repeat left side
4) then hips, lower back, belly, torso
5) lastly do heart area

WILD RICE: an aquatic grass; purchase varieties that are hand-harvested if you can; color varies from dark to woody grain-like; do not soak, rinse in cool water, drain, for 1 cup boil 2½ cups water, add a pinch of salt, the rice, simmer 1 hour, let steam in covered pot 10-15 minutes when done.

Resources

The Kushi Institute located in Beckett, Massachusetts, a leading source of healing through macrobiotics; kushiinstitute.org

Kaare Bursell's website providing a wealth of information on healing through macrobiotics; alchemycalpages.com

NOW Foods, natural products company in Bloomingdale, Illinois, to purchase agar powder; nowfoods.com

Goldmine Natural Foods, in San Diego, California, for macrobiotic and organic foods, it is where the knife I use can be purchased; goldminenaturalfoods.com

> **knives:** NHS Professional Vegetable Knife, the one I recommend and use, 6½" carbon steel blade, clean and dry after each use; purchase a sharpening stone too, I got mine in china town in San Francisco for $2, and still have it 20 years later!, they do not need to be expensive. Learn to care for and sharpen your knife and it will last decades.

The Natural Import Company, located in Biltmore Village, North Carolina, a great online company for macrobiotic foods (bulk sea vegetables, kukicha tea, umeboshi vinegar, etc.). Prices tend to be inexpensive, I purchase items here most often; naturalimport.com

Eden Foods, an online source of organic, macrobiotic foods. They have recipes too; edenfoods.com

Parchment paper, I purchase unbleached parchment paper by the company, Beyond Gourmet, available in most health food stores.

Following are books that provide recipes, food preparation/methods, healing journey's, information on food and its impact on us and the environment, and insightful experiences of people who have completely over-hauled their diet and lifestyles:

Prevent and Reverse Heart Disease, Caldwell B. Esselstyn, Jr., M.D.

The End of Medicine, Kaare Bursell

Diet for a New America, John Robbins
My Beautiful Life, Mina Dobic – her healing journey through Macrobiotics in overcoming cancer. Mina is a leading macrobiotic counselor.

Nourishing Traditions, Sally Fallon (she advocates a lot of meat, fat, and raw dairy products, but her information on the preparation of whole grains, nuts, etc. is very informative as well as other recipes for the home cook).

Nourish, Holly Davis

Eco-Cuisine and *Friendly Foods,* Brother Ron Pickarski, O.F.M.

Cookbook author Lorna Sass, recipes and information on pressure cooking.

Complete Guide To Macrobiotic Cooking, Aveline Kushi. There are many other macrobiotic books by Michio and Aveline Kushi, Alex Jack, Wendy Esko, etc. for information, recipes, and healing techniques.

The Master Cleanse (a.k.a Lemonade Diet), Stanley Burroughs

Paavo Airola, his many books on cleansing and healing through juice fasting and natural food.

Bernard Jensen, a pioneer of health, his books are incredible fountains of information on holistic health, nutrition, fasting and exercise.

N.W. Walker D. Sc., one of the original fresh juice nutritional therapists.

Geneen Roth, her many books on cravings, addiction, and the emotional causes of over-eating or eating junk.

The China Study, Dr. T. Colin Campbell

Fast Food Nation, Eric Schlosser

Natural Medicine, A survivor's Guide (DVD), Dr. Gwen Scott; gwenscottnd.com

And Films: *Fat, Sick, Nearly Dead; Forks Over Knives; Food, Inc.; Food Matters; Eating*

Index

D

E

F

U

V

W

Y

Z

1237173R00150

Made in the USA
San Bernardino, CA
02 December 2012